D1564676

¡SÍ, ELLA PUEDE!

Inter-America Series

Edited by Howard Campbell, Duncan Earle, and John Peterson, series editors

In the new "Inter-American" epoch to come, our borderland zones may expand well past the confines of geopolitical lines. Social knowledge of these dynamic interfaces offers rich insights into the pressing and complex issues that affect both the borderlands and beyond. The Inter-America Series comprises a wide interdisciplinary range of cutting-edge books that explicitly or implicitly enlist border issues to discuss larger concepts, perspectives, and theories from the "borderland" vantage and will be appropriate for the classroom, the library, and the wider reading public.

¡SÍ, ELLA PUEDE!

THE RHETORICAL LEGACY OF DOLORES HUERTA AND THE UNITED FARM WORKERS

STACEY K. SOWARDS

University of Texas Press 〜 Austin

Requests for permission to reproduce material from
this work should be sent to:
    Permissions
    University of Texas Press
    P.O. Box 7819
    Austin, TX 78713–7819
    utpress.utexas.edu/rp-form

♾ The paper used in this book meets the minimum requirements of ANSI/NISO
Z39.48–1992 (R1997) (Permanence of Paper).

Library of Congress Cataloging-in-Publication Data
Names: Sowards, Stacey K., author.
Title: ¡Sí, ella puede! : the rhetorical legacy of Dolores Huerta and the United Farm
    Workers / Stacey K. Sowards.
Other titles: Inter-America series.
Description: First edition.
    Austin : University of Texas Press, 2019.
Series: Inter-America series
Includes bibliographical references and index.
Identifiers: LCCN 2018018115
    ISBN 978-1-4773-1766-2 (cloth : alk. paper)
    ISBN 978-1-4773-1767-9 (pbk. : alk. paper)
    ISBN 978-1-4773-1768-6 (library e-book)
    ISBN 978-1-4773-1769-3 (non-library e-book)
Subjects: LCSH: Huerta, Dolores, 1930-
    United Farm Workers—History.
    Women labor leaders—United States—Biography.
    Mexican American women labor union members—Biography.
    Migrant agricultural laborers—Labor unions—United States—History.
Classification: LCC HD6509.H84 S68 2019
    DDC 331.4/7813092 [B]—dc23
LC record available at https://lccn.loc.gov/2018018115

doi:10.7560/317662

FOR VIOLETA MARIETTE

CONTENTS

ACKNOWLEDGMENTS

This book has been several years in the making, and of course, I could not have completed it without both the direct and indirect support of countless people and organizations. Most importantly, I want to thank Dolores Huerta for her tireless work, both then and now, in promoting social justice and activism. When I first met her in 2003, she took the time to let me introduce myself and tell her about my project and her letters to César Chávez that I had collected while living in Detroit from 1999 to 2000. I then arranged for her to speak at my institution in 2006, and she not only came but also stayed at my house and gave countless speeches and inspirational messages over the span of two days to students, staff, faculty, local farm workers, undocumented immigrant detainees at an undisclosed location in El Paso, local politicians, and community members. A few months later, she was back again to speak at the Chamizal National Memorial, then a couple years later at New Mexico State University, El Paso Community College in 2013, and finally, back to El Paso in 2017 to promote and speak about the documentary film *Dolores*. Each and every time I heard her speak, I was profoundly inspired by her work and the very substantial obstacles she had to overcome to become the social justice icon that she is today. My personal and professional life, career, motherhood, and activism have been significantly informed and shaped by what she was able to accomplish starting in 1955 and her legacy that has shaped a generation of Chicanx and Latinx activists and academics. In our current political climate, it is so important for me and so many others to have Latina advocates in whom we can believe and who can inspire us to do more. That optimism and hopefulness is what will push the next generation of activists forward.

This project started when I first visited the official United Farm Workers archives at Wayne State University in Detroit, Michigan.

Kathy Schmeling at the Walter P. Reuther Library of Labor and Urban Affairs at Wayne State was so helpful every time I visited the library or requested information from afar. I also want to thank Lizette Guerra, at the Chicano Studies Research Center at the University of California, Los Angeles, who assisted in the transcription of taped speeches (they are now available in CD and print form through the library). Anne Marie Menta at the Beinecke Library at Yale University was also instrumental in gathering materials from the Jacques E. Levy collection in the middle of a major snowstorm that closed the campus for two days.

I am also thankful for the financial travel assistance and research assistant support from California State University, San Bernardino (my first real academic job), and The University of Texas at El Paso (UTEP, my academic home). I am grateful to both universities for supporting my career in general and, in particular, the research for this book. The accomplishments made in the El Paso community and in higher education by UTEP's president, Dr. Diana Natalicio, and Dr. Patricia D. Witherspoon, the former dean of the College of Liberal Arts, have always been huge inspirations. I thank both for their continuous encouragement. At UTEP, I also deeply appreciate my colleagues' support of my work: Arvind Singhal, Roberto Avant-Mier, Tarla Peterson, Frank Pérez, Sarah de los Santos Upton, Mary Trejo, Sabiha Khan, Eli García, Michael Lechuga, Beth Brunk-Chavez, Zita Arocha, Kate Gannon, Dino Chiecchi, and Irasema Coronado. I especially have to thank my former student, and now colleague, Carlos Tarín for his assistance as an undergraduate research assistant and then for reading and proofreading the entire manuscript. My former graduate student and advisee Joseph Flores also spent many hours transcribing letters and speeches. I am deeply indebted to both.

Many colleagues and friends in the communication and history disciplines were also supportive and helpful in the completion of this project. Mario García and Angharad Valdivia encouraged me over several years to complete this manuscript and wrote letters of recommendation to support grant applications. Angharad was also the editor of *Communication Theory*, the first outlet for my work on Dolores Huerta, an essay I thought would never get published. Her editing of that journal essay, as well as the insight of anonymous reviewers, contributed to the rest of this book. Bernadette Calafell, Michelle Holling, Catalina de Onís, and Darrel Wanzer-Serrano have been good colleagues, friends, and supporters. I owe big thanks to Lisa Flores, Karma

Chávez, Alberto González, and Manny Campbell for reading parts of or the entire manuscript. Their insights have substantially improved the end product. Writing is a painful process for me, and editing my own work even more so. I am lucky to have such fantastic thinkers who read and helped improve this book.

One of the best writing activities I have ever done was the Rhetoric Society of America's session for midlevel career scholars in 2013. At that workshop, I met my future writing group partners, Sue Hum and Rae Lynn Schwarz-DuPre. For five years (and hopefully many more), we have checked in with each other on a monthly, weekly, and sometimes daily basis to push one another to get our writing projects done. I still would not be done with this book if it were not for them. They also read many early (and terrible) drafts of this manuscript. Their suggestions, feedback, and motivation were essential in both starting and finishing this project, as was their friendship and camaraderie.

My comadres and closest friends, Valerie Renegar, Jonna Perrillo, Rosa Alcalá, Olga Avant-Mier, Marion Rohrleitner, Maryse Jayasuriya, and Gina Núñez-Mchiri, were essential for moral support and love. Not only have these brilliant women attended Dolores Huerta events with me, but they have been there through thick and thin in just about everything else. Valerie has been with me since the start of my academic career and is one of my favorite favorites (as a friend, colleague, and co-author). The birth of my daughter in 2015 was one of the most special moments I shared with them. My other dear friends, Becky Bunn, Rachel Hollander, and Lowry Martin, have also been supportive in too many ways to list. I am indebted to Eli, Lowry, and Jonna for coming to the hospital during my emergency surgery the day before I left for the ill-fated trip to Yale's Beinecke Library. Paulami Banerjee and Katie Wedemeyer-Strombel, two doctoral students at UTEP and good friends, have been so amazing in helping me with childcare. Marion and Paulami also took care of my daughter during my surgery, and I will never forget their willingness and generosity to help out on a moment's notice. Paulami also has become my daughter's best friend, and they spent many evenings hanging out while I worked on this project and others.

Finally, I owe everything to my family. Everything. My siblings, Heather, Matt, and Chad (and their spouses Dan, Kelaine, and Mio), have always been people I know I can count on. All my grandparents loved and supported me, but my grandma, Mary Kay Fleming, did so much for me so that I could go to college and then to graduate school; she has always been my biggest cheerleader in supporting my education. My parents, Michael and Wayne, are truly the best. I have awesome parents who pushed me to achieve my educational dreams and supported me my whole life, but especially during my darkest moments and greatest joys. I am especially thankful and grateful for all my parents have done for me over the past five years. My daughter, Violeta Mariette, was born in the midst of all this writing, research, and life drama, as were her two cousins, Maggie and Reyo. This book is about the past, but it reflects and inspires courage and optimism for my daughter's (and her cousins') future and her generation. If Dolores Huerta's life can teach us anything, it is that we need those moments of hope, bravery, and support to keep us moving forward, toward a more just world.

The author and the publisher gratefully acknowledge permission for use of the following material, published originally as: "Rhetorical Functions of Letter Writing: Dialogic Collaboration, Affirmations, and Catharsis in Dolores Huerta's Letters." *Communication Quarterly* 60, no. 2 (2012): 295–315. Reprinted by permission of Taylor & Francis.

"Rhetorical Agency as Haciendo Caras and Differential Consciousness through Lens of Gender, Race, Ethnicity, and Class: An Examination of Dolores Huerta's Rhetoric." *Communication Theory* (2010): 223–247. Reprinted by permission of John Wiley & Sons.

ABBREVIATIONS

AB	Assembly Bill (State of California)
AFL	American Federation of Labor
ALRA	Agricultural Labor Relations Act (State of California)
ALRB	Agricultural Labor Relations Board (State of California)
AWA	Agricultural Workers' Association
AWOC	Agricultural Workers Organizing Committee (under AFL-CIO)
CAWIU	Communists' Cannery, and Agricultural Workers Industrial Union
CIO	Congress of Industrial Organizations
CSO	Community Service Organization
FWA	Farm Workers Association (precursor of the NFWA)
NFLU	National Farm Labor Union
NFWA	National Farm Workers Association

NLRA   National Labor Relations Act

PL   Public Law

UCAPAWA   United Cannery, Agricultural, Packing, and Allied
                Workers of America

UFW   United Farm Workers

UFWOC   United Farm Workers Organizing Committee

INTRODUCTION

Don't be a marshmallow! Walk the street with us into history. Get off
the sidewalk. Stop being vegetables. Work for justice. Viva the boycott!
(Huerta, quoted in Baer, 1975)

As a farm worker organizer and a cofounder of the United Farm
Workers union, Dolores Huerta has demonstrated a lifelong commitment and social justice orientation to fighting for the rights of the poor
and oppressed. Her work for the United Farm Workers (UFW) spans
four decades, from the early 1960s to the early 2000s when she retired
and started the Dolores Huerta Foundation for community organizing
(www.doloreshuerta.org). It is surprising that her work for the UFW is
not better known in both academic and public communities given her
lifelong commitment to farm worker issues and her extended working
relationship with César Chávez, dating back to the mid-1950s. While
César Chávez has become an established public figure for his work
on behalf of farm workers (as evidenced by state holidays in Texas
and California, for example), Dolores Huerta has received relatively
little attention in historical and rhetorical scholarship. Her status as a
Chicana and Latina icon, as well as her role as (arguably) the most important Chicana/Latina activist of the 20th century (and into the 21st
century), warrants much greater attention to her life stories, leadership experiences, and rhetorical legacy. In particular, her rhetorical
practices reveal much about underrepresented and marginalized lives,
motivations for social justice activism, and individual actions from
community organizing to broader social movements.

Born in 1930, Dolores Huerta spent much of her life fighting for
the rights of farm workers in California and throughout the United
States. Huerta was (and still is) an outspoken, confrontational, and

assertive union leader. In 1955, Huerta founded the Community Service Organization's (CSO) branch in Stockton, California, where she met César Chávez. Huerta and Chávez decided that farm workers deserved the right to unionize for greater protection than what the CSO could offer (Ferriss & Sandoval, 1997), so in 1962, Dolores Huerta and César Chávez cofounded the Farm Workers Association (FWA), which eventually became the UFW. FWA activities started with membership drives and, beginning in 1965, quickly moved to a series of strikes and boycotts. The UFW obtained successful collective bargaining agreements between farm workers and growers; established union contracts that provided rest breaks, toilets, drinking water, protections against pesticide exposure, and farm worker seniority and job security; and developed programs for a farm worker health plan, pension plan, and credit union. The UFW became the strongest and best-known advocate for farm workers' rights, helping to ensure greater protections for US farm workers. Dolores Huerta played an integral role in the UFW, as cofounder; vice president; key negotiator with growers; advisor to Chávez; lobbyist in Washington, DC, and Sacramento; and boycott organizer.

As the president of the FWA, César Chávez served as the primary spokesperson for the organization, but Huerta's commitment and assertiveness drew attention to her vice-presidential role, especially within the union. Griswold del Castillo and Garcia (1995) explain that

> César Chávez and Dolores Huerta had a symbiotic relationship. Chávez was the visible leader and Huerta was the "hidden" one. He functioned as the catalyst; she was the engine. Most people did not realize the qualities Huerta brought to the Farm Workers Association: personal strength, communication skills, an ethic of work, an intellectual approach, and a strong sense of self. Farm workers listened to her; young Chicanas followed her. . . . To understand Chávez and the union, we must also understand Huerta. (p. 59)

Huerta was well known for her stamina, often working eighteen-hour days, earning between five and thirty-five dollars a week, and living on donated food, clothing, and shelter (Felner, 1998; Rose, 2004). She also raised and supported eleven children and was twice divorced. While she traveled throughout California and the East Coast supporting boycotts, membership drives, and lobbying efforts, many of Huerta's children lived with union families or the Chávez family. Juggling her career as a social justice activist, community organizer, and union leader was no small feat along with her role as a mother, and at times, as a single (divorced) mother.

Part of Huerta's recognition came from her charismatic and assertive leadership style, as evidenced in numerous reports (e.g., Baer, 1975; "A Life-Time Commitment," 1979; Speer, April 19, 1977; April 26, 1977). She was referred to as Adelita ("the symbolic *soldadera* [female soldier] of the Mexican Revolution") (Ruiz, 1998, p. 134), "La Pasionaria (the passionate one)" (M. T. García, 2008, p. xv), General Patton, and the Grand Lady of Steel (Foster, 1996). She was described frequently as a powerful, dynamic, and eloquent speaker (Speer, April 19, 1977; April 26, 1977). Her speeches usually began with gratitude to the organizers. The content that followed was tailored to the specific audience, ranging from farm workers to student activists to politicians. If speaking to farm workers, she often spoke entirely in Spanish, whereas for non-Spanish speaking audiences, she might use only a few Spanish language words, translating or explaining the meaning to her audience. Her speech content focused on contextual issues of the moment for each particular audience. For example, a 1974 speech for the American Public Health Association included specific references to health care policy and the health concerns facing farm workers (Huerta, "Keynote Address," 1974). The speech was entirely in English, except at the very end, when Huerta closed in the way that she always did, with gritos (yells) such as "Viva La Causa!" (long live the cause!) and "Abajo! Down with lettuce and grapes!" (p. 8). These gritos were part of audience engagement and inspiration to take action on farm worker causes and other social justice issues. In other speeches, depending on the audience, Huerta talked more about her personal involvement and experiences in farm worker organizing. The adaptation, engagement, and personal narrative were all signature aspects of her speaking style.

This book seeks to understand Huerta's rhetorical legacy and iconic status, as well as the reasons for her obfuscation in historical and contemporary accounts of the farm worker movement. The extensive historical, political, rhetorical, sociological, and biographical writings on Chávez often overlook the vital role that Huerta played in the UFW's movement. In many Chávez biographies and UFW histories, Huerta is barely mentioned (e.g., full-length books on Chávez and the

UFW include Bardacke, 2012; Ferriss & Sandoval, 1997; Ganz, 2009; M. T. García, 2007; Garcia, 2012; Griswold del Castillo & Garcia, 1995; Levy, 2007; Hammerback & Jensen, 1998; Jensen & Hammerback, 2002; Pawel, 2009, 2014; Yinger, 1975). Furthermore, no full-length book about Huerta has been written besides a few children's books (M. Brown, 2010; Warren, 2012). While the 2014 film about the UFW featured a character role of Dolores Huerta, the film was titled *Cesar Chavez* (Cruz et al., 2014). The only significant works about Dolores Huerta are the documentary film *Dolores* (Bratt & Bensen, 2017) and Mario García's (2008) reader on Dolores Huerta. This inattention often suggests that as a leader, Chávez single-handedly achieved the successes of the UFW, when in reality, there were many other actors who contributed to the movement in significant ways. This book expands extant UFW and Chicana/o movement[1] documentation and histories to account more fully for Huerta's role as a leader in the UFW.

This project also addresses how she was able to negotiate dominant stereotypes of the era regarding race, ethnicity, gender, class, language, and religion to become one of the UFW's top leaders. During the height of the farm worker movement in the late 1960s and early 1970s, Huerta was a strong speaker, negotiator, lobbyist, and UFW spokesperson, but she also faced considerable material, political, and social constraints. Her citizenship, upbringing, fluency in English and Spanish, college education, and family afforded her some privileges. Yet her racial and ethnic background as a Mexican American woman meant that she also faced significant gender and racial discrimination throughout her life and activism on behalf of the UFW. Furthermore,

---

1. I use the phrase "Chicana/o movement" to describe the movements of the 1960s and 1970s that were really comprised of a number of activist gestures, such as Reies Tijerina's Alianza land movement in New Mexico, Rodolfo "Corky" Gonzáles's work in Colorado, the walkouts/blowouts in California led by Sal Castro and his students, the farm worker movement, and other social justice initiatives (see Delgado, 1995; M. T. García, 2015; Hammerback & Jensen, 1980; Jensen & Hammerback, 1982). Many scholars, activists, and writers at the time called these activists' work the Chicano Movement, which it is still often called today. Because I am writing about the historical context of the UFW, I also have not used the more contemporary term, Chicanx. Much scholarship on and about social movements was not gender neutral, and *Chicanx* and *Latinx* are terms that emerge in the 21st century as ways to move beyond gender binaries (e.g., de Onís, 2017).

many social movements at the time were male-led; female leaders were often criticized for complaints about sexism or gendered aspects of social movements. A number of Latina and Chicana scholars have addressed the tensions for female leaders during the 1960s and 1970s. For some Chicanas, as Catherine Ramírez (2009) contends, feminism and women's rights conflicted with other social justice issues, such as racial discrimination and the plight of the poor. There was also the association of feminism with white and middle-class women. Chicanas who labeled themselves feminists were often considered sellouts or traitors to the Chicana/o movement. Vicki Ruiz argues that Chicana feminists were called agringadas (acting white) for focusing on women's issues when other Chicanas and Chicanos were saying, "Our enemy is the gavacho [white man] not the macho" (Ruiz, 1998, p. 108). Anna NietoGomez, in her seminal essay "La Feminista," explains that many in the Chicana/o movement saw feminism as a white women's cause.

Vicki Ruiz (1998) further notes that many male leaders in the Chicana/o movement did not acknowledge the problems women faced within the movement, such as gendered assignments, lack of recognition for their work, or playing behind-the-scenes roles, even though women were very active and worked hard for various causes:

> Women did not stand on the sidelines. They distributed food, formed picket lines, taunted scabs, and, when attacked by the police, fought back. . . . As they did in labor camps and colonias, women's networks offered physical and emotional support. As channels for political and labor activism, they also fused private life and public space in pursuit of social justice. (p. 75)

Chicanas were expected to remain in the shadows of their male counterparts in the Chicana/o and UFW movements (Pesquera & de la Torre, 1993). Chicana leaders also faced gender discrimination and threats of sexual violence from within the Chicana/o movement (M. T. García, 2015). While many leaders of the Chicana/o movement focused on class and racial inequities, the intersectional aspects of gender were important to Chicana feminists and were not easily separated from other practices of discrimination. Chávez played a critical role in Huerta's leadership legacy, but he also engaged in (often gendered) name-calling and criticisms of her. He has been considered a soft-spoken leader who embraced nonviolence, but journalists and historians have revealed other aspects of his internal leadership of the UFW (e.g., Bardacke, 2012; Garcia 2012; Pawel, 2014).

In order to more fully understand Dolores Huerta's life and rhetorical legacy, this book advances three arguments. These arguments form the crux of the overarching theoretical goal of this book, to examine the nature of rhetorical agency and its relationship among individual actors and broader social justice activism. I understand rhetorical agency as the interplay of three facets: intersectional habitus that shapes identities, identities that solidify public personae through differential bravery, and public personae that enable collaborative social activism. First, Huerta's iconic status originated in her early family life, in which habitus, or one's early life experiences, has profound impact on the people we become. Her familial and educational influences, coupled with her complicated yet supportive relationship with César Chávez, as illustrated in their private communication, reflect the many ways in which habitus plays a role in one's identities and activities. However, that intersectional habitus is only one component of rhetorical agency. The second key argument in this book focuses on how private identity lays the groundwork for a public persona. In the case of Huerta, her public persona involves two components: her womanhood/motherhood and her optimistic, social justice orientation. Taken together, her rhetoric of family/motherhood and optimism/justice form the basis of Huerta's public rhetoric and leadership styles and what I call differential bravery. Finally, I argue that habitus, along with private communication and an identity that leads to the development of a public persona, is the foundation for actors who become icons within social movements.

Situating Dolores Huerta in Rhetorical Scholarship

Rhetorical scholars have studied the Chicana/o and farm worker movements of the 1960s and 1970s (Delgado, 1995; Hammerback & Jensen, 1980, 1994, 1998; Hammerback, Jensen, & Gutierrez, 1985; Jensen, Burkholder, & Hammerback, 2003; Jensen & Hammerback, 2002; Yinger, 1975), yet these studies focus on male leadership and overlook women's roles in these movements and other types of political activism. This scholastic gap effectually erases women like Dolores Huerta, Helen Chávez, Jessica Govea, Hope López, and others from Chicana/o and farm worker movement history. For example, John Hammerback and Richard Jensen have written extensively about the rhetorical legacy of César Chávez, yet their work gives only passing reference to Dolores Huerta. In their 1985 book (written with Jose Angel Gutierrez), *A War of Words: Chicano Protest in the 1960s and 1970s*, Huerta is mentioned once. In their 1998 book, *The Rhetorical Career of César Chávez*, Huerta is mentioned six times, cited for her comments about Chávez's leadership style. None of these references elaborate on Huerta's contributions or her leadership within the UFW. One recent study examines Huerta's rhetorical style through the lens of the shifting transcendent persona (Doss & Jensen, 2013), and my own work has examined the rhetorical aspects of letter writing (Sowards, 2012) and rhetorical caras (faces) through an analysis of Huerta's words, speeches, interviews, testimonies, and other documents (Sowards, 2010). Building on these works, this book seeks to provide a more nuanced understanding of Huerta's rhetorical legacy and role as a Chicana leader.

Not only has Huerta been overlooked in rhetorical scholarship, but César Chávez has received credit for ideas that Huerta claims were hers, suggesting that she has also been overlooked in historical scholarship, with a few exceptions (Griswold del Castillo & Garcia, 1995; Rose, 1988, 1990a, 1990b, 2004). For instance, Jensen and Hammerback discuss how Chávez converted the name of a neighborhood he had lived in, "*Sal Si Puedes* (get out if you can)," to "*Si, se puede* (Yes, we can),"[2] which has long been used as a rallying cry for the UFW (Jensen & Hammerback, 2002, p. xix). Yet Huerta has said that she was the person who initiated "Sí, se puede" as a rallying cry (Huerta, 2003; Godoy, 2017), and Chávez himself gave credit to Huerta for using "Sí se

---

2. Spanish grammar conventions require an accent on *sí* when translated to mean yes (*si* means if). Because many writers in the United States did not have access to typewriters or computer programs that allowed the insertion of accents, often accents were/are not included in Spanish language words. In cases where authors did not include accents, I have not included them either, when quoting their materials. Here, Jensen and Hammerback (2002) do not include the accent on "*sí*," nor do they note that "*sí, se puede*" can be translated as "yes, we can," "yes, one can," or "it can be done." "*Se puede*" in Spanish is generally used to reflect the absence of an actor or the passive voice; in this case it can be translated in several different ways. This phrase is a registered trademark of the UFW, even though it is a common rallying cry for Spanish speakers in the United States and Spanish-speaking countries like Mexico.

puede" in the farm worker movement (Levy, 2007). Many of Huerta's contributions may have been misattributed to Chávez, without recognizing her role in those union activities. As Margaret Rose observes, "Such male-centered interpretations have distorted the history of the UFW and the role of women in its development" (Rose, 1990a, p. 26). Biographies and histories that focus on Chávez as the leader of the UFW also erase a history of collaboration and how such leaders become the face of movements, social justice causes, and organizations. Margaret Rose (2004) has also made similar arguments in her studies of Chicana and Mexican women's participation in the farm worker movement, as she calls the union formation and subsequent movement a collaboration between Huerta and Chávez.

Dolores Huerta's rhetorical styles are especially useful exemplars of how women from places of marginality negotiate intersectional identities of gender, race, ethnicity, language, and class. Several scholars have argued that women, especially historically, often employ different rhetorical styles, such as "feminine" styles that include practices like relying on personal experiences and tone, structuring arguments inductively, inviting audience participation, addressing the audience as peers, basing authority on experience, creating identification with audience, and focusing holistically on relationships (Blankenship & Robson, 1995; Campbell, 1989; Daughton, 1995; Dow & Tonn, 1993; Hayden, 1999). Michael Calvin McGee (1980a) discusses the "feminization" of power, which focuses on leadership styles that emphasize gentleness, caring for others, and goodwill of the people. Karlyn Kohrs Campbell (1986, 1989, 1995) has also observed that some women enact diverse rhetorical styles. For example, Mari Boor Tonn (1996) examines what she calls "militant motherhood" in the rhetoric of Mother Jones, who used both feminine (mothering) and masculine (militant) rhetorical styles (see also Hayden, 2003; Japp, 1985).

However, Raka Shome (1996) problematizes "the generalized notion of a 'woman's or feminist rhetorical or communication perspective,' which is often articulated by feminists in the discipline" (p. 53). She argues that nonwhite women may negotiate rhetorical situations very differently because of their diverse cultural backgrounds. Shanara Rose Reid-Brinkley (2012) also critiques theories of feminine style for failing to consider and include intersectional aspects of identity, such as race. Black women, for example, may have to employ double voice because "[s]uch a rhetorical strategy is dependent on simultaneity:

training in black discourse communities, its values, beliefs, and socio-linguistic rituals, but also a mastery of the discursive practices of white-ness" (p. 39). Similarly, other communication studies interrogate the assumptions of Chicanas' rhetorical practices, suggesting that feminine style theory and analysis must, at the very least, consider intersectional identities or must be questioned altogether as useful theories (Flores, 1996; Holling, 2000; Palczewski, 1996). Recovery of women's rhetoric has been an important project for several decades (e.g., Blankenship & Robson, 1995; Borda, 2002; Campbell, 1989; Zaeske, 1995, 2002), but few rhetorical studies have examined Latina/Chicana voices in social movements, with a few exceptions, such as Enck-Wanzer's (2010) anal-ysis of women's roles and rhetoric in the (Puerto Rican) Young Lords movement in New York and Michelle Holling's (2012) study of Emma Tenayuca. As this book demonstrates, Dolores Huerta's rhetoric pro-vides a compelling example of how marginalized women might nego-tiate their circumstances in different ways and questions the value of theories of the feminine style. Huerta drew on gendered aspects of identity, such as motherhood, as a key rhetorical tactic, complicating how we understand intersectional rhetoric and rhetorical agency.

Overview of *¡Sí, Ella Puede!*: The Rhetorical Legacy of Dolores Huerta and the United Farm Workers

As the most famous Chicana leader of the 1960s and 1970s whose legacy continues today, understanding Huerta's rhetorical and historical con-tributions is essential for knowing more about intersectional issues re-lated to class, race, gender, ethnicity, and national origin, as well as cul-tural and political icons, social movements, social justice, civil rights, and the history of the Chicana/o and UFW movements themselves. Huerta's lower- to middle-class background and status as a Mexican American resident of the US Southwest and California speak to the experience of many Chicanas and Latinas in the United States. Few of these women's lives have been well documented; Huerta provides an opportunity to look at the life and rhetorical legacy of one such Chicana who came from both typical and atypical circumstances, in that she and her family knew farm workers intimately but were mostly not farm workers themselves. Her family was not wealthy, but she did go to college to earn an associate's degree. In essence, Huerta's life runs against the stereotype of the downtrodden farm worker, yet she experienced significant racism, sexism, classism, ethnocentrism, and other forms of discrimination.

To better understand the rhetorical legacy of Dolores Huerta, this book relies on a wide range of primary texts that were obtained through archival research (including public statements, speeches, congressional testimonies, UFW organizational documents, and private letters) and publicly documented interviews, speeches, books, and articles. This project started when I was living in Detroit, Michigan, and I stumbled across the UFW archive at Wayne State University in 2000. Some of these archival materials can be found in Mario García's 2008 book, which is a collection of articles, interviews, and a few letters about or by Huerta. Much of this book's analysis stems from studying the texts in the archival materials obtained from the UFW archive at Wayne State University's Walter P. Reuther Library; the Beinecke Library at Yale University; the Farmworker Movement Documentation Project at the University of California, San Diego, library; and the University of California, Los Angeles, Chicano Studies Research Center.

More recent materials from the 2000s were used for analysis as well. These include public speeches, interviews, and articles. To understand how Huerta remembers her own contributions and the history of the UFW, I attended some of her speaking events in California, New Mexico, and Texas from 2001 to 2017, recording and documenting those speeches. In 2006, at the height of the immigrant rights protests and marches, I arranged for her to speak at my university and in the El Paso community. I also formally interviewed her and spoke with her in casual conversation. Archival materials, ethnography, and interviews are the three methodological approaches employed for the analyses in this book. Attending her speeches and having Huerta stay at my house deeply informed my understanding of her positionality as an activist, mother, and Chicana. For example, one speech I attended on March 9, 2002, was at a Mexican restaurant in Rialto, California, and sponsored by the Mexican American Political Association's Rialto chapter. I vividly remember the birria (Mexican stew type dish) that was served for breakfast and the prayer that started the meeting. The audience consisted of about fifty people, and Huerta spoke about political organizing and UFW history. The breakfast, combined with the small audience, created an intimate and connected setting.

By contrast, the speech that I organized at The University of Texas at El Paso in 2006 had an audience of over 500 people and was very emotionally charged because of the immigrant rights protests that were happening at the time all over the United States. Another speech I organized during this same trip to El Paso was at a dinner held at La Mujer Obrera; mole enchiladas were served. Huerta spoke to an audience of about 200 people. I picked her up from the airport, and she stayed at my house, at her request. She told me at the time that she preferred to stay in people's homes to save money and because it was more comfortable. The following night, she stayed at her cousin's home in El Paso. These events were different in scope, context, and audience but represented different aspects of her life philosophy in small ways. Over coffee in the morning at my house, she told me that raising her children was her most important accomplishment and subtly encouraged me to have children of my own (at the time, I had not yet had my daughter). She was daytime fasting in solidarity with the immigrants' rights protestors, a long time UFW strategy to call attention to the cause. These aspects of meeting Dolores Huerta and talking with her informed the way that I think about her as an activist and a person but are not directly discussed in the analysis of her private and public personae for this book. They also are part of how I understand Huerta's rhetorical legacy and iconic status as a civil rights leader. In meeting her and hearing her speak, it is clear that a broad sense of civil rights and social justice has infused every moment of her life from a very early age to today. She is generous and caring to those who face social injustices. When she came to El Paso for the screening of the *Dolores* film, I was struck by her energy and tirelessness. She took pictures with every single person who wanted one, often for hours after the film's screenings. She seemed to understand what she represents to the El Paso community, a mix of people who include activists in the Chicana/o and UFW movements, millennial Chicanx and Latinx, children and their parents, local politicians, and those interested in social justice.

In addition to pursuing ethnographic participation and participant observation as an audience member at Huerta's speeches and in interviews with Huerta, I also analyzed her rhetorical (speaking and writing) styles, her words, and her embodied performances. As several scholars contend, this type of field and textual methodological approach reveals more about the different kinds of texts, contexts, audiences, judgments, and ethics involved in analyzing someone like Huerta (McKinnon, Asen, Chávez, & Howard, 2016). Phaedra Pezzullo and Catalina de Onís (2017) argue that situating rhetorical studies within an understanding of culture, interconnection ("location matters"), and voice (listening and amplification) is important for providing deep and nuanced meanings of texts (2017, pp. 7–9). The analysis of historical documents and texts is also important for recovering Huerta's voice and uncovering her dynamic personae of the 1960s, 1970s, and 1980s, periods in which I did not have the opportunity to see Huerta speak. Rhetorical criticism also relies on theoretical analysis; in this case, I use Pierre Bourdieu's concept of habitus to examine the influence of her early life and how it shaped her private and public communication as an adult. To better understand her public persona, I use the work of Gloria Anzaldúa on haciendo caras (making faces) and Chela Sandoval's concept of differential consciousness to illustrate how leaders who become iconic come to see themselves, particularly within social movement contexts. Huerta's public persona also speaks to the importance of such public figures in how others remember civil rights movements. Furthermore, I argue that Huerta's rhetoric illustrates a form of rhetorical agency—that is, how one uses communication (of all types) to create space and advance social justice, enabled by contexts and relationships with others.

While the first chapter provides an overview of the history of farm worker organizing and the inception of the UFW union, the remaining chapters of this book focus on how Huerta became such an important civil rights leader for both the UFW and other social justice movements. To understand Huerta's leadership in the UFW, chapter two develops a theoretical framework related to rhetorical agency. Specifically, using Pierre Bourdieu's (1990) concept of habitus, the social circumstances that enable and/or prevent one's sense of agency, I explore the importance of actors and their relationships within the concept of rhetorical agency. Put differently, rhetorical efficacy originates in social contexts in which the rhetor[3] resides and is not simply a product of the self. Intersectional habitus considers the way in which race, gender, class, language, and other social standings enable and constrain rhetorical agency. This chapter also provides more biographical information about Huerta's life, showing how early influences shaped her habitus and adult persona, which is particularly important for Huerta, as she became known for her outspoken leadership style.

---

3. The rhetor is the person or people who create rhetoric, such as a speaker, writer, producer, director, or other creator.

In chapter three, I analyze how Huerta's habitus informed the development of her private persona as an activist and a leader in the letters she wrote to Chávez, particularly in the early days of the UFW. Huerta wrote numerous letters to Chávez to document organizational activities, to request and give advice, and to ask for assistance. Specifically, in this chapter I argue that her letters function collaboratively, affirmatively, and cathartically. Huerta used these letters as a primary form of communication to collaborate with Chávez on UFW activities as well as other social issues. She also used these letters to affirm her commitment to and role within the UFW by outlining her numerous accomplishments. Finally, she used the letters as cathartic release from the financial, emotional, and familial problems she faced, given that she was trying to raise her children while working eighteen-hour days for the UFW.

Chapter four moves to Huerta's creation of a public persona as an outspoken leader and savvy negotiator for the UFW. An examination of her public speeches demonstrates how she crafted this persona in various ways, strategically employing emotionality, motherhood, and familia. For example, crying has long been a disavowed rhetorical style, yet Huerta regularly used tears to connect with audiences or to make a point. Similarly, she used her own family as a way to construct the union as a metaphorical family. Since many UFW members thought of union families as part of their own, Huerta's children often stayed with the Chávez or other union families. She also brought her children to picket lines, protests, boycotts, and bargaining sessions. In essence, she constructed and expanded her public persona through her work and family simultaneously. In this chapter, I also employ Gloria Anzaldúa's (1990) term haciendo caras (making face, making soul) to explain the physical and psychological aspects of negotiating social circumstances.

The following chapter addresses Huerta's persona centered on collaborative social justice and optimism. In particular, UFW chants of "viva la causa" (long live the cause) or "abajo con injusticia" (down with injustice) reflect collaborative speech making that embodies Huerta's approach to getting farm workers and other people involved in social justice causes. The topics of her public discourse have concerned a wide range of issues, such as farm workers' rights, women's rights, gay and lesbian rights, environmental issues, and health care access. In addition, she often included calls for greater public participation in social movements, social justice causes, and politics, observing that people at all levels of society can get involved. Related to her commitment to social justice and egalitarianism, Huerta also strongly believed in the UFW campaigns and made those goals her personal mission. This chapter also explores the role of optimism, hope, and faith in Huerta's rhetoric. Her interviews and speeches demonstrate how she developed a sense of courage to voice her strong opinions. Huerta became one of the most powerful union negotiators and lobbyists through her ability to speak confidently and optimistically, relying on her faith and Catholicism to connect with herself, farm workers, and broader audiences. As such, her rhetoric forms the basis for understanding differential bravery, expanding concepts of differential consciousness, belonging, and vision.

Chapter six explores how Huerta's early life and relationship with Chávez (chapters two and three) shaped her public persona (chapters four and five), which, in turn, created a rhetorical legacy and, in the case of Huerta, established her as a Chicana leader and social movement icon. However, Huerta's iconic status has led to criticisms of her, Chávez, and the UFW. This chapter outlines those criticisms, Huerta's responses to those criticisms, and her contemporary status as an icon to explore the complicated nature of icons in relationship to social movements.

The epilogue concludes the book and theorizes how rhetorical agency functions beyond Huerta's rhetoric and her ability to negotiate barriers related to race, ethnicity, gender, motherhood, class status, language, and cultural expectations. Huerta's rhetoric shapes understandings of rhetorical agency through intersectional habitus, flexibility, optimism, differential bravery, and transformative effects for both self and other. Huerta's negotiation of social and material forces stems from the social, economic, and political aspects of her upbringing, as well as her relationships with people like César Chávez. Such familial and social relationships also helped her to create a private and public persona of collaborative transformation, expanding beyond herself as individual to her significant contributions to larger social movements. Although Huerta was an exceptional and unique UFW spokesperson and leader, the study of her discourse facilitates deeper understanding of rhetorical agency, social movements, and how women might relate to and capitalize on their intersectional identities to engage in rhetorical agency through some of the rhetorical options Huerta employed, such as courage, optimism, faith, family, and motherhood.

Chapter 1

FARM WORKER ORGANIZING AND THE ADVENT OF THE UFW: 1900 TO 1993

By the time I was 25 years old, I had been married and gotten a divorce. I was still living in Stockton [California] when Fred Ross came into town and he started telling us about forming this organization, the Community Service Organization (CSO). And he told us about how in Los Angeles they had sent these policemen to San Quentin for beating up a Mexican. At that time, I didn't even talk about things like that publicly. Everybody knew that the cops did it, but you just accepted it. Now these two cops were sent to San Quentin and Fred had organized it. . . . But I always thank the day that I met Fred. I always hated injustice and I always wanted to do something to change things. Fred opened a door for me. He changed my whole life. (Huerta, January 25, 1973)

Dolores Huerta came to farm worker organizing in a historical context that provided the impetus for strike and boycott success. As she noted in the essay published in *La Voz del Pueblo* in 1973 excerpted above, the 1950s were the beginning of social change in terms of civil rights for Mexicans, Mexican Americans, and Chicana/os living in Los Angeles and elsewhere, in part, because of the community organizing efforts of the CSO, headed by Fred Ross. It was this organization, buttressed by changing social and political contexts, as well as her hatred of injustice, that led to her involvement in first the CSO and later the UFW.

This chapter explores three crucial contexts that undergird Dolores Huerta's rhetorical legacy in the UFW and beyond. First, I trace a brief history of farm worker organizing from the 1900s to the end of the 1950s to establish the rhetorical context from which the UFW emerged. Then, I discuss a brief history of how the UFW evolved into an organized social movement in the period from 1960 to 1972. The final time period marks the UFW's declining influence beginning in 1972 until the death of César Chávez in 1993. These three time periods frame Huerta's life from childhood almost through to her retirement from the UFW at the turn of the 21st century. Understanding these contexts also illustrates the challenges, opportunities, constraints, and enabling factors that Huerta faced as one of the most important Chicana leaders of the 20th century.

Farm Worker Organizing: 1900 to 1960

After California achieved statehood in 1850, the privatization of public land led to large-scale properties used for, first, ranching and then, later, agriculture (Ganz, 2009). At the turn of the 20th century, California had yet to become the major agricultural center that it is today, but farm workers still faced significant obstacles in obtaining workers' rights and benefits, in part because many farm workers were immigrants who did not have high levels of education or English-language skills. During this period, there were some attempts to organize farm workers, but it was not until 1962 that such efforts were successful, when Dolores Huerta, César Chávez, and others came together to organize as the Farm Workers Association (FWA). In the late 19th century and early part of the 20th century, expanding land use and agricultural markets (such as wheat) increased the numbers of farm workers needed, many of whom came from some 12,000 unemployed Chinese laborers who had worked on building the railroads that were completed in 1869. According to Ganz, the Chinese workers were not allowed to become US citizens or to work in most other industries, so they did not have many options for earning a living: "Growers, in other words, learned how to recruit a workforce too powerless to give them much trouble—a workforce of impoverished new immigrants, noncitizens, and people of color" (2009, p. 24). As Natalia Molina argues, rising capitalistic labor markets created more opportunities for low-end employment of nonwhite and noncitizens: "capitalism needs race and gender to create endless new forms of seemingly natural divisions that allow exploitation to take place" (2014, p. 10). Markets for wheat and then fruits and vegetables east of California opened with the increased use of railroads, refrigerated transport, and these unemployed Chinese laborers. However, the 1882 Chinese Exclusion Act prevented additional Chinese migrants from coming to the United States; many also returned to China to their families (who were barred from migrating to the United States). To fill these labor shortages in the early part of the 20th century, Japanese migrants, Sikhs, and southern Europeans were also recruited for farm work.

By 1920, California agriculture had expanded from 1 million to 4.2 million acres of irrigated farmland (Ganz, 2009). The four major agricultural valleys in California (the Imperial, Coachella, San Joaquín, and Salinas Valleys) also benefitted significantly from investment in damming major rivers (Bardacke, 2012; Garcia, 2012). These changes in the Californian topography led to significant agricultural output and a large number of workers employed in the industry. However, this growth also created labor shortages, which became one of the factors that enabled effective organizing, even if such efforts were not able to achieve long-term unionization and other farm workers' rights until the 1960s (Ganz, 2009). Ganz identifies three key periods of organizing in which workers were able to capitalize on labor shortages before the advent of the UFW: 1900–1920, 1933–1942, and 1946–1951. These three periods were somewhat successful because labor shortages provided leverage to organizers, but ultimately, either the short-term nature of such shortages or other aspects of the social and cultural contexts prevented long-term success.

In the first wave of organizing during the first twenty years of the 20th century, Japanese and Filipino migrants formed effective organizing groups (Ganz, 2009). Since racial exclusion (through both legislation and socioeconomic discriminatory practices) prevented widespread organization, these migrants mostly organized through piecemeal approaches. Ganz contends that they had two strategies: First, the Japanese workers gained control of the market by accepting low wages and getting a lot of their people into the farms, giving them the power to later advocate for a strike or higher wages. A second approach used by Japanese farm worker groups was to save money and then purchase their own farms. If the Japanese immigrants were not eligible to own land due to laws prohibiting Japanese ownership, then their American-born children or other agents were employed as title-holders. As for Mexican farm workers, the 1917 Immigration Act restricted Mexican immigration through "requirements of literacy and the payment of a head tax" (Rose, 2004, p. 212). But when the United States entered World War I in 1917, white farm workers started moving to urban jobs. Agricultural growers effectively lobbied for wartime exclusions that led to the suspension of the 1917 Immigration Act. This allowed the Mexican farm worker labor market to expand to over

71,000 new workers and resulted in further ineffectiveness in attempts to organize farm workers since there were so many available (Ganz, 2009; Rose, 2004). During and after World War I, growers continued to be extremely effective at keeping a steady workforce by recruiting Mexican and Filipino farm workers. Mexicans were exempt from immigration quota laws, and the Immigration Act of 1917 was rarely enforced, enabling Mexican and Filipino farm workers to flood the workforce. This facilitated growers' move away from Japanese farm workers, who had been more effective in their organizing efforts. The Johnson-Reed Immigration Act of 1924 was also significant in defining, limiting, and outright banning immigrant groups, such as southern and eastern Europeans and Asians (Councilor, 2017; Molina, 2014).

The Depression era (1929–1942) also significantly impacted California's agricultural industries, but as Ganz notes, the passage of President Roosevelt's National Industrial Recovery Act (1933) revived efforts to organize and unionize workers. In California, this meant the rise of organizers and leaders in the Communist Party's Trade Union Unity League, the American Federation of Labor (AFL), and the Congress of Industrial Organizations (CIO). Ethnic leaders who represented different ethnic communities of farm workers were encouraged to participate in such organizing efforts through organizational subsidiaries, such as the Communists' Cannery and Agricultural Workers Industrial Union (CAWIU) and the United Cannery, Agricultural Packing, and Allied Workers of America (UCAPAWA). Ethnic leadership was essential to the success or failure of such movements, since many farm workers were of nonwhite backgrounds, unlike their counterparts in other industries, such as canning, packing, and transport. The 1933 strikes led by CAWIU were quite successful, especially the Pixley cotton strike, but contributed to the death of three strikers (Ganz, 2009; Ruiz, 1998). However, other CAWIU strikes, such as the 1934 lettuce strike, were not as productive because the growers were more prepared to respond violently. The growers then organized themselves to put pressure on politicians to support the agricultural industries and prevent such labor organizing efforts.

In 1935, the National Labor Relations Act (NLRA) was passed, but agricultural workers were excluded from protections under the NLRA because of growers' successful lobbying efforts with senators from the southern and western states, demonstrating increased racial discrimination in labor organizing, since most industrial workers were white (Bardacke, 2012; Ganz, 2009; Garcia, 2012; Pawel, 2014). As the CIO and AFL competed to organize mostly white cannery workers, they abandoned farm workers, in part because such workers were not covered under the NLRA. In 1937, California began to experience internal migration from other parts of the United States, such as Oklahoma and Missouri, as part of the Dust Bowl migration (resulting from severe drought in the central US states) and the Great Depression. By 1939, many farm workers were white, a circumstance that attracted public support and sympathy through the documentation projects of famous authors and photographers such as John Steinbeck, Dorothea Lange, and others (Bardacke, 2012; Ganz, 2009; Ruiz, 1998). Bardacke (2012) notes that "[s]ome 400,000 of these Okies came to California between 1935 and 1939, and many of them headed directly for the fields, where they competed for disappearing jobs with the 200,000 mostly Mexican farm workers who were already there" (2012, p. 46). However, by 1941, with the pending US entry into World War II and labor markets shifting to wartime production, Congress passed legislation to allow growers to recruit braceros, or workers from Mexico, who could cover the growers' needs as the white Dust Bowl migrants returned to their home states or migrated to urban areas (Rose, 2004). While the country focused on production to fight in World War II, tight labor markets in agriculture once again appeared, but farm workers lost opportunities for effective mobilization as braceros from Mexico began to take over agricultural labor markets.

The post–World War II era led to the third wave of organizing attempts by farm workers from the late 1940s through the early 1950s. Again, competition for laborers was central to the AFL's effort to create a farm workers' union, then called the National Farm Labor Union (NFLU). According to Marshall Ganz (2009), the NFLU used two approaches: secondary boycotts and government lobbying to constrict labor markets. The bracero program played a major role in the failure of these approaches, as evidenced by the strike against the DiGiorgio Fruit Corporation, a large fruit distributor and wine company (Ganz, 2009). The braceros were threatened with deportation if they continued the strike, so most of them went back to work. Similar NFLU strategies also failed as the federal government continued to support growers' needs and demands to produce agriculture. This wave of organizing ended when Congress passed Public Law 78 which ensured the continuation of the bracero program through 1965 (Garcia, 2012). These three periods shaped organizing efforts that failed because growers were able to find alternative sources for their workers (e.g., the braceros or Dust Bowl migrants), and organizers were not able to come together and join forces to successfully organize.

The 1950s saw continued efforts to organize farm workers despite the powerful bracero program, which prevented groups from capitalizing on labor shortages. The AFL and CIO had merged into the AFL-CIO by this point, and the joint organizations launched the Agricultural Workers Organizing Committee (AWOC) in 1959. The Community Service Organization, an organization focused on voter registration and other issues facing poor communities, expressed some interest in helping farm workers. Fred Ross, the head of the CSO, recruited Dolores Huerta, César Chávez, and Gilbert Padilla (all of whom would go on to cofound the FWA in 1962) to work at the CSO. The International Brotherhood of Teamsters, an organization long focused on transport workers and related industries, also started to organize farm workers, as they were involved in a number of operations related to agriculture. These three organizations, the Agricultural Workers Organizing Committee (under AFL-CIO), the CSO, and the Teamsters, became central to farm worker organizing success in the 1960s and beyond.

Another significant factor in supporting farm workers and other impoverished workers was the community organization. Throughout the period leading up to the civil rights movements of the 1960s, many Mexican and Mexican American communities in the United States relied on community organizations such as mutualistas. As Vicki Ruiz (1998) explains, the mutualista was (and still is) a place of community self-help that connected communities and families to services such as health care, medical clinics, educational services, libraries, and help with immigration problems. In particular, these organizations were a big draw for women, as Ruiz contends: "Women, through *mutualistas*, sought to help their neighbors; they worked within their communities in a public way, although their labor generally remained invisible outside the barrio" (1998, p. 88). The mutualista, then, functioned as a space where women could be active, politically and socially, albeit somewhat behind-the-scenes. Unlike Chicana and Mexicana activists in public protests, women's involvement in mutualistas was encouraged and respected (Ruiz, 1998).

Despite these efforts to organize and gain protections, farm workers still faced many problems in the fields. As Miriam Pawel (2014) explains, older workers had no job security, safety provisions were few and far between, women were sexually harassed, and there were no bathrooms or drinking water available in the fields. Growers set wages at uncompetitive rates; undercounted production when farm workers were paid by the piece, box, or pound; and changed wages depending on the season and type of produce. Furthermore, workers were not entitled to minimum wage rights and unemployment benefits. Workers often lived in poor housing conditions in growers' labor camps that had not been updated since their construction in the 1930s (Garcia, 2012). The housing units were essentially made out of tin, and the communities had very little access to bathrooms or running water. The work itself was very taxing. Workers put in long, hard days—they started early and ended late. Using the cortito, a short-handled hoe, required bending over virtually all day long. Even though some crops required skill and specialization with tools, such as the aperios or celery cutters, many growers of other crops were able to hire workers to fill their labor demands without making any accommodations at all (Bardacke, 2012). Given these circumstances, the FWA became an important force for farm worker rights.

The Rise of the United Farm Workers: 1960 to 1972

The 1960s and the 1970s became an important era for organizing farm workers, in part because of other social movements developing at the time, such as the Chicana/o movement, American Indian movement, women's rights movement, gay liberation movement, Black Power and freedom movements, environmental movement, student group protests, and Vietnam War protests (see M. T. García, 2015; Morris & Browne, 2013; Ramírez, 2009). Dolores Huerta remembered that there was "an ambience all around you that you could change the world" (in Bratt & Bensen, 2017). This era placed civil rights issues at the forefront of many people's minds, not only because of movement leaders themselves, but also because of news media coverage of events and issues (Ganz, 2009; Morris & Browne, 2013). Without these other movements simultaneously advancing their causes, a single movement or union would have seemed much more radical and been less likely to succeed. The extensive calls for civil rights reform during this time period also inevitably influenced and inspired Huerta and Chávez as they built their union and movement.

The 1965 farm worker strike has been called a starting point for the Chicana/o movement, although Chicana/o activists had been advocating for rights long before that (M. T. García, 2015; Ramírez, 2009). As Mario García (2015) contends,

> The Chicano movement was the largest and most widespread civil rights and empowerment struggle by Mexican Americans in US history. It combined the more traditional civil rights issues of the earlier Mexican American generation (1930–1960)—which pioneered struggles to desegregate the so-called Mexican schools in the Southwest, where the majority of Mexican Americans resided—with efforts to break down discriminatory barriers in jobs, housing, the legal system, and political representation and to eliminate cultural stereotyping. (p. 3)

Yet the farm worker and Chicana/o movements had their differences (Delgado, 1995; J. Brown, 1972). Student activists concentrated on issues beyond the labor focus of the UFW and worked to develop strong Chicana/o identities, taking a much more radical approach to organizing and protesting than the UFW. Still, the movements were both deeply invested in social justice for Chicana/os, Mexicana/os, and other marginalized peoples.

In addition to the civil rights movement context, the bracero program, which had formally started in 1942, was diminishing in popularity in Congress even though many agricultural lobbyists and growers still pushed for the use of temporary Mexican laborers because they filled temporary labor needs. As the bracero program was essential for alleviating tight labor markets (which also prevented successful organizing efforts), its eventual decline over the first half of the 1960s and end in 1965 meant that farm workers could more effectively organize. Braceros were also harder to organize than stable communities who lived near the agricultural fields long-term (Ganz, 2009; M. T. García, 2007; Garcia, 2012).

The emergence of three groups from within farm worker organizing efforts also created competition and leadership issues and the eventual formation of the UFW (Ganz, 2009). The AFL-CIO started the Agricultural Workers Organizing Committee (AWOC) in 1959, led by Al Green and Clyde Knowles (Garcia, 2012). However, one of the major problems for AWOC was its lack of involvement with farm workers and the communities themselves. One of the few ethnic minority organizers in AWOC was Ernesto Galarza, a Mexican American academic; however, he did not have strong ties to farm worker communities (Ganz, 2009). The Teamsters, expelled from the AFL-CIO for corruption issues in 1957, began their own organizing efforts in 1961. As Marshall Ganz (2009) contends, since the Teamsters controlled transport and management positions related to farm work, they were more interested in jurisdiction issues than in farm workers' rights. By attempting to organize farm workers, the Teamsters wanted to ensure their dominance in union organizing in the related industries that they already controlled.

The third group of farm worker organizers was initiated by César Chávez and Dolores Huerta, after Chávez's decision to resign from the CSO in protest of their decision to not develop a plan of action for farm worker organizing (Bardacke, 2012). On March 31, 1962, at a meeting of CSO leaders, Chávez thought that board members were going to support efforts to give more attention to farm workers. When they changed their minds, he resigned. This date, also coinciding with César Chávez's birthday, is considered the founding date of the FWA (which was later known as the National Farm Workers Association and then as the United Farm Workers). By September 1962, a temporary election of officers was held in which a president and eight vice presidents were elected. Although neither Huerta nor Chávez was part of this first election, Chávez served as the general director. In the permanent election in December of 1962, Chávez was elected president, and Huerta was elected vice president (one of ten vice presidents). Chávez noted the importance of Huerta's contributions, contending, "While Dolores and I were the architects of the National Farm Workers Association, Fred [Ross] helped us, and Manuel [Chávez's cousin] played a large role" (quoted in Levy, 2007, p. 166). Even though Huerta and Chávez resigned from their positions at the CSO and cofounded the FWA together, the CSO, along with Fred Ross, remained a major influence and supporter of the fledgling organization. Another major player was Chávez's wife, Helen. Although she operated more as a behind-the-scenes leader than Huerta did, she was instrumental in the formation of the new organization and activities that followed. She also acted as one of Chávez's key advisors and confidantes (Bardacke, 2012; Rose, 1990a, 1990b). As Huerta, Chávez, and another CSO organizer, Gilbert Padilla, became the leaders of the newly formed FWA, they continued to focus on the key principles, activities, and strategies of the CSO, including community-style organizing, such as house meetings, storytelling, and one-on-one organizing (Bardacke, 2012).

To grow into a fully functioning membership-based organization, the FWA focused on recruiting and providing services to its members, who were mostly Mexican or Mexican American. Some key contributions included the development of a credit union in January of 1964 and the establishment of a family death benefit. The official newspaper, *El Malcriado*, helped spread the word about farm worker organizing. Published in both Spanish and English, *El Malcriado* was distributed to grocery stores and other locations frequented by local area farm workers. Ganz argues that during these years, the NFWA "began to define itself not only as a union but also as a farm worker civil rights movement, a far more effective approach" than what AWOC and the Teamsters were doing during this same period (2009, p. 117). As the NFWA built momentum, they began to threaten agricultural growers with strikes. One of the important early strikes, which utilized an innovative strategy, was the Tulare County rent strike (Garcia, 2012). Instead of striking and picketing growers, the NFWA organized workers who lived in substandard conditions in labor camps to withhold rents in order to protest violations of tenants' rights. This rent strike increased support for the NFWA (Garcia, 2012) and calls for further strikes, such as those among rose and lettuce workers. Although those early attempts were not always successful, the groundwork was being prepared for the famous Delano strike of 1965–1966 and subsequent boycott efforts.

By 1965, the NFWA was still a fledgling organization trying to recruit members. However, the end of the bracero program, an excess of grape supply, and the context of the civil rights movement led to more favorable conditions for strike success. The NFWA itself was not ready to take on a massive strike effort, but Filipino workers who were organized under the AWOC went on strike on September 8, 1965, and asked the NFWA to join them. As Matt Garcia explains, "The AWOC action caught Chavez by surprise and forced upon him a decision about striking that he was not prepared to make" (2012, p. 40). Dolores Huerta was a key connection between the two groups, as she had long worked with Filipino farm workers while growing up in her mother's hotel and restaurant businesses (Garcia, 2012). This first AWOC strike targeted J. D. Martin's Rancho Blanco, and subsequently eight other grape growers in the Delano area. In a crucial meeting, held strategically on Mexican Independence Day (September 16, 1965) with AWOC and NWFA members, the NFWA leadership found that its members were ready to strike and willing to join AWOC's efforts. The strike began. Toward the end of this strike, the successful partnership between the AFL-CIO's AWOC group and the NFWA led to the proposed merger of the two groups, which became the United Farm Workers Organizing Committee (UFWOC) under the AFL-CIO in 1966.

A crucial aspect of the grape strike was the implementation of a consumer boycott in key US cities as well as in Europe. Jerry (Jerald) Brown, a doctoral student at Cornell University, came to work for the farm workers in 1966, convincing leaders that the boycott would be most productive if it were targeted at the ten cities that received 50 percent of California grapes: New York, Los Angeles, Chicago, San Francisco, Philadelphia, Boston, Toronto, Detroit, Montreal, and Cleveland (Brown, 1972; Garcia, 2012). In addition, volunteers and UFW workers needed activities to do during the off-seasons, so the boycotts became the perfect avenue for promoting the cause. The boycott initially targeted specific growers, but by 1968, all table grape companies were included, in part because of the consumers' difficulty in distinguishing between different companies' grapes in supermarkets. Dolores Huerta was the director of the New York boycott house and made decisions as how best to implement the boycott. In New York, Huerta first engaged in secondary boycotts, earning the support of the Central Labor Council, Amalgamated Meat Cutters, and the Seafarers International Union. This secondary boycott and the support from these other unions meant that they would not move grapes across the Hudson River, significantly reducing the number of table grapes that reached New York City supermarkets (Brown, 1972; Garcia, 2012).

Although such secondary boycotts were deemed illegal under the Taft-Hartley Act (also known as the Labor Management Relations Act of 1947, which generally restricted the power of unions) and the grapes were eventually released, substantial damage had been done to the grape market. Huerta then shifted to the consumer boycott, as she explained:

In each of the five boroughs, we organized neighborhood coalitions of church, labor, liberal and student groups. Then we began picketing A&P, the biggest chain in the city. For several months we had picket lines on about 25 to 30 stores and turned thousands of shoppers away. A lot of the managers had come up through the unions and were very sympathetic to us. In response to consumer pressure, the store managers began to complain to their division heads, and soon they took the grapes out of all of their stores, 430 of them. (quoted in J. Brown, 1972, p. 205)

However, in other cities, Huerta's tactics did not work as well, and other leaders had to adjust their boycott strategies depending on the local market. The boycott then expanded beyond those ten cities. For example, Elaine Elinson, a US graduate student living in London, developed the European market boycott in the United Kingdom, the Netherlands, Sweden, Norway, Denmark, and Finland and recruited volunteers in those countries who were sympathetic to the plight of the farm workers (Garcia, 2012).

While the strike and boycott were two of the UFW's most useful strategies, the union also employed a number of other tactics to recruit volunteers and raise awareness about farm workers. For example, scholars have identified a number of cultural and ethnic rhetorical strategies that worked particularly well in the recruitment of nonwhite farm workers to participate in pickets and as members of the union (Bardacke, 2012; Ganz, 2009; M. T. García, 2007, 2008; Garcia, 2012). Unlike the Teamsters and AFL-CIO's AWOC, the UFW was led by mostly Mexicans or Mexican Americans who were former farm workers. In telling their stories, they created ethnic identities and personae that fit well with the Chicana/o movement that was playing out in more urban settings, such as Los Angeles. As many farm workers were Catholic, part of the UFW story was narrated through Catholic masses and organizations such as the Migrant Ministry and Luis Valdez's Teatro Campesino (Bardacke, 2012; Pawel, 2014). In 1966, a peregrinación, or pilgrimage, from Delano to Sacramento, the state capital, was planned and implemented (Bardacke, 2012; Ganz, 2009). As Hammerback and Jensen (1994) contend, the peregrinación, along with the Plan of Delano, which was read at each stop along the way, drew upon ethnic and religious Mexican heritage to connect with Catholic and mostly Mexican farm workers.

The convergence of the strikes, boycotts, and strategies to connect with union members, as well as the broader public, contributed a supportive context to the negotiations of consumer awareness, contracts with growers, and legislative victories in California and nationally during this time frame. Marshall Ganz contends that the UFW's strategic capacity, based on targeting, tactics, and timing, during the epoch of the civil rights movement was a factor in its success. As Ganz (2009) explains,

> NFWA leaders had to keep figuring out, with new urgency and limited resources, how to proceed and what to do next. It was an ongoing task that drew deeply on their strategic capacity. Their tactical choices, in turn, began to reshape the contours of the organization and its leadership in ways that expanded that strategic capacity still further. (p. 126)

The farm workers and their leaders proved adept at implementing their strategic capacities, but as the UFW entered into the 1970s and beyond, eventually they came to rely on tactics that no longer worked as effectively in different political climates and social contexts.

The Decline of the UFW's Influence: 1972–1993

From 1970 to 1978, the UFW experienced increased competition in farm worker organizing and faced other contextual issues that made it difficult for the fledgling organization to maintain its operations. It was not until 1972 that the UFWOC was officially renamed the United Farm Workers (UFW). During the early 1970s, the rise of the Teamsters once again threatened the UFW's stability in recruiting and maintaining members and contracts with growers, as they had previously attempted to do in 1961 and 1966. As Matt Garcia (2012) explains, President Nixon's relationship with the Teamsters, including his pardon of one of their leaders, Jimmy Hoffa, increased their input in decisions regarding labor issues, which created a more powerful base for them at national and state levels. The Teamsters had become the most powerful union in the United States, with 1.9 million members by 1970, compared to the UFW's membership base of 12,000 grape workers in the same year (Garcia, 2012). As the Teamsters sought out contracts with growers, they were increasingly in competition with the UFW and used any means, including violent approaches, to gain such contracts. Several UFW leaders were beaten, threatened, and intimidated by the Teamsters during this time period. The Teamsters gained contracts with growers by employing strikebreakers and other intimidation tactics. Ganz (2009) reports that "[w]hen it was all over [by 1973],

UFWOC was left with 10 contracts, 6,000 members, a shattered dues income, and a fight for its life" (p. 232). Furthermore, Filipino UFW members became increasingly disillusioned with what they felt was the unfair approach of UFW hiring halls, and they joined up with the Teamsters. The resignation of Larry Itliong, the leader of the original 1965 strike led by Filipinos and AWOC under the AFL-CIO, also demonstrated the divide between the Filipino and Mexican farm workers (Garcia, 2012).

The longevity of the boycott and national and state politics also contributed to the decline of UFW's influence. The Teamsters employed a strategy of getting contracts from companies such as lettuce producer InterHarvest by convincing sellers not to use boycotted lettuce. Consumers were increasingly confused by which group was doing what; knowing that produce was under a union contract was perhaps enough to encourage consumers to start purchasing grapes and other vegetables again. In other words, they did not care which organization was providing union-contracted fruit and vegetables (Garcia, 2012). In addition, Republican leaders such as Richard Nixon and Ronald Reagan further diminished UFW influence by supporting advocacy for growers' rights. Reagan, then the governor of California, restricted social services and did little to alleviate the disputes between the UFW and the Teamsters (Garcia, 2012). Both politicians created an atmosphere that made it more difficult for the UFW to succeed in obtaining contracts and maintaining union membership.

The 1974 election of Jerry Brown as California governor offered the UFW a more favorable political climate. Dolores Huerta was instrumental in the passage of the 1975 Agricultural Labor Relations Act (ALRA), which provided farm workers protections such as the rights to unionize and to file complaints about unfair labor issues (Garcia, 2012). The Agricultural Labor Relations Board (ALRB) opened offices across the state to support farm workers' rights. However, the ALRA and the ALRB were short-lived, since California's Legislative Assembly failed to approve appropriations that would enable the ALRB to do its job. The lack of training and qualified staff also further hampered the success of the ALRA. To make matters worse, in 1976 the UFW became financially and politically embattled in the passage of Proposition 14, which would have provided more funding for the ALRB. The proposition was defeated after an intense campaign led by Harry Kubo, a Japanese American farmer who lost everything during the World War

II internment of Japanese Americans and advocated arduously on behalf of individual property rights (Garcia, 2012).

These three factors—the Teamsters, UFW debt and loss of face due to the failure of Proposition 14, and the political climate of the 1970s—created contexts in which it was very difficult for the UFW to gain stronger footholds with growers, farm workers, and the general public. The UFW might have succeeded despite these changing cultural and political forces if it had not been for the internal issues that the organization began to experience around this time. Several scholars have documented Chávez's strange and paranoid behaviors starting around 1976, which had lasting effects on the UFW until his death in 1993 (Bardacke, 2012; Ganz, 2009; Garcia, 2012; Pawel, 2014). As Ganz (2009) argues, the strategic capacity of the UFW was compromised as loyal followers replaced seasoned UFW leaders. As a result of Chávez's increasing suspicions of longtime UFW leaders and volunteers, many were fired or left the organization, as happened with various leaders on the executive board, including Philip Vera Cruz, Eliseo Medina, Jessica Govea, Gilbert Padilla, Marshall Ganz, and the entire legal team (seventeen lawyers and forty-four other employees) (Ganz, 2009; Garcia, 2012; Pawel, 2014). As Ganz (2009) contends,

> Between 1977 and 1981, Chavez undid the UFW's strategic capacity. The changes irrevocably altered the character of the UFW leadership. Instead of a diverse team with both strong and weak ties to multiple constituencies, it became a narrow circle of people with strong ties, often Chavez family members or dependents. (p. 247)

However, some of Chávez's mistrust and paranoia was completely understandable, given that the FBI had been monitoring his and other UFW leaders' activities for some time. Perhaps his focus on loyalty was a response to the UFW's national visibility and subsequent scrutiny as well as conflicts with the Teamsters.

Beyond the so-called strange behaviors of Chávez and the UFW as an organization, the UFW also began to shift away from boycotts, strikes, and general labor-organizing strategies. Ganz (2009) reports that from 1981 to 1993, the UFW focused more on direct marketing, political campaigns, and public advocacy. Pawel (2014) outlines three problems of this era: (1) a lack of financial accountability and possibly malfeasance; (2) the failure of California political campaigns in which thousands of dollars were spent; and (3) court losses on key legal decisions, such as the 1987 decision in which "the UFW was found liable for $1.7 million in damages" for the 1979 strike against Maggio, a vegetable agribusiness (p. 434). In 1993, Chávez passed away during one of his infamous fasts while in the middle of testifying on another court case in Arizona involving libelous publicity. After Chávez's death, many thought that Dolores Huerta would become the face of the UFW, but the board did not support her, and eventually she retired from the UFW. Although the UFW still operates today under the direction of Arturo Rodríguez, Chávez's son-in-law, its power is much diminished. Yet the UFW, Chávez, Huerta, and other leaders still symbolically represent the success of both the farm worker and Chicana/o movements.

Conclusion

The rise and decline of the UFW's influence is more nuanced and complicated than presented here, but this brief history and overview contextualize the importance of the UFW and the difficulties in creating social change. Achieving social justice requires the right context, people, strategies, tactics, and timing. However, a change in any one of those factors can create different circumstances in which failure is the result. While journalists and historians have well documented what they call the decline of the UFW (e.g., Ganz, 2009; Garcia, 2012; Pawel, 2014), this project is more interested in how Huerta, along with Chávez, created rhetorical legacies as part of this social justice organization and movement. Because of their work, they have both become icons not just for Mexican Americans, Chicanx/a/os, and other Latinx/a/os but for many more who want and demand social justice in the United States and around the world. Understanding this underlying context helps frame Huerta's early life, the subject of the next chapter, as well as her life as a community activist, which is documented in later chapters.

Chapter 2

DOLORES HUERTA'S LIFE

INTERSECTIONAL HABITUS AS
RHETORICAL AGENCY

On April 6, 1969, approximately seven years after Dolores Huerta and César Chávez cofounded the Farm Workers Association (FWA), the journalist and Chávez biographer Jacques Levy interviewed Huerta to get a deeper understanding of Chávez and the union (Levy, 1969). This interview reveals a great deal about Huerta at the time; she talked about her own life, contributions to the United Farm Workers (UFW), and her relationship with Chávez. Early in the interview, she discussed the challenges she faced as a community organizer, from family members, farm workers, and her colleagues, such as Father McCullough, one of the religious leaders connected to the farm worker movement. She noted that "the priest, Father McCulloagh [sic], then he didn't want me to be involved so I kind of had to work under cover, I had to work through my husband and my brother and do all the work through them because Father McCulloagh [sic] said that farm labor organizing was no place for a woman. It's very difficult" (Levy, 1969, p. 9). Her comments reveal the intersectional challenges she faced and the ways in which she navigated such resistance to her work. Instead of giving up, she capitalized on her relationships with others, such as her brother and her husband (at the time), to engage in community organizing and the inception of the union. She also observed that there were others, such as Fred Ross and César Chávez, who were deeply supportive of her efforts: "[T]he only two people that really had faith in me that I can do anything as a woman, were Fred and Cesar because everybody else kept knocking me down all the time, no place for a woman" (Levy, 1969, p. 10).

Huerta's own words illustrate the importance of context, relationships, and rhetorical maneuvering for engaging in social action. Actors like Huerta may face many challenges but also have the encouragement of a few key people that somehow enable, motivate, and inspire them to continue forward. This chapter thus explores theories related to rhetorical agency, the social and material circumstances that both hinder and enable social activists such as Huerta, and how those contexts can be navigated through Pierre Bourdieu's concept of habitus, the early life context and relationships that lay the groundwork for one's identity, positionality, and social orientation. I argue that, in part, Huerta's early family life, her mother's role in her life, and her relationship with Chávez were major factors that enabled her to become a powerful leader of the UFW and, later, an outspoken advocate for Chicana/o/xs, women, and other marginalized groups and social movements. Habitus is a precursory element in how one navigates and negotiates social circumstances, bolstered and constrained by the context and relationships within that person's life. As such, this chapter proceeds to unpack the concepts of rhetorical agency as it relates to habitus and then focuses on biographical details from Huerta's life that played a significant aspect in her UFW work to understand habitus through intersectionality. Addressing intersectional issues means examining not just one aspect of identity but rather the way identities work together in context and over time (Crenshaw, 1991; Griffin & Chávez, 2012). Recognizing the instabilities of identities and thinking of constitutive intersectionality as the "meeting place between discourse and subjectivity" helps us understand how intersectional identities do not reside in one place, in one person, or at one time (Hahner, 2012, p. 153). I then conclude by working through and expanding that rhetorical scholarship to illustrate what I call "intersectional habitus," which reflects the negotiation of agency through concepts such as flexibility, resistance, optimism, and transformation, and is rooted in understanding the material, political, and social constraints of gendered, racialized, and classed contexts.

Rhetorical Agency as Habitus:
Negotiating Social Constraints

Rhetorical agency is a slippery term that, to invoke Lloyd Bitzer's (1968) "rhetorical situation," depends on rhetorical exigence, audience, and constraints, while also considering the context and actor(s) involved. To begin to understand agency requires an examination of how rhetors or groups of rhetors reach a moment in which they want or are invited to speak, write, and/or perform. Emirbayer and Mische define agency as a multifaceted concept that includes

> a temporally embedded process of social engagement, informed by the past (in its "iterational" or habitual aspect) but also oriented toward the future (as a "projective" capacity to imagine alternative possibilities) and toward the present (as a "practical-evaluative" capacity to contextualize past habits and future projects within the contingencies of the moment). (Emirbayer & Mische, 1998, p. 962)

As Emirbayer and Mische suggest, this process is gradual and largely shaped by social forces. Darrel Enck-Wanzer (2011) further explains that "agency leaves traces of itself on the scenes, acts, and agents involved, which means that its residue is always-already present and constantly being renewed and reformed" (p. 350). Agency is constitutive, contextual, and performative; it does not occur just anywhere but must occur somewhere (Shome, 2003). Karlyn Kohrs Campbell suggests that the very nature of rhetorical agency is "promiscuous and protean" because it "can refer to invention, strategies, authorship, institutional power, identity, subjectivity, practices, and subject positions, among others" (Campbell, 2005, p. 1). Isaac West maintains that agency is "not completely born anew in response to a rhetorical act and/or situation but is instead a psychic reservoir constantly and dialectically renewed against the accumulation of one's experiences" (2008, p. 247; see also Enck-Wanzer, 2011). These scholars demonstrate the roles of the individual, past and present contexts, and the material and social conditions, among other factors that shape an individual's relationship to rhetorical agency.

Pierre Bourdieu's work on habitus illustrates how agency is influenced by the past and habitual elements, the first aspect of Emirbayer and Mische's definition and the focus of this chapter. While Bourdieu's work draws from his observations and experiences in France, his discussion of how intersecting life experiences and identities often relate to social, class, and educational standing is quite relevant in the context of farm workers' rights in the United States because of his interests in how societal power dynamics are reinforced and resisted. Habitus relates to the dispositions that originate in childhood, as individuals are socialized by parents, family members, educational systems, and others who teach them the unspoken and unwritten rules of appropriateness and inappropriateness. Bourdieu suggests that agency emerges from these dispositions, in the act of balancing opposing forces, such as "possibilities and impossibilities, freedoms and necessities, opportunities and prohibitions" (Bourdieu, 1990, p. 54). Individuals base their expectations on "the accessible and inaccessible, of what is and is not 'for us', a division as fundamental and as fundamentally recognized as that between the sacred and the profane" (Bourdieu, 1990, p. 64). Habitus, and these opposing forces, influences our abilities to speak, invent, perform, act, and resist in ways that may not be consciously recognized.

Habitus, as Bourdieu describes it, also places agency both within and beyond the individual, as the individual is shaped by other people, organizations, ideologies, and politics. Marilyn Cooper (2011) argues that rhetorical agency is emergent and enacted but not possessed, in that it is "a response to a perturbation that is shaped by the rhetor's current goals and past experiences" (p. 426). María Lugones (2003) extends this notion of active subjectivity:

> It is adumbrated to consciousness by a moving with people, by the difficulties as well as the concrete possibilities of such movings. It is a sense of intentionality that we can reinforce and sense as lively in paying attention to people and to the enormously variegated ways of connection among people without privileging the world or monological understanding of sense. We can reinforce and influence the direction of intention in small ways by sensing/understanding the movement of desires, beliefs, and signs among people. (p. 6)

Individuals who enact resistance, according to Lugones, are active subjects, but not agents, emerging through and within collective and collaborative spaces. They learn to resist through "epistemic shifts" and ways of moving, such as traveling to other worlds, trespassing, pilgrimages, streetwalking, hanging out, and playfulness (2003, p. 12). Passing along such tactical strategies to other potential active subjects is part of the act of resistance and how collaborative action takes place. As such, Dolores Huerta's early life and relationships with key people illustrate how habitus plays such an important role in the understanding of rhetorical agency; she was not an acontextual, individual agent but rather an active subject empowered by some aspects of her life while constrained by others. Historians such as Margaret Rose (2002, 2004), Alicia Chávez (2005), and Vicki Ruiz (1998) have historicized Huerta's early life and career with the UFW, but what follows examines her early relationships and how they contributed to a sense of rhetorical agency that, in part, shaped her leadership within the UFW and other social movements, moving within and beyond these historical accounts of her life and contextualizing intersectional habitus through race, ethnicity, language, class, and gender.

Dolores Huerta's Life before the United Farm Workers

Dolores Fernández (Huerta) was born on April 10, 1930, in Dawson, New Mexico, but grew up in Stockton, California, raised by her mother and grandfather. Her parents' divorce when Huerta was five years old and subsequent move to Stockton resulted in little contact with her father, Juan Fernández. After working in coal mines and beet fields, he later became a politician, and in 1938, he won a seat in the state legislature of New Mexico; his political career and social activism may have inspired, at least in part, Huerta's social justice organizing. He was reportedly very proud of her activist work (A. Chávez, 2005; Rose, 2004).

However, the real influences in Huerta's childhood were her mother and maternal grandfather, who significantly shaped her worldview and, later, her social activism (Griswold del Castillo & Garcia, 1995; "A Life of Sacrifice," 1990; Rose, 2004). According to Huerta, her childhood, her relationships with her mother (Alicia Chávez Fernández) and grandfather (Herculano Chávez), and the educational opportunities she was afforded as a child and a young adult were leading factors in what enabled and motivated her to become a powerful spokesperson for the UFW and a civil rights leader. Bourdieu explains that "[e]arly experiences have particular weight because the *habitus* tends to ensure its own constancy and its defence against change through the selection it makes within new information by rejecting information capable of calling into question its accumulated information, if exposed to it accidentally or by force, and especially by avoiding exposure to such information" (Bourdieu, 1990, pp. 60–61). That is, as we become older, we may become more resistant to new ideas; what we are exposed to in our early experiences can have a profound influence on how we interact with the world.

Huerta has reported that her mother played an influential role in how and why she became a strong and outspoken woman: "We were close—like sisters. She was a very gentle woman. . . . She was absolutely influential in my life. She was very strong and she called the shots" ("A Life of Sacrifice," 1990, p. 257). According to Huerta, "My mother was a very good cook and when we came to California, she worked in a cannery and as a waitress. It was during the depression. She eventually borrowed money and opened her restaurant, and, when world war two came, she opened a hotel and catered mostly to farm workers" ("A Life of Sacrifice," 1990, p. 256). She described her mother as a "Mexican-American Horatio Alger type" (Huerta, quoted in Coburn, 1976, p. 12). Huerta also said, "My mother was always pushing me to get involved in all these youth activities. . . . We took violin lessons. I took piano lessons. I took dancing lessons. I belonged to the church choir. . . . And I was a very active Girl Scout from the time I was eight to the time I was eighteen" (quoted in Rose, 2004, p. 217).

Because Huerta's mother worked so much, her children were often left in the care of relatives, especially Huerta's grandfather (Rose, 1988, 2004). According to Huerta, this reversal of traditional gendered caretaker roles allowed her to see that independent and assertive women could succeed in the US American workforce and society. Huerta's grandfather called her Seven Tongues, because she talked so much and with great ease (Rose, 2004), foreshadowing her assertive persona as an adult. Not only did Huerta experience a reversal of gender roles in her family life, but she reports, "My mother was a very assertive woman—not aggressive, assertive. . . . My brothers were raised to be self-sufficient. We all had to wash the laundry, clean. My mother always worked. We had to chip in and share the work. From very young, she taught us how to work. She brought us up all the same" ("A Life of Sacrifice," 1990, p. 257). Huerta's somewhat middle-class upbringing and closeness with her mother enabled her to see opportunities for Mexican American women and herself that she might not have otherwise pursued. These early experiences, combined with Huerta's family's sense of social justice, contributed significantly to Huerta's later roles in civil rights activism.

During the era of Huerta's childhood, significant social, cultural, political, and economic changes were taking place in the United States. Born in 1930, she was a young girl during the Great Depression. Because work was in short supply and it was a time of deep poverty for many, there was a lot of anti-Mexican and anti-foreigner sentiment (Ramírez, 2009). By the time Huerta was a teenager, the United States was deeply involved in World War II, another major historical event that influenced cultural and social forces for Mexicans and Mexican Americans. Although World War II changed the workforce for women during the era in which Huerta was growing up, Mexican and Mexican American women, particularly first-generation immigrants, still faced social expectations of traditional gender roles. For second- or third-generation (and beyond) Mexican Americans, there was more tension and conflict with tradition and expectation. As Catherine Ramírez (2009) notes in her book about women and zoot suits, "Many of these youngsters were the first in their families to be born and/or reared in an urban setting, to speak English, and to attend school for an extended period of time" (p. 3). Yet Mexican Americans also faced racism, classism, segregation, and anti-immigrant sentiments in school, the workplace, and many other institutions.

Not only did US American events, such as the Great Depression and the country's entry into World War II, influence Mexican American organizing, but an earlier historical event, the Mexican Revolution (1910–1920), increased the number of Mexican immigrants coming to the United States (Hammerback & Jensen, 1994; Ruiz, 1998). Many Mexicans came to the United States either during or after the Mexican Revolution and then had children in the United States, creating the stage for Mexican American (and later Chicana/o) identities with strong ties to farm worker movements. As Vicki Ruiz (1998) writes, regarding early organizing efforts in the 1930s, "Borne out of material conditions, class consciousness provided the leavening for labor activism. Mexican men and women proved enthusiastic union members. Some acted out of socialist convictions nurtured during the Mexican Revolution; others viewed the union solely as a vehicle for decent wages and conditions" (p. 77). However, while there were some Mexican and Mexican American activists in the 1930s, such as Emma Tenayuca and her work with the Pecan Shellers Strike in Texas (see Holling, 2012), opportunities for union strikes and other avenues of activism were hampered by the Great Depression because so many people were looking for any kind of employment, including farm work (Ganz, 2009). For Huerta, coming of age during this era was undoubtedly influential in how she viewed the world, as evidenced in her own recollections. For instance, Huerta recounted, "When I got into high school, . . . it was really segregated. There were the real rich and the real poor. I later realized we were poor too, and I had got hit with a lot of racial discrimination" (cited in Griswold del Castillo & Garcia, 1995, p. 65).

Huerta also grew up with a middle-class understanding of the world, even if her mother was working all the time to make ends meet. At the same time, she witnessed poverty from a young age in her mother's restaurant and hotel work, as well as in the schools she attended. She grew up surrounded by working-class Mexicans, Mexican Americans, Filipinos, and other farm worker groups, and her mother's sense of social justice became infused in Huerta's life (Rose, 2004). Huerta reports, "I was also raised in Stockton in an integrated neighborhood. There were Chinese, Latinos, Native Americans, Blacks, Japanese, Italians, and others. We were all rather poor, but it was an integrated community so it was not racist for me in my childhood" (quoted in Griswold del Castillo & Garcia, 1995, p. 64). After graduating from high school, Huerta attended University of the Pacific's Stockton College (now San Joaquin Delta College), where she studied in the teaching certificate program and graduated in 1953 (A. Chávez, 2005; Lori de Leon, personal communication, June 14, 2006; Rose, 1988, 2004). Huerta's childhood, adolescence, and college education during the period of the Great Depression and World War II shaped how she thought about education, injustice, and social activism.

Such social, political, and economic forces, like those that Huerta encountered, are most influential as early life experiences because they become our "practical hypotheses based on past experiences," and the *habitus*—"embodied history, internalized as a second nature and so forgotten as history—is the active presence of the whole past of which it is the product" (Bourdieu, 1990, p. 56). While family relations are a key part of the habitus, Bourdieu also contends that habitus is class based, as what individuals come to know are situated in the life experiences of their families and those around them of the same class. For example, symbolic capital and power constitute a class status that is gained either by birth or a gradual adoption of practices that lead to such power, or what Bourdieu calls the "slow process of co-option and initiation" (1990, p. 68). Symbolic capital is acquired not just by attention to language and cultural practices but also in how one expresses the body, face, and emotion. As Bourdieu explains, "Symbolic power works partly through the control of other people's bodies and belief that is given by the collectively recognized capacity to act in various ways on deep-rooted linguistic and muscular patterns of behaviour, either by neutralizing them or by reactivating them to function mimetically" (p. 69).

Habitus is a strong force that shapes the individual and the collective in conscious and unconscious ways through recognized symbolic capital and power that circulates at different levels. It can thus have both a constraining and liberating effect because of how people interact their pasts with their presents and their futures: "The tendency of groups to persist in their ways, due *inter alia* to the fact that they are composed of individuals with durable dispositions that can outlive the economic and social conditions in which they were produced, can be the source of misadaptation as well as adaptation, revolt as well as resignation" (Bourdieu, 1990, p. 62). Racial, ethnic, and gendered habitus are also factors in Huerta's life, something that Bourdieu's work does not account for, although his analysis of symbolic capital is omnipresent in racial, ethnic, and gendered relationships and how people experience such circumstances. Huerta learned to be an assertive and strong woman from her mother, but her deep commitment to social activism emerged as she entered adulthood.

Huerta's Early Activism through Teaching and the Community Service Organization

In the 1950s and 1960s, Mexican and Mexican American women faced significant rhetorical constraints related to the intersectional aspects of their gendered, classed, and ethnic status in both Mexican and Mexican American culture as well as within the dominant hierarchical structures (M. T. García, 2008). Such social constraints, connected to Mexican and Mexican American traditions, called for women's subservience and obedience to men within the family structure, the Catholic Church, the institution of marriage, labor markets, educational systems, legislative and legal systems, and heterosexual relationships (Saldívar-Hull, 2000; see also Holling, 2000, 2006; Williams, 1990; Zavella, 1987, for discussions on familia [family]). Many Mexican farm workers were traditionalists and Catholic, expecting Mexican women to be reserved and to care primarily for family (Alarcón, 1989; Hurtado, 1998; Rose, 1990b). Huerta's early activist life revolved around traversing these cultural and gendered norms.

By the early 1950s, Huerta had married her first husband, Ralph Head, and had two children (Celeste and Lori), a job teaching elementary school, and an associate's degree, a life that represented the American dream (Abalos, 1998; Castillo, 1995; Martinez, 2000). However, Huerta recognized, as Jacqueline Martinez argues, the effect of failing to achieve the American dream meant that many in US-American society believed that "those who have not made it up the socioeconomic scale deserve to be at the bottom. And it removes social accountability to even the most horrifically poor, destitute, and socially isolated communities within society" (2000, p. 21). Huerta eventually rejected the idealized version of the American dream so that she could help others, such as the students in her classes and working-class Mexicans and Mexican Americans in her Stockton community, to achieve a higher standard of living. The early 1950s were an important time for her in this regard, as she felt increasingly dissatisfied with her job as a teacher and role as a housewife and mother because she felt she was not doing enough. According to Huerta, several years passed before she was able to reconcile her identity in relationship to familial expectations in order to organize for farm workers' causes: "I knew I wasn't comfortable in a wife's role . . . but I wasn't clearly facing the issue. I hedged, I made excuses, I didn't come out and tell my husband that I cared more about helping other people than cleaning our house and doing my hair" (quoted in Baer, 1975, p. 39). By the mid-1950s, Huerta had given up her teaching job, divorced her first husband, and started working for social justice organizations. She married her second husband, Ventura Huerta, and had five more children (Fidel, Emilio, Vincent, Alicia, and Angela); her second marriage would end in 1961, just before she and Chávez cofounded the FWA (Baer, 1975; A. Chávez, 2005; Rose, 2004).

In 1955, Huerta became involved in the Stockton branch of the Community Service Organization (CSO), a group that worked to protect poor people's rights and assist them in acquiring basic public services (Coburn, 1976; Ferriss & Sandoval, 1997; Rose, 1994). Her husband, mother, and aunt were also involved in CSO work. The women focused on activities such as "registering voters in the barrio, teaching citizenship and naturalization classes, pressuring for neighborhood improvements such as better streets, lighting, parks, and playgrounds, and engaging in the typical behind-the-scenes tasks of preparation for local and regional CSO meetings" (Rose, 2004, p. 218). Huerta then became involved in farm worker issues, especially when she became a part of the Agricultural Workers Association (AWA), which led to her involvement with the AFL-CIO Agricultural Workers Organizing Committee (AWOC) in the late 1950s. But, as Margaret Rose explains,

Huerta "soon grew disenchanted with the group's leadership, direction, and top-down policies and resigned" (2004, p. 219), a decision that shaped her eventual work as a leader in the UFW.

These experiences in Huerta's young adult life were formative in her social justice organizing. Habitus thus resides in how the individual responds to life's early experiences in relationship to the social collective, as well as the present and the future. However, as Michel de Certeau (1984) contends, it is not enough to have a social justice disposition (habitus); the actions to address injustice do not always emerge from disposition alone. In the study of sociological structures, practices, and habitus, the epistemological concern is in how gaps between practices and structures are addressed. As he explains:

> [T]he *acquisition* of knowledge; this is the sought-for mediation between the structures that organize it and the "dispositions" it produces. This "genesis" implies an interiorization of structures (through learning) and an exteriorization of achievements (what Bourdieu calls the *habitus*) in practices. A temporal dimension is thus introduced: practices (expressing the experience) correspond adequately to situations (manifesting the structure) if, and only if, the structure remains stable for the duration of the process of interiorization/exteriorization; if not, practices lag behind, thus resembling the structure at the preceding point, the point at which it was interiorized by the *habitus*. (1984, p. 57, emphasis in original)

As Bourdieu acknowledges, active subjectivity (to use Lugones's term) can both be limited and freed by practices that emerge from one's sense of habitus. It is this tension between the constraining and enabling factors of habitus that Dolores Huerta illustrates so effectively, in both her achievements (exteriorization) and engagement of structures (interiorization), especially as she navigated intersectional habitus and moved into leadership roles in the founding of the UFW union.

Huerta and the United Farm Workers Union

During her time working and organizing for the CSO, Huerta met Chávez, and both agreed that there was a need for farm worker protections beyond what the CSO could offer (Ferriss & Sandoval, 1997;

Rose, 2001, 2004; Shaw, 2008). Although many attempts to create organized protests and union-like groups existed long before the inception of the UFW (Ganz, 2009; Ruiz, 1998), these attempts failed for various reasons, such as the size of labor markets; social, economic, and political conditions; and the strength of organizers and unions. Huerta and Chávez mutually agreed to quit the CSO and start the FWA. César Chávez called Huerta's involvement in the founding of the FWA critical and her eventual effectiveness in collective bargaining and lobbying, essential. Along with Chávez, Huerta was also responsible for organizing the grape boycott on the East Coast (Rose, 1988; Shaw, 2008) and initiating *El Malcriado*, the union newspaper ("Cultivating creativity," n.d.). Another major legislative and organizing project that Huerta tackled was the passage of the 1975 California Agricultural Labor Relations Act (Coburn, 1976; Rose, 1988). Also during this time, Huerta became romantically involved with Richard Chávez (César's brother), a relationship sustained until his death in 2011 (Bardacke, 2012). Although they never married, they had four children together, Juanita, María Elena, Ricky, and Camilla (Rose, 2004); Huerta had a total of eleven children from her first two marriages and her relationship with Richard Chávez. Although César Chávez disapproved of her divorces and approach to child-rearing and did not always back her in decisions related to her personal life (Cram, 1981), he significantly supported her in many other ways.

Chávez was instrumental in enabling and motivating Huerta's negotiation of habitus and move from a social justice life orientation to activist and leader. He also established a set of cultural dispositions within the UFW through which most organizers came to respect Huerta. Huerta's voice was authorized, in part, because of Chávez's leadership in the UFW and his encouragement for her to take on leadership roles. Huerta was also equally supportive of Chávez; their relationship was reciprocal. As Huerta reported, "I told Cesar one time, 'Seems like the workers know more about organizing than I do.' But Cesar said, 'Dolores, if they didn't need you, they would have organized themselves long ago'" (Huerta "Martin Luther King Farm Workers Fund," 1976, p. 12). The repeated actions of practicing leadership create the grounds for charismatic leadership: "I think people develop charisma in trying to reach people, in trying to get to them. Gradually and before you know it, you become a charismatic leader" (Huerta, quoted in Griswold del Castillo & Garcia, 1995, p. 70). Chávez, who had great respect for Huerta's leadership abilities, observed, "No march is too long, no task too hard for Dolores Huerta if it means taking a step forward for the rights of farmworkers" ("A Life of Sacrifice," 1990, p. 266), and "Dolores is absolutely fearless, physically and emotionally" (Coburn, 1976, pp. 12–13).

Huerta looked to Chávez to confirm her ideas, actions, and self, which, in turn, may have fostered her sense of agency and motivation to continue her work with the UFW and vice versa. Huerta explained her relationship with Chávez as almost like family:

> Cesar and I have a lot of personal fights, usually over strategy or personalities. I don't think Cesar himself understands why he fights with me. We have these heart-to-heart talks every six months or so on how we're not going to fight anymore, and how demoralizing it is to everybody else that we do. But then, like the next day, we'll have another fight. . . . He still gets that way when he's under a lot of tension, and uses me to let off steam, as I would do with my own family. He says, "I know that I treat you very mean, like I treat Richard [Chávez's brother] and treat Manuel [his cousin] and Helen [his wife], all very mean." But I understand it. He knows I might get angry or feel bad about it, but I'm not going to leave the Union. . . . He worries about my health, and bugs me all the time. I do get myself worked up and tense, but I'm better now than I used to be. I can relax more. (quoted in Levy, 2007, p. 265)

In Huerta's words, they fought a lot with each other, like a familial relationship, as if they were brother and sister. As Rose observes, "Huerta and Chávez had developed a dynamic partnership. Although disagreements arose, they had a comfortable working relationship, displayed mutual respect, and shared an unshakable commitment to unionizing farmworkers" (2004, p. 222).

Huerta also was one of Chávez's most trusted advisors and collaborators; he delegated important union tasks to her, such as negotiations with growers, the direction of the New York City boycott on grapes, and lobbying activities with politicians. Although Chávez has been credited for inventing the UFW slogan, "sí, se puede," he also readily attributed that idea to Huerta:

> We had just come from California where everywhere we went, farm workers were fighting. In Arizona the people were beaten.

You could see the difference. Every time we talked about fighting the law, people would say, "No se puede, no se puede—it's
not possible. It can't be done." My brother Richard mentioned
that at a staff meeting in the motel at Wickenburg, and when
it was Dolores's turn, she said, "From now on, we're not going
to say, 'No se puede,' we're going to say 'Si se puede!'" I picked
up on it immediately. "Okay, that's going to be the battle cry!"
(Chávez, quoted in Levy, 2007, p. 464)

As this example illustrates, Chávez helped to authorize and create her
own rhetorical space by giving credit to her accomplishments and ideas.

Huerta and Chávez had a symbiotic partnership, focused on farm
worker issues as a collective and communal struggle (M. T. García,
2008; Griswold del Castillo & Garcia, 1995). Chávez's influence as the
primary leader of the UFW is well documented, but Huerta was also
quite influential with Chávez and the UFW. Griswold del Castillo &
Garcia (1995) argue:

Chávez had asked Huerta to be cofounder of the Farm Workers
Association because he recognized her leadership abilities, her
powerful character, her intellectual toughness, and above all her
self-assuredness. . . . Her role in shaping César Chávez's life and
the farm-worker movement was crucial, especially during the
early organizational years . . . she was a key negotiator, a nontraditional Mexicana, and a loyal follower. (p. 59)

Understanding how Huerta and Chávez collaboratively communicated
is important for moving outside of individualistic frameworks, since
their identities and discourses were shaped by cultural norms and
forces rooted in collectivism and collaboration. In effect, Huerta's collaborative relationship with Chávez (and others) reciprocally, reitera-
tively, and incrementally produced an authority for rhetorical agency.

Other people also influenced Huerta's worldview on many topics.
For example, Huerta reported that she was influenced by feminist
leaders such as Gloria Steinem, even though during the early period
of the union's formation, Huerta was not active in gender, feminist,
and women's issues. As Huerta became more aware of gender issues,
she began calling out sexist practices and comments from her male
colleagues in the union and in negotiating sessions and was clearly

aware of the role men played in decision-making and organizing (Rose, 2004). In a 1976 interview for *Ms.* magazine, Huerta explained her position on feminism:

> I consider myself a feminist, and the Women's Movement has done a lot toward helping me not feel guilty about my divorces. But among poor people, there's not any question about the women being strong—even stronger than men—they work in the fields right along with the men. When your survival is at stake, you don't have these questions about yourself like middle-class women do. (Coburn, 1976, p. 13)

Later in this same interview, it is noted that Huerta had spoken out against the use of contraceptives and abortion, two cornerstones during the women's rights movement. Huerta called herself a feminist, but that label was fraught with social expectations of what feminism meant at the time. However, as Aída Hurtado (1998, 1996) argues, acts of disruption that dispelled stereotypes of women, and particularly Chicana women, were essential to recognize the "joys of struggle" over victimhood and to celebrate agency so there is hope for the future rather than the despair of the past (1998, p. 145).

Studies of the Chicana/o and the UFW movements in the 1960s and 1970s have reported that leadership roles were limited for women or were gendered, in that women were often assigned to do secretarial and entertaining work (Blackwell, 2003; Cram, 1981; Rose, 1994, 2004). Vicki Ruiz and John Chávez's 2008 book, *Memories and Migrations*, documents how families and husbands limited Latinas' participation in the work force even as they desired better lives and politicized their positionalities (see also Vicki Ruiz's 1998 book, *From Out of the Shadows*; Alma García's edited collection *Chicana Feminist Thought*, 1997). Gabriela Arredondo (2008) contends that from the 1920s through the 1940s, for example, some Mexican feminists and activists thought that greater freedoms for women threatened the sense of family and that women had few job opportunities, mostly related to cooking, cleaning, and caregiving. On the other hand, Mexican and Mexican American women who worked in the fields in the 1940s and 1950s were often encouraged by their mothers and other family members to move out of farm work, to obtain an education and then the better jobs and lives that also led to increasing public participation in the later farm worker and Chicana/o movements, even amid the gender discrimination in both movements (M. Chávez, 2008; Salas, 2008).

Rose (1990a) has identified different roles that women played within the farm worker movement, using Huerta and César Chávez's wife, Helen Chávez, as examples. She contends that Huerta took a non-traditional path as a major leader within the organization as well as a key negotiator, lobbyist, and boycott organizer. Helen Chávez, by contrast, played a more traditional role similar to the participation that many other women undertook. She worked in the office, participated in strikes, and took care of the Chávez children; her activism was central to her life, but she prioritized her family over the union, whereas Huerta integrated her family into the union so that they were one and the same (Rose, 1990a). As Rose (1995) argues elsewhere regarding Chicana activists in the farm worker movement, "the sexual division of labor gave more prominence to their husbands' leadership and community-organizing activities. As a result, Chicanas' commitment to the boycott remained obscured because they juggled domestic concerns and child-rearing with picket line duty, participation in demonstrations, and work in the local union boycott offices" (p. 7).

Huerta also noted that many farm workers refused to take her seriously as a leader. Even though she was a cofounder and vice president of the FWA, she struggled with male farm worker attendance at house meetings and participation under her leadership, especially when meeting with new groups (Rose, 2004). Furthermore, she faced resistance from growers and politicians. Highlighting the social expectations for and stereotypes of Mexican American women, one grower's representative problematically stated that Dolores Huerta was "a violent woman, where women, especially Mexican women, are usually peaceful and pleasant" (quoted in Baer, 1975, p. 40). Vicki Ruiz (1982) explores how (usually white) employers paradoxically stereotyped Mexican and Mexican American women working in canneries both as unreliable, ignorant, and lazy workers and as quiet, submissive, hard workers, particularly those who did not speak English.

Huerta was one of the most important Chicana figures of her generation because she challenged not only notions of stereotyped gender roles for Mexican American women but also expectations and constraining elements of habitus related to ethnicity, race, gender, and class. Empowered by her upbringing and relationship with her mother, her visibility in the UFW movement defied stereotypes of Mexican

American women. As Rose argues, "Huerta's rebellion against traditional gender ideology led to major improvements for an exploited ethnic minority. Her accomplishments were a great source of pride for both men and women in the UFW" (Rose, 1988, pp. 102–103). Huerta has often identified her mother, Chávez, and several others as key supporters who facilitated her sense of leadership and agency through support and collaboration with others. María Lugones argues that "[o]ne does not resist the coloniality of gender alone. One resists it from within a way of understanding the world and living in it that is shared and that can understand one's actions, thus providing recognition. Communities rather than individuals enable the doing; one does with someone else, not in individualist isolation" (2010, p. 754). Huerta was able to navigate the contours of her social standing within her own communities and the larger social movements of the era. She maneuvered relationships so that instead of constraining her, they enabled her, as Anjali Vats explains, through a sense of agency that is "a fluid and situated set of possibilities for invention, constrain[ed] and enabled by existing rhetorics, representations, and materialities" (Vats, 2014, p. 117). Although Huerta retired from the UFW at the age of seventy, she is still very active as a speaker, organizer, and campaigner, especially through the work of her foundation, the Dolores Huerta Foundation. A 2017 documentary film, *Dolores*, illustrates her lifelong contributions to many social justice causes and finally recognizes her social justice work on behalf of farm workers and others.

Conclusion

What does rhetorical agency mean in relationship to Dolores Huerta's early life and career? This chapter has explored the nature of intersectional habitus and its influence, for which Dolores Huerta is a good illustration because she comes from a context of gendered, racialized, classed, and segregated social groups and movements that seemingly would have prevented her leadership. If anything can be gleaned about such an activist, it is that one can be productive in the most challenging of contexts, with just a few enabling factors. Still, care should be taken in making this sound easy. Huerta grew up understanding the social world in a specific context of major events including the Depression, World War II, and the social movements of the 1960s, as well as social activism on behalf of and by Mexicans and Mexican Americans in the 1930s, 1940s, and 1950s. In addition, her family structure, especially her mother's and grandfather's roles, provided a sense of social justice, entitlement, and self-esteem that enabled her to become assertive as a student and later as community organizer and leader. She was able to overcome judgments about her divorces and style of motherhood, despite charges that she often focused more on organizing and the union than on her kids. She trusted that they were being taken care of in her community, even while many accused her of being a bad mother.

Huerta's community leadership was fostered by the social and political context of the time, as well as support from key people, such as her mother and César Chávez. However, Huerta's authority did not exist only in connection to Chávez, as they had a reciprocal relationship. Writing about the UFW, Marshall Ganz (2009) contends, "The motivation, knowledge, and learning practices of a leadership team grow in part out of the combined *identities* of its individual members. By identity, I mean the way each person has learned to reflect on the past, attend to the present, and anticipate the future" (p. 14). The UFW's success was because of strategic capacity, which Ganz contends comprises three factors: motivation, knowledge, and the ability to learn. Some of this success was clearly related to the diversity of the UFW leadership team, their various social networks and relationships with one another, and tactical repertoires.

Rhetorical agency is not limited to one's past dispositions, but also functions as a continual, reflective negotiation of rhetorical styles within the present. Each "subject" encounters social and material constraints relating to gender, ethnicity, class status, and sexuality, or their intersectional habitus. As Michelle Holling (2000) explains, agency exists in relationship to other subjects, so that for Chicanas, socialization (e.g., related to family), social contracts of marriage (e.g., related to Catholicism), and sexuality can limit rhetorical options, voice, and construction of one's identity. To negotiate these social and material constraints, Lisa Flores argues, Chicana feminists create a rhetoric of difference through their writing that includes rejecting mainstream rhetoric and shaping their own constitutive rhetoric. This rhetoric of difference allows for the "creation of discursive space [that] means that the margins are transformed into the center of a new society, and the disempowered find power" (1996, p. 152). Carrillo Rowe (2009) further explains that "the formation of the subject is never individual, but is forged across a shifting set of relations that we move in and out of, often without reflection" (2009, p. 3).

Rhetorical agency is not just the process of negotiating one's individual and social habitus but also the way in which the agent embraces enabling mechanisms, such as collective and collaborative efforts for social organizing and elements that facilitate the constitution of identity from past and present dispositions, while resisting rhetorically constructed social conventions that limit or foreclose rhetorical options. María Lugones suggests it is in how one moves with other people. To think about rhetorical agency in other contexts is difficult because, as Margaret Rose (1990b) has observed in her research on traditional and nontraditional styles of female farm worker organizing, Huerta is unusual. Bourdieu and de Certeau claim that the habitus enables and/or constrains, but we are not always aware of the ways in which our past influences our present and future choices and actions. Still, given that Huerta is a Chicana, feminist, and social movement icon for many, understanding her rhetorical legacy has inspired others to pursue a path like hers, in seeing that she was able to overcome, at least in part, rhetorical barriers and obstacles. In other words, she found the right people within her intersectional habitus and capitalized on key contexts and relationships. Intersectional identities related to class, gender, race, ethnicity, and language could have been major constraining factors in her life (and sometimes, if not often, were). Sara Ahmed describes "how power works as a mode of directionality, a way of orienting bodies in particular ways, so they are facing a certain way, heading toward a future that is given a face" (2017, p. 43). Huerta navigated these social and material circumstances to move within and outside of such normative and directive forces. Huerta's intersectional habitus and resistance to directionality illustrate the suturing of disposition and practice. The next chapter delves more fully into Chávez's and Huerta's foundational relationship and how it moved both Huerta's leadership and the UFW forward.

Chapter 3

LETTERS TO CÉSAR CHÁVEZ

BUILDING COLLABORATIVE AGENCY

Dear Cesar,
This is the fourth attempt [I] have made to write this letter, I hope this time I finish it. [I] hope your family had a nice Christmas, we did. Only one drawback, [I] caight [sic] the flu and was in bed for two days, Christmas and yesterday, but [I] am OK now. . . . Bob McLaine (remember him from Sacramento, Joe Gunterman's side kick,) sent his 17 year old daughter to live with me, and she is a whiz with kids and loves to cook. She is now home for the holidays, but was here a week before she went home for Christmas. She is coming back next week maybe Sunday. So you see, it will be possible for me to work on the road , [sic] so just lay out your map and I will hit it. . . . Please give my love to all of your family, we were thinking of you all, and I wish it would have been possible to send them some Christmas presents, but you know how the pickle squirts - Acido [acidic, bitter]. . . . As far as the kids were concerned, Santa came out like gang busters. . . . Well, hasta luego [until later], and let me know if I should plan to stay an extra day to help either with your book work, or else to plan our AB 59 campaign. I shall work on a [xxxx] leaflet and try to get it [xxxx] to you over the weekend. . . . Dolores. (Huerta, "This is the fourth attempt," December 196[x])[1]

The extant letters that Dolores Huerta sent to César Chávez, mostly in the 1960s, illustrate aspects of her life, the United Farm Workers (UFW) social movement, and her role within that movement. Building from chapter two's examination of intersectional habitus, such as the early life dispositions and relationships that influence social actors in

---

1. The last digit in the year of the date of this letter is not visible on the letter, so the year is sometime in the 1960s, hence: 196[x]. It was the early 1960s, based on the reference to the AB 59 (Assembly Bill 59, state of California) campaign.

racialized, gendered, and classed contexts, Huerta's letters also reveal how writing to someone who holds that important relationship status can enable and empower. Her frustrations, setbacks, achievements, and sense of self emerge in her letters to César Chávez and others involved in the UFW movement. Furthermore, such letters also provide insight into Huerta's relationship with Chávez as well as how they (and other UFW organizers) went about their work in recruiting members, lobbying politicians, negotiating with growers, and developing boycott strategies.

This chapter examines Dolores Huerta's letters to better understand her life and letter writing as a private rhetorical form in the UFW organization and movement. As with the previous chapter on intersectional habitus, the role of private communication and private aspects of relationships illustrate and reveal where a public, iconic persona comes from and how that contributes to a broader social movement. Huerta was well known for her UFW public speaking events; this analysis of her private letters to Chávez provides insight into how she developed this assertive public persona. In what follows, I first provide a brief overview to rhetorical scholarship on letter writing. I then explore how Huerta's letters expand our understanding of letter writing through the rhetorical functions of documentation, collaboration, affirmation, and catharsis. Finally, I conclude that these rhetorical functions illustrate letter writing as a rhetorical form, one that fosters social justice identities related to gender, race, ethnicity, nationality, and class.

Letter Writing as a Private and Public Rhetorical Form

The historical and rhetorical study of letter writing focuses on two types of letters, those that are intended for a public audience and those that are meant for a single person to whom the letter is addressed. In social movements and protests, public letters have often been used to highlight injustices and causes. For example, Martin Luther King Jr.'s "Letter from Birmingham Jail" offered a response to eight clergymen in Birmingham, Alabama, who wrote a public letter urging protesters to cease their activities (see Fulkerson, 1979; Gaipa, 2007, for further analysis). Catherine Palczewski also discusses the nature of letters intended for public audiences in her analysis of one of Gloria Anzaldúa's letters to an audience that includes "third world women writers" and others who are interested in Anzaldúa's work (1996, p. 3). The personal nature of the letter reflects a presentation of self through accounts of the writer's daily activities, goals, frustrations, and reflections by way of embodied rhetoric (Palczewski, 1996). The letter, then, has been used with rhetorical efficacy to create identification and what Kenneth Burke (1969) calls consubstantiality, or shared substance, in letters to public audiences.

However, a private letter is usually directed to a much smaller audience, often one other person, and is never intended to be publicly distributed. Rhetorical studies of private letters illustrate that such letters recount personal stories and create narratives or arguments for the person to whom the letter is addressed (Carlson, 1995; Forbes, 2004; Gring-Pemble, 1998; McCormick, 2008). Gring-Pemble (1998) has further observed that letters between members or organizers of a movement can function as the pre-genesis stage of that social movement by clarifying and discussing ideas in letter form. The private communication that functions as a pre-genesis to a social movement operates initially in the private sphere, but as these private ideas become more clearly articulated, they begin to appear in public rhetoric, such as speeches, political lobbying, and other forms. For marginalized groups, this precursory discussion function in letter writing is especially important (Gring-Pemble, 1998; Holling, 2000) and can function as an enclave, a form of hidden communication in a safe place (K. Chávez, 2011; Squires, 2002). Flores (1996) argues that for marginalized groups, such as Chicanas and Latinas, private discourse can play an important public role because it validates personal experience tied to real lives and the self. Catherine Squires (2002) explains that such organizing work may function as an "enclaved public sphere," which "requires the maintenance of safe spaces, hidden communication networks, and group memory to guard against unwanted publicity of the group's true opinions, ideas, and tactics for survival" (2002, pp. 457, 458). Karma Chávez (2011) further elaborates that coalition building often takes place behind the scenes, allowing for allied meaning making and the invention of new tactics and strategies.

In the rest of this chapter, I analyze letters written by Dolores Huerta addressed to César Chávez, obtained from the UFW official archive at the Walter P. Reuther Library of Labor and Urban Affairs at Wayne State University in Detroit, Michigan. I have purposefully not included Chávez's letters in this analysis for several reasons: First, there are only a few Chávez letters available that are specifically addressed to Huerta. Since Huerta's letters are not dated, it is also difficult to determine which Chávez letters are responses to specific letters from Huerta. In addition, because Chicana activists from the UFW and the Chicana/o movement have been obscured in historical and rhetorical analyses (Pesquera & de la Torre, 1993; Rose, 1988; Ruiz, 1998), this chapter foregrounds Huerta's voice to provide a richer analysis of her discourse.

This analysis of Huerta's letters reveals four rhetorical functions that extend the understanding of letter writing as a rhetorical form. First, her letters to Chávez are often reports of her activities that serve as documentation of her UFW work and establish accountability for financial and other resources that the UFW provided (e.g., use of gas credit cards). Second, her letters worked through problems and UFW activities collaboratively. Although Gring-Pemble (1998) has explored how letters function as collective consciousness raising and move social change from the private to the public sphere, this project expands Gring-Pemble's work to explore how letters also create space for collaborative dialogue to foster union activities and self-building. In addition, building on Carlson's (1995) study of character invention and differentiation through letters, Huerta used her letter writing for (self-) affirmation by illustrating how she found solutions to her own problems as well as her accomplishments in organizing farm workers and other UFW activities. More specifically, Huerta's letters did not invent character through narrative, as Carlson (1995) illustrates; rather, these letters outlined her accomplishments, providing an affirmatory process through written documentation. Through this written affirmation, Huerta reminded both Chávez and herself that she was a competent and committed organizer. Finally, her letters functioned cathartically in the process of describing her daily life and, specifically, the problems she encountered as a social activist, organizer, and primary caregiver for her children. These functions helped Huerta to construct and negotiate identities related to race, ethnicity, class, and gender, as well as her public persona.

Rhetorical Functions of Letter Writing: Documentation, Collaboration, Affirmation, Catharsis

As scholars such as Carlson (1995), Palczewski (1996), and Gring-Pemble (1998) have observed, letters, whether intended for public or private audiences, employ a personal tone. As such, Huerta's letters were personal in nature, especially because she had an intimate relationship with Chávez as a longtime friend and collaborator. Huerta regularly used the first person, signed letters with her first name only, wrote in the active voice, and failed to correct or notice spelling and grammatical errors. Additionally, she regularly used informal language such as "your favorite paper xxx," "thru" instead of "through," and "ha, ha" to signify a joke (e.g., "Just a few short lines . . .," n.d.; "This letter has been a week in the making," 1962; "You have probably thought," n.d.). Huerta also frequently asked about the Chávez family (e.g., "Thank you very much," n.d.) and made other personal inquiries in her private discourse.

Huerta also used Spanish and English code-switching, using Spanish words on occasion to express a concept that poorly translated into English or when it better suited her choice of words (see Jensen & Hammerback, 2002, for further discussion on how César Chávez similarly used code-switching in his public addresses). These characteristics of Huerta's letters exemplify the personal nature of letter writing and how she tailored letters to their recipients, such as César Chávez. However, beyond their rhetorical style of personal tone, Huerta's letters also express her motives for writing these letters to Chávez, revealing how letters function beyond the sharing of information or relationship building, including documentary, collaborative, confirmatory, and cathartic rhetorical purposes. These functions also illustrate the intertwined purposes of a pre-genesis stage for social movements (Gring-Pemble, 1998), an enclaved safe place to share ideas (K. Chávez, 2011; Squires, 2002), and the sharing of personal stories (Carlson, 1995) to demonstrate the complicated and multifaceted nature of letter writing. Gring-Pemble (1998) contends that letter writing served "to test ideas, challenge opposing views, refine opinions and build consensus" for 19th-century women's rights activists (p. 50). While Huerta's letters to Chávez illustrate these pre-genesis functions of letter writing, her letters also demonstrate a more collaborative, collectivist aspect of letter writing through an exchange of ideas and a tone of uncertainty. The very personal nature of these letters also demonstrates Huerta's epistemological standpoint, particularly reflected in her letters about her everyday family life and life as a farm worker activist. Indeed, Mario García (2008) notes that "Huerta's life tells us something about the condition of farm workers" (p. xx). This agency of voice and this space for marginalized voices are important for understanding these perspectives (Córdova, 1999; Holling, 2000) and also for building an understanding of how these rhetorical functions in Huerta's letters contributed to her social justice identities related to race, gender, class, ethnicity, and nationality.

Letter Writing as Documentation

Huerta's letters and other documents, such as memos and reports, written to Chávez, highlight important activities of the UFW union, from its inception as the Farm Workers Association (FWA) through the early 1970s. These UFW materials bear witness to Huerta's internal organizational work on lobbying, negotiating, and boycotting activities and reveal information far beyond her public rhetoric, such as interviews, speeches, and published writings. Much scholarship of social movements, especially in rhetorical studies (e.g., see Morris & Browne's *Readings on the Rhetoric of Social Protest*, 2013; Cox & Foust, 2009), has focused on public address, performances, and texts; these letters allow for a deeper understanding of and insight into the goals, strategies, and rhetoric of the UFW by reporting Huerta's activities, discussing UFW work, and establishing accountability to the organization.

REPORTING HUERTA'S ACTIVITIES

One of the most interesting illustrations of Huerta's UFW activities is her political negotiations with outsiders, such as politicians and growers. As the previous chapters note, the 1962 Farm Worker Association began as Chávez and Huerta maneuvered within the Community Service Organization (CSO) to generate more support and services for farm workers. Both eventually resigned over this issue when the CSO did not move to take on more organizing activities on behalf of farm workers; Chávez and Huerta agonized and strategized incessantly over the move to form the FWA. As they shaped the new organization with very few members, how they portrayed it to outsiders mattered a great deal. The following letter illustrates why organizational image was so important:

> I spoke to the guy in the Insuance [sic] deal again. He is still unsure about the organization as an organization, I think. He will be meeting with you the first week of May either in Delano

or in Los Angeles. I guess you understand that in acting through an agent, it will be more expensive. I am sticking to my original lie that we have x [sic] 1000 members. I gofed [sic] though, when he asked me if I was a salaried employee, I said no, I should have said yes. He wned [sic] to know how any [sic] of our mebrs [sic] were Anglos, I told him 1% (Ericka Maclane). So he knows we are a bunch of greezers [sic]. (for oiling machines, that is). ("Enclosed is an application for an estate loan. . . .," n.d.)

In this letter, Huerta indicated that she was exaggerating their membership number to make the organization seem more influential, and she acknowledged that she should have said she was salaried because such information would mean that the organization was well-established and supported. Her mention of the racial slur "greezers [greasers]," in response to the insurance representative's question about the number of Anglo members, suggested that an organization comprising mostly Mexican and Mexican American members would not be taken seriously by outsiders. Chávez, Huerta, and others were clearly aware of the need to have (white) outsider support of the farm worker cause, and although the organization consisted of mostly Mexican and Mexican American farm workers, the move to include and welcome Marshall Ganz, Chris Hartmire, Jerry Brown, and other "Anglos" into the UFW leadership may have been a strategic response to such inquiries.

Even among friends and supporters, such organizational strategizing was important. In the letter excerpted below, Huerta wrote about giving a report that would incite a response from Gil, probably Gil Padilla, one of the cofounders of the FWA. The letter suggested that there was a lot of political maneuvering in the early days as the organization was beginning to form:

> I had a long talk with Fred [probably Fred Ross] on the phone, and naturally he wants me to go to the Convention to give a report with the hopes that Gil will attack me and lose points, but I don't know yet. I plan to go down be it either to Delano or Hanford on Friday after the hearing. ("Enclosed are dues for a new member . . .," n.d.)

The reference to dues for members indicates that this letter was written after the initial formation of the organization but still in the early days of organizing, as Gil Padilla became one of the primary leaders of the UFW.

In another letter, Huerta documented her transition from the CSO to the FWA and her recognized leadership status in community organizing. She wrote about serving on a committee because of her role within the CSO, noting that she would do so only if she could represent the FWA:

> Oh, the reason I am calling Jerry Sampson, the sectary [sic] of State Social Welfare Board is that I have been asked to serve on Chris Hartmires [sic] sub committee [sic] on Social and Economic Problems .[sic]Professor Aller is Chairman, Chris Hartmire, Vice Chairman. They meet Thursday on the day of Our Lady of Lupe. (Thats [sic] the way Emilio says it) I am going to tell Samspon [sic] that I am no longer with CSO and if they want me anyway, I shall go represet ing [sic] FWA however if they want someone from CSO, I thought of proposing, Cirilio Lopez of Madera. ("Thank you very much," n.d.)

Huerta also wrote about working in the state capitol on farm worker issues such as the minimum wage and number of hours per workweek, demonstrating, again, her influence in the state of California:

> I went to Sacto yesterday monring, [sic] they have some varoyuo [sic] about setting 40 hour work week as a standard for Farm Workers. Now they are going to set up a minimum or prevailing wage (remember my bill) but I couldn't get ahold of the guy who is doing the settng ,they [sic] were in a meeting. . . . I hope they are the prevailing or minimum under AB 59 at xxx [sic] twenty-five cents per hour, don't you? I told them off at Social Welfare, because they never let one in on anything until the decisions are made. Tom Moore of the State Welfar [sic] Board office told me that our "competitors" were working in Merced Co., (Al Green of AWOC) but that the County had refused to take any of their applicants. ("I hope this letter finds you well and recuperated," n.d.)

Writing about such requests, strategy sessions, and political maneuvering shows how influential Huerta was in California state lobbying, committee work, and leadership, especially on behalf of Mexican and Mexican Americans, particularly farm workers. The letters reported her activities, which seems normal in the personal tone of the letter format; discussing such activities might seem boastful in a more public setting, so the letters reveal activities that would not be talked about at all in public rhetoric.

DOCUMENTING UFW ACTIVITIES

Huerta's letters also document the internal activities of the UFW as well as the organization's relationship with other organizations, including the Agricultural Workers Organizing Committee (AWOC, the AFL-CIO group that eventually merged with the UFW), state officials, farm owners, and those with whom they negotiated contracts. They reveal significant information about the organization and Huerta's contributions to it. A few examples here illustrate the importance of such documents in understanding the UFW's history. One of the major issues that the FWA faced was competition from AWOC and the Teamsters, as the first chapter discusses. Huerta confirmed and critiqued this competition in a letter in which she wrote, "The AWOC is having meetings in the camps. It seems they copy everything I do. But they are as usualy [sic] going in with their false promises, and the worker are [sic] already kicking" ("You have probably thought that the FWA . . . ," n.d.). The union also had to be strategic about membership because of the risks farm workers were taking in signing up as members. In another letter, Huerta wrote:

> I hope you noticed in the last memberships I sent that the ones on MacDonald Island were to be sent in Blank Envelopes. This is very important because these guys will get the boot if they are known to belong to any kind of workers/association [sic], and with John Zuckerman, their boss they have year round employment (Mike Leon and Pablo Castillo). ("Hope this letter finds you all in the best of health," 1964)

The personal connection and observation in these letters, even though the problems with membership and AWOC and the Teamsters at the time were well known, communicated Huerta's perspective on the challenges of union organizing and the UFW's competition, such as the reference to AWOC copying her strategies and making false promises.

Another good example of UFW activity detail in Huerta's private, internal organizational communication concerns negotiations with other union organizers and growers. As evidenced in many accounts, there was a lot of conflict among union and community organizers, such as the CSO, the AWOC, the California Agricultural Workers Union, the Teamsters, and the UFW. Each group had different ideas about whom to target, as the following letter illustrates:

> Otto [Estrada, from the CSO] works in a canery [sic], and he said he had a long discussion with the local organizer. It seems they are concentrating on the Filipinos at present because the Mexicans are too unreliable and hard to organize. Their dues are $6.00 (he was not sure on this) and they are looking for a group ins [sic] for their members. Also they are goin [sic] to concentrate on sheds rather than the fields. ("Thank you very much . . .," n.d.)

The reference to Mexicans being too hard to organize and the focus on sheds (probably fruit and vegetable packing and the loading of trucks) also indicate the kind of racial and ethnic division that these organizations faced and how they thought about union organizing. In another memo, Huerta described various internal discussions regarding a strike at the Santa Maria Berry Farm in 1970:

> The people had a work stoppage because they wanted to have a smaller box limit of 10 boxes to the hour and a higher wage of $1.70 per hour. They received their increase of wages to $1.70. The people there negotiated with the xxx [sic] foreman a guy named Mr. Segura, who is the general foreman. They told the foreman they wanted to meet with the main officials of the company and this request was denied. Mr. Segura told them to write a letter to the Company telling them why how [sic] good the union would be for the Company. They have drafted a letter telling them that the Union would be good for the company because it would increase production because when the workers are contented [sic] they produce more. (Memorandum, 1970)

This memo detailed specific negotiations between workers and the company, with advocacy for workers to become members of the union. The memo reveals that one rhetorical tactic used to convince growers to allow union membership was to persuade them that the union was good for the company itself because, as the last sentence explained, satisfied workers produced more.

Huerta's letters also provide insight into her personal views on other UFW activities, such as the national boycott of grapes. In a detailed memo dated 1973, Huerta explained activities in New York as well as other cities. As the director of the New York boycott, this memo outlined strategies for campaigning in New York. New York was one of the more successful boycotts; other city directors tried to emulate her leadership and strategies with less effectiveness, especially in Montreal (Garcia, 2012). As the memo reports:

> FARM WORKERS—Morale is good We have split up the group Two crews of 4 in Queens and Brooklyn to do the Queens Brooklyn Long Island Area One crew to Philadelphia to work with Rut h [sic] Shy. One crew to New Jersey to work with Dave Cormier but he needs direction on how to put muscle on the chains One crew works in the Bronx with Richard [Chávez] although Richard is now extended to the Westchester area above the Bronx and Two [sic] crews work in Manhatten [sic] We are running out of chains to Picket in manhatten [sic] as most of them are clean with the exception of Grand Union. Bohacks, Sloans whom we have a meeting with on Tuesday and of cousrse [sic] A & P who is carrying only Union (UFW) lettuce Meeting with A & P for Friday (East Coast Boycott Report, 1973, punctuation in original)

The memo continued to detail clean chains in New York: International, E & B, Fedco, Royal Farms, King Kullen, Key Foods, Pioneer, Met Foods, and Associated. Huerta then gave updates on the boycott in Chicago (planned march, picket lines, and television coverage), Pittsburgh (support of butchers and steel workers and continued work on smaller stores), Philadelphia (picket lines and church support), Cleveland (picket lines and a newsletter on pesticides), Baltimore (stores carrying union lettuce), Boston (distribution of leaflets and stores carrying union lettuce), Detroit (college campus support), St. Louis, smaller towns in New Jersey, and a few cities in Iowa (East

Coast Boycott Report, 1973). The list of other locations beyond the boycott's top ten cities is significant, suggesting that the boycott happened in many locations, not just in top targeted cities; in other words, it truly was a national boycott.

Huerta's letters and private internal communications within the UFW (such as memos) contain many more details on the inner workings of the organization, and these examples demonstrate the rhetorical importance of such letters in documenting UFW history, providing unknown details or confirming other public reports of union activities. In this sense then, the letters helped record UFW history in important ways, such as providing insider information on how the organization operated.

ESTABLISHMENT OF ACCOUNTABILITY

Huerta's letters to Chávez also served as accountability, beyond a simple reporting of her own activities and UFW activities. The letters and memos she wrote to Chávez function as documentation of a promise to do something or to avoid temptation of some kind. For example, she used the letters as a way to ensure her own financial accountability to the organization, as the following letter indicates:

> I am enclosing a check of my for [sic] $61.00 which is reimbursement for expenses on my Washington trip. Please keep it for me so I will not be tempted to spend it. If you want you can put it in the bank but then I would have to borrow some to pay rent, utilities, etc. So if you think that is not wise, just keep it. I'm afraid I'll be tempted to spend it if I keep it here. ("At long last I am sending you another letter . . .," n.d.)

Avoiding temptation to spend money is one way she held herself responsible, but she also wrote about avoiding other kinds of temptation, for example, about where she would stay the night:

> I am going to Washington again tonight for anotherEqual [sic] Opportunities Conference, but I am coming right back after the meeting. I have a house meeting scheduled for Wednesday night, so I won't get tempted to stay over. ("I hope this letter finds you and yours in the best of health," November, 1963)

These letters illustrate the kind of action she took to keep on track with the UFW's goals; the temptation she described was not illicit, but writing these letters or taking action such as scheduling a house meeting to ensure her timely return helped her keep track of her priorities.

Another common reference in Huerta's letters was about membership dues, again maintaining financial accountability to herself, the members, and the organization. While there are many examples of Huerta's documentation of financial accountability in her letters, the membership dues are perhaps the most important because of the financial hardships so many farm workers faced. Facing many economic obstacles herself as well, Huerta understood the importance of making sure that dues were accurately recorded and paid, as evidenced by the following excerpt:

> Enclosed are dues for a new member Salvador Salas and for Filemon Lepe. I hope you get the new member in time to submit him for March. I mentioned to you that ISAAC TORRES of Acampo is paid for the month of February, ad [sic] I asked you not to charge him, but I guess you did. I gave you his dues on one of my trips to Delano (I think or else I sent hm [sic] in in [sic] one batch after one of my trips along with Dolores Gozales [sic]. However it may be, I am sure he paid me, and I will send in the dues for him if need me [sic]. If you remember, please send him a corrected reminder with March ownng [sic] only, and I will send in his dues for Feb, because he did pay! ("Enclosed are dues for a new member . . .," n.d.)

Similarly, in another letter she wrote about the attention she needed to put toward dues collecting, to ensure the accountability of the members themselves: "Well, dear leader, the time has come to stop this chatter, and I will set my nose to the grind-stone and dues co lection [sic]. I left my list and receipt books with Jose Soto and Gabino , [sic] but havenot [sic] seen them yet to see how they made out as collectors of delinquent dues" ("Well, dear leader . . .," n.d.).

Financial accountability also extended to the organization itself, which often struggled financially. The following account refers to the UFW bank account balance, as well as credit union membership:

ON THE BANK—I'm glad you/did [sic] not invite Correa or Louie to help with the bank, because I've been telling everyone that we have $10,000 in our bank and I would hate to be found out a mentirosa [liar] (this was due to one of your typographical errors). I'm sorry not to be able to send any but f [sic] I can get the CSO to pay that tax, then I can send in at least $50.00 Does it cost anything extra for the member to join the credit union? Or is he automatically a member if he pays his dues? ("This is the fourth attempt," n.d.)

As illustrated by this and other letters and UFW documents written by Huerta, the worry of finances was constant. A $10,000 bank account balance for an organization like the UFW, which had to support numerous activities (ranging from boycott and strike support to regular everyday office work) and staff salaries and expenses (even though they were quite low), was probably considered healthy by the UFW staff but would be considered low by most for-profit and even nonprofit organizations. This letter suggested that they might not even have that much money.

These are just a few examples of how Huerta established accountability within her written correspondence with Chávez. This accountability is especially important as her letters highlight financial hardships that farm workers and the union organizers (as well as Mexicans, Mexican Americans, Filipinos, Chicana/os, and other marginalized groups) encountered in the 1960s and 1970s. Her letters, then, reveal racialized, classed, and gendered aspects of their lives in significant ways. Concretizing these experiences in written form with specific reference to members' and her own needs demonstrates intersectional identities (e.g., Carrillo Rowe, 2009; Griffin & Chávez, 2012), particularly class status. Protecting and accounting for small sums, such as sixty-one dollars, membership dues, and the organization's bank account reveal moments within the UFW's history and Huerta's financial struggles, personally and professionally.

Letter Writing as Collaboration

While Chávez and Huerta generated many of their organizational ideas working together in the CSO and in meetings when they managed to find time and the transportation to get together, Huerta's letters are one of the few recorded documentations of how she and Chávez privately discussed UFW activities and ideas. Letters were an important safe space for building the movement (e.g., enclaves, in Squires, 2002). The nature of the United Farm Worker movement and organization was more collectivistic and communal; for example, entire families and their children were involved in boycott strategies and picket lines (Rose, 1990b; Ruiz, 1998). Fernando Delgado's (1999) study of Rigoberta Menchú's testimonial style reflects this kind of collective understanding: "In the collective frame, ingroupness, community, and interdependence are organizing cultural concepts that structure communication and discourse" (p. 19). Huerta's letters to Chávez suggest a collective, collaborative rhetoric in which she sought opinions and discussed ideas with Chávez through her focus on interdependence within the UFW organization.

When writing about the union, which was almost always the focus of Huerta's letters, three aspects demonstrate how her letters function as collaboration through written dialogue. First, Huerta's letters represent discussions of possible directions the UFW was headed in and what objectives they wanted to pursue. Many policies and objectives implemented in the UFW were discussed as vague ideas in letters. For example, the establishment of the UFW newspaper, *El Malcriado*, was discussed in Huerta's letters to Chávez before the implementation of the idea:

> Cesar, I think we should get that show on the road. I mentioned-to [sic] you before if you wanted me to get adds [sic] to start out with, I think I can get them. What we should do, is budget for a three month out-put [sic] of the paper, get the adds [sic] for a three month period, xxxxxxxxx [sic] and also plan the content of the paper for that length of time, then go out and get the adds [sic]. We can probably write most of the stuff ourselves and plan what phototts [sic] we want to use, etc. I wish I could get to Delano to discuss all this with you . . ." ("This letter has been a week in the making," 1962)

Huerta also used the collective "we" to coordinate actions, expressing her desire to meet in person for further discussion about how to take action to establish the union newspaper, which was first published in 1964 by Chávez and Huerta. The first issues of the newspaper illustrate some of the ideas mentioned above, especially the use of artwork, cartoons, photographs, and a large number of advertisements from local businesses that were included in each issue ("Cultivating creativity," n.d.; *"El Malcriado,"* n.d.). Further demonstrating the collaborative nature of the UFW movement, none of the early issues of *El Malcriado* have author attributions, including each issue's editorials (*"El Malcriado,"* n.d.).

Additionally, Huerta's letters reflect an uncertainty not found in her more public rhetoric. Huerta imbued her letters with a personal tone while writing about policy issues. She frequently wrote with uncertainty about the future actions of the organization. In another letter discussing the feasibility of starting *El Malcriado*, she expressed this uncertainty, asking for Chávez's input:

> I don't know what we are going to do about the newspaper. It all really hinges on you and what you are going to do. If you want me to move down there and take over your duties of paper work, I guess I can . . . I guesstheonly [sic] alternative to freeing you for the newspaper is to get xx [sic] more members so we can hire some clerical help. Am iI [sic] right in xxxxx [sic] this assumption.? [sic] If you have xxxx [sic] other thoughts let me know. ("Since I had not heard," 1964)

Huerta supported the implementation of the newspaper, but her verbal hedges and uncertainty—"I don't know what we are going to do," "It all really hinges on you," and "I guess"—also demonstrate that they were working through ideas about the actual work of putting the newspaper together in a collaborative approach.

Another way Huerta's private letters function as collaboration is through the reciprocity of offering and asking opinions concerning a variety of issues. Huerta used these letters as a way to articulate those issues and develop ideas and possible solutions; she discussed them with Chávez, invited his feedback, or worked through her own plan of action through the process of writing the letter. For example, in the following letter, she discussed some ideas for membership recruitment, one of her key contributions in the early years of the UFW:

I had a brain storm==[sic] on the ab 59, when it goes into effect now in January, lets [sic] try to get some of the members with large families that can't join now for lack of funds in to [sic] the Welfare to make the applications. If we dd [sic] this in each town, we could add—probably double our membership in the month of February, when the going is to be a lot roughter [sic] than it is now. . . . During these next two months we could dedicate ourselves to hunting these people up and making a list of them so they wou d [sic] be rready [sic] to apply in January/ [sic]. Que te parece? ("I hope this letter finds you and yours in the best of health," November, 1963)

In this letter, Huerta illustrates how she was working through potential ways around the effects of proposed legislation (California Assembly Bill 59), as well as ways to simultaneously increase membership. "Que te parece? [What do you think/how does it seem to you?]" asked for Chávez's feedback or engagement, but by putting these ideas on paper, she was also able to develop and work through these ideas.

In another example, she suggested, "Maybe a letter should go out on the FWA stationary [sic] too. What do you think. Originally, I thought we could wait till the session here was over, but now I don't know" ("Received your concise communication," n.d.). She often proposed ideas and then asked for feedback, using qualifiers such as "I hoped we could . . ." and "What I hoped we could do . . ." ("I'm goinf [sic]," n.d.), followed by a plan of action. In other letters, she also told Chávez about similar problems as a way of writing to work through solutions or to create ideas about how to lobby and work with members more effectively, as well as about projects related to the UFW newspaper or radio. Huerta made this very point to Chávez: "[A]s always in these reports to you I am thinking out loud, and out of this confusion must come our plan of action [sic] Looking at this from a more objective stand, I hope you will help me to prepare the plan of action out of the observations I send" ("Capitol Capers," n.d.).

These examples illustrate that such letters played an important role in articulating ideas in the planning stages of various union activities. Exchanging opinions also demonstrates the collaborative element in where they stood on emerging organizational and movement issues (e.g., Gring-Pemble, 1998). This process of uncertainty and reciprocating opinions was absent in Huerta's public rhetoric (e.g., Huerta, 1973; Huerta, "Keynote Address, 1974;" Huerta, "Stanford University," 1974; Huerta, 1987). As Delgado (1999) explains, this type of collaborative, collectivistic rhetoric "privileges the whole and demands an ethos of mutual dependence and shared identity. Collectivists share a cultural and symbolic substance that pervades their social interactions and organization" (p. 19). Huerta's letters clearly demonstrate how personal letters function in this collectivist fashion, through their complete integration of farm worker causes and personal matters, collapsing personal and professional lives into one cause that became the UFW's symbol of shared identity.

Letter Writing as (Self-)Affirmation

Not only did Huerta use her letters as a way to discuss and collaborate on ideas with Chávez, but the letters served a more personal function as well. In many ways, reports of her UFW activities to Chávez functioned to affirm her successes, sacrifices, and roles within and outside the UFW. Huerta's letters allowed her to share her union activities and accomplishments with Chávez. Richard Gregg argues that protest rhetoric often involves an ego-function; although Huerta's letters are not written as protest rhetoric per se, her protest-related work for the UFW may have contributed to this ego-function in her letters. Specifically, Gregg contends that this type of rhetoric involves self-persuasion because of the need for "psychological refurbishing and affirmation" and self-constitution, or "*constituting* self-hood through expression; that is, with establishing, defining, and affirming one's self-hood as one engages in a rhetorical act" (1971, p. 74, emphasis in original). Gregg explains that it is the process of verbalization and repetition that enables self-realization, selfhood, and self-identities. Huerta's letters reported her numerous accomplishments, affirmed proposed ideas, and noted her sacrifices for the union. Given the challenges and barriers that Chicana activists faced during the 1960s, this approach in her letters may have played an important role in persuading both herself and Chávez that she was a highly skilled negotiator, lobbyist, and organizer. Although Chávez emerged as the public face of the UFW, Huerta skillfully negotiated the male-oriented activist movements of the 1960s and 1970s and took on a leadership position in the UFW from the beginning.

This rebellion, however, took confidence and courage, and her written documentation of her accomplishments illustrates one way in which she may have engaged in an affirmatory process, particularly because she felt "a sense of guilt about inadequacy," something that Gregg contends is a key feature of the need for ego affirmation (p. 81). In a 1975 interview, Huerta noted, "I know I have a terrible temper. It might be that I'm still suffering from guilt about my divorce, and from the feeling that I shouldn't really be the leader people see in me. . . . I guess I just haven't forgiven myself the divorce, and if you haven't forgiven yourself something, how can you forgive others" (Baer, 1975, p. 40)? This interview reflects Huerta's sense of guilt and insecurity; as Gregg (1971) maintains, "to be aware that one has an ego, to know of the existence of one's self-hood, there must be not only a feeling of being noticed, of being attended to, but a perception of being able to control at least a portion of the situations in which one finds himself [or herself]" (p. 79). Huerta's letters serve as an example of exerting control through self-affirmation.

Because Huerta and Chávez used letters to discuss UFW business, her letters and reports fulfilled the collaborative function of informing Chávez of her activities. They also allowed her to think through her activities, write them down, and send them to Chávez, verbalizing and repeating her accomplishments. For example, in one six-page letter, Huerta discussed her many accomplishments during a trip to Sacramento by noting:

> Being a now (ahem) experienced lobbyist, I am able to speak on a man to man basis with other lobbyists and am being continuously over-flattered by having other lobbyists, legislaters [sic], government folk and complete strangers come and speak to me congratulating me and asking me about CSO's legislative program and begging to know 'What We Want.'" ("Capitol Capers," n.d., p. 1)

In introducing her accomplishments with her experiences working as a lobbyist in the state capitol, Huerta shared her success with Chávez. She then continued, in great detail, with what she called "Personality Portraits," which introduced key players in Sacramento, discussing proposed actions and strategies for negotiating with them. Throughout this letter, she demonstrated her strong understanding of the political situation in Sacramento and ideas for proposing legislation and working with key lobbyists.

The letter functions to establish Huerta's competence as a lobbyist and ability to network and connect with important legislative decision makers. Not only did the letter emphasize her work in Sacramento, it also confirmed her aptitude for this kind of work. In the process of describing her accomplishments, she demonstrated to Chávez and other UFW members that she was a talented lobbyist and negotiator and simultaneously affirmed those accomplishments. Given Huerta's recognition for her contributions to UFW lobbying and negotiating (Coburn, 1976; Rose, 1988), these letters not only evidence her early successes but also demonstrate the process of self-affirmation in letter writing.

In other letters, Huerta often highlighted her interactions with not only legislators but also with potential UFW members. For example, she wrote to Chávez in 1962 that "the membership pledges are coming in much easier than I thought. I have 15 more to send you & and I really have not begun as yet" ("Please excuse my long delay," October 19, 1962). In another letter, she gave a specific example of how union activities were influential for membership drives:

> The Union had a big meeting (of wins and palapatoys [sic]) in St. Mary's Hall. Teresa Lopez (one of my unexpected callers) was so inspired by the Union's proposals of "Strike now, eat later", Call on us and we will go talk to your boss to increase your wages", etc., that she came right over and paid her dues to us. Furthermore she said some of the other ladies that were present at that meeting also want to join us the non-striking Union. ("I received you [sic] penitent letter," February 29, 1964)

Although in this letter Huerta does not directly take credit for recruiting new members, she calls Teresa Lopez "one of my unexpected callers," implying that she was indeed responsible for recruiting her for union membership. She was not simply reporting union activities but sharing her accomplishments, which functioned as self-affirmation through the process of writing. Furthermore, her membership recruitment spoke directly to her contributions to the farm worker social

movement, since membership in the union was essential for negotiating contracts with the owners of the farms that started in 1965, after
the first grape strike.

Finally, many of Huerta's letters highlighted the great sacrifices she
made for the union, whether related to her health, family, or financial
difficulties. These numerous narratives of sacrifice may have been conscious or unconscious rhetorical choices, but the reader understands
from these letters that she sacrificed herself for the union. For example,
she wrote to Chávez:

> Yes, I am still breathing, although I got a bad scare last week. I
> kept feeling worse and worse so I went to the County Hospital
> and hey [sic] shook me up because they said I have to have an
> operation. . . . I have a tumor in one of my ovaries. . . . The only
> reason I hate to get operated on is because I hate to lose the
> time. My health, plus no bay [sic] sitter is one of the reasons
> things hav [sic] not been moving, so help me Cesar, without
> someone to watch my kids, i [sic] just can't find enough time
> to work, especially in the evening when it counts. . . . Also my
> finances have been terrible. I only drew $20.00 on my last U.I.
> check and have two weeks for my next check. ("Yes, I am still
> breathing," n.d.)

In this letter, she concluded by telling Chávez that she was planning
to go to Delano and then Los Angeles for meetings and that she had
addressed problems with delinquent union members. Her narrative of
personal problems related to her health, finances, and child care emphasize not only the issues she faced as a Chicana activist and sometimes single mother but also the sacrifices she had made for the farm
worker cause and the UFW mission of social justice for farm workers.
In effect, she used the letter as confirmation of her sacrifices for the
union and to bolster her own commitment, best illustrated in the line
"The only reason I hate to get operated on is because I hate to lose the
time." This line also may reflect the sense of guilt she felt in not getting
more done, reflecting feelings of inadequacy as well. The letter functioned to reframe that guilt, in that she demonstrated what she had
accomplished even with her health problems and lack of babysitters.

The process of writing these letters to Chávez enabled Huerta to
highlight her accomplishments, proposed ideas, and sacrifices, which
allowed her to constitute self and create an identity as a social justice

activist and organizer for the farm worker cause. Gregg (1971) explains that ego-function of such rhetoric is based on three general stages of ego formation, ego maintenance, and ego destruction. Huerta's letters represent these three stages in which she built ego through the writing and verbalization of her work, maintained ego through proposing plans and asking for feedback, and destroyed ego through personal sacrifice to the union, which, according to Gregg, becomes a repetitive and ongoing cycle. Carlson's (1995) study of letters illustrates that letters can function to constitute identity on one's own terms through self-description, revealing the affirmatory aspect of letter writing that can carry over into interpersonal and public rhetorical acts. While Carlson focuses on the constitutive aspect of letter writing in terms of character invention through a rhetorical strategy of differentiation, Huerta's letters are more about the process of recording her accomplishments and plans, which played a constitutive as well as an ego-function role. For Huerta, these letters to Chávez may have functioned as precursory ideas to UFW movement rhetoric, but they also empowered her to become a UFW negotiator and lobbyist. Holling notes that Chicana identity is constructed through a woman's "conception of her self which is communicated through the names or labels she attributes to herself, the stories she tells and the experiences she conveys, and it involves a process of becoming" (2000, p. 17). Mario García (2008) further explains that Huerta developed intersectional identities related to gender, ethnic, and class consciousness through her work with the UFW. The process of writing letters allowed Huerta to claim her own names, stories, and experiences, facilitating this intersectional identity constitution through affirmation of self.

Letter Writing as Catharsis

In the process of using letters as collaboration and confirmation, Huerta constantly wrote about issues that affected her personally. These personal narratives also rhetorically functioned as catharsis, or a way for her to negotiate the various personal and professional stresses in her life, while at the same time, often proposing solutions to her own problems. Aristotle defined catharsis as the process of cleansing or purification, whereas Kenneth Burke (1966) called catharsis a transcendence or transformation. As I have argued elsewhere (with my co-author, Valerie Renegar), the "writing process reflects a self-oriented activism that is more about self-affirmation, catharsis, and expression than generating social change" (2006, p. 67). While Huerta was certainly motivated to work for social change, the process of writing these letters also functioned as catharsis for her.

Frequently, she wrote about her financial difficulties in arranging shelter, food, clothing, transportation, and other basic necessities for her children and herself. Huerta earned very little money from union paychecks and lived on mostly donated food, clothes, transportation, and childcare (Coburn, 1976; Felner, 1998; Foley, 1974; Rose, 1988). Because Huerta worked as many as eighty hours per week, she had to either rely on family and friends for childcare or take her kids with her to meetings and negotiations. Huerta's letters illustrate her constant concern about her children: where they would live, what schools they would attend, and who would care for them. Her children were often separated, living with various family members and friends' families.

Although Huerta had two ex-husbands, her letters also indicate that she was responsible for childcare and financial support. In the following letter excerpt, Huerta detailed how she typically arranged her children's living situations:

> I am now working on having my kids stay with various assorted relatives for the next month and one half until school starts. If all goes very well, I will still be left with maybe one or two kids, depending on whether Ventura [Huerta's second ex-husband] can make arrangements to keep the boys. . . . Then do you suppose I could make living arrangements with someone to put me and my one kid up for a month and one half, then I could pay room and board. That means I would not be paying rent, or a baby sitter or utilities, at least until school begins. ("Just a few short lines," n.d.)

One of Huerta's biggest issues was determining where each of her children would live, often only for a few months at a time. The letter reflects a problem-solution thought process, as she wrote about her childcare arrangements and proposed how she might address them.

Similarly, Huerta also constantly looked for ways to create more time so that she could work on various union activities. Babysitters were an expensive necessity that provided her the time to commit to lobbying and traveling, but as the following and the previous excerpts illustrate, she was in constant negotiation to find family-provided or free childcare, reduce her living expenses, and participate in ongoing union meetings:

> I spoke to my step-father about giving me 6 months rent free. I expect to fire my babysitter, Sunday, so then my living expense will be cut down about half. I am again going to propose my plan to CSO that they pay just for two days a week for lobbying, instead of a weekly salary. On $30 a week, I should be able to survive, if I don't have to pay a baby sitter. Maybe I can [sic] get some ne [sic] to watch the kids for me just two days a week, free, then I can have the house meetings at night, for the Association. ("You have probably thought that the FWA," 1962)

This pattern is repeated in many of Huerta's letters to Chávez. Although her ex-husbands ostensibly did support their respective children financially and sometimes provided a home, Huerta assumed most of the responsibility for planning and ensuring that her children had a place to live, food to eat, and a school to attend, issues that other UFW leaders (mostly male) did not have to face. For example, Helen Chávez took care of the Chávez children, so childcare was not an issue in the same way for César Chávez. In fact, Huerta's children sometimes stayed with the Chávez family (Rose, 1990a). This problem-solution format in Huerta's letters represents catharsis through the transformation of the problem itself into a workable solution, as she began the letter discussing the difficulties of finding childcare but then explained the steps that she had already worked out to cover childcare to provide her time for union activities.

Not only did Huerta write about her personal financial problems, she also openly expressed her frustrations with various people, including Chávez himself. Huerta, who had a reputation for being assertive, was often confrontational with Chávez in her letters, even though they both respected one another for their own strengths and contributions to the UFW movement (M. T. García, 2008). This ability to be confrontational comes from an open discursive space in which Huerta felt confident and comfortable in expressing herself assertively with Chávez. For example, she wrote to Chávez in 1964:

> To furth r [sic finish up with my peeves, since I am not the xxxxx [sic] quiet long suffering type, I also resent it when you are not

honest with me. . . . I do not mind playing the part of the heavy
if If [sic] I know why and when I am supposed to take this role
—please remember this for any future conspiracies. This is what
I mean by your "honesty" of sin cerity [sic] if it sounds nicer
thatway [sic]. ("Since I had not heard from you," 1964)

This letter illustrates Huerta's ability to cleanse or purify herself of a
possible interpersonal conflict with Chávez by expressing her peeves
in letter format. In the above letter, she addressed these peeves at the
beginning, and after half a page of typewritten peeves, she wrote, "All
of the above is old business, but now I want to get to the new developments" ("Since I had not heard from you," 1964), and quickly moved
into a report of her union activities.

Furthermore, Huerta may have used the writing process to (sub)
consciously construct new identities as she wrote about her struggles
to provide for her family. Although it is difficult to pinpoint the ex-
act moment when someone evolves into a new identity, her letters reflected a consciousness of her social standing and the struggles she
faced as mother, activist, organizer, and female leader. Palczewski
(2001) draws from Kenneth Burke's notion of terministic catharsis to
explain how such definitional shifts occur, enabling guilt redemption,
"'rebirth,' transcendence, transubstantiation, or simply for 'transformation'" (Burke, 1966, p. 367). In Huerta's case, terministic catharsis
functions as identity formation, as her letter writing process reminded
both the recipient and herself of her social justice awareness and her
own struggles. Huerta believed that it was important to focus on key
principles: "first, to establish a strong sense of identity; second, to develop a sense of pride; third, always to maintain the value of service to
others; and fourth, to be self-reflective and true to oneself" (Griswold
del Castillo & Garcia, 1995, pp. 69–70).

Huerta's personal stories, frustrations, and hardships reflected in
her letters exemplify how those letters function cathartically and constitutively. Huerta used the letters to Chávez to write about her problems as a way of purging the stresses she was facing on a daily basis
but also as a way to balance tensional guilt about her children and the
farm worker cause. Indeed, the union became Huerta's family, and her
children were raised by the union. Rose (1990a, 1990b) observes that
work related to the union became family affairs, whether related to
bargaining with growers, participating in protests or picket lines, or
lobbying in Sacramento or Washington, DC.

Her letters to Chávez may have functioned cathartically to purge and cleanse anxieties about balancing family and union activities, as well as to address interpersonal issues with Chávez, or as a way to create space for self-expression and constitutive identity. Lisa Flores explains that "Chicana feminists begin the process of carving out a space for themselves where they can break down constraints imposed by other cultures and groups" (1996, p. 143). Although Flores writes about Chicana novelists and writers, Huerta used these letters as one way to create her own space for expression, agency, and identity. The manner in which Huerta's letters were written reflect a style of cathartic stream of consciousness rather than one of carefully planned, edited, and revised writing, since her letters were written on a typewriter and contain typographical errors and colloquial language. This style suggests that she felt free to express her thoughts and concerns without restraint. Huerta's sense of agency came from years of developing the self-confidence to speak out and originated in her social and family networks, which enabled her sense of confidence and rhetorical agency, as explored in the previous chapter. Huerta's cathartic writing style is just one manifestation of her sense of rhetorical agency. The symbiotic relationship between rhetorical agency and constitution of identity that emerges in Huerta's letters is especially important, given the rhetorical constraints that Huerta faced as a Chicana and labor activist.

Conclusion

Huerta's letters reveal three important conclusions about the rhetorical process of her letter writing. First, the four functions of Huerta's letters—documentation, collaboration, affirmation, and catharsis—are intertwined features that contributed to Huerta's social justice identities, especially related to race, class, ethnicity, nationality, and gender. While I have separated these four functions for analysis, Huerta's letters illustrate how documentation, collaboration, affirmation, and catharsis often occurred simultaneously in her narratives and appeals. Delgado (1995) explains that collectivistic rhetoric emphasizes interdependence and the need to share common experiences; Huerta's letters focus on that kind of collaboration with Chávez. While this chapter focuses only on Huerta's letters, there was a great deal of reciprocity in their relationship; they collaborated and affirmed each other.

Building from Gring-Pemble's (1998) work, this analysis also reveals that letter writing in social movements can be more than conscious-ness raising and a transition from the private to the public sphere. That is, Huerta's letters demonstrate a collaborative and collectivistic function for organizational activities and ideas, such as her thoughts about *El Malcriado* or membership drives. Her language, like her use of the plural "we," and requests for exchanging opinions further illus-trate this collectivistic approach. Huerta's letters also reflect a need for affirmation and catharsis to address her insecurities and the guilt that she experienced, whether about her role as a mother or as a labor or-ganizer (Baer, 1975). Her letters were both simultaneously other and self-directed, expanding Gregg's (1971) and Stewart's (1999) under-standing of the ego-function in social movements through the study of letters. Furthermore, as Carlson (1995) explains, letter writing can function as character invention; for Huerta, the cathartic aspect of her letters may have also played a role in identity formation and aware-ness, as well as a reminder of her sacrifices for and commitment to the union way of life. Huerta's letters, then, build an understanding of the purposes of letter writing, especially within social movements, through these interrelated concepts of documentation, collaboration, affirmation, and catharsis.

Furthermore, Huerta's letters provide insight into the UFW union in ways that scholarship about public discourse does not reveal. Specifically, Huerta's letters demonstrate not just the difficulties of her own life, especially as a mother, but also the challenges facing UFW activists during the 1960s. Other scholars have studied the public rhetoric of Puerto Rican and Chicano activists such as César Chávez, Reies Tijerina, Rodolfo "Corky" Gonzáles, and the Young Lords Organization (Delgado, 1995; Enck-Wanzer, 2006, 2010; Hammerback & Jensen, 1980, 1994; Jensen, Burkholder, & Hammerback, 2003; Jensen & Hammerback, 1982), but the focus on the personal experience of what it means to be a social activist in these movements has been missing. Huerta's letters reveal her personal struggles as a woman participat-ing in the UFW union and how she negotiated and survived these struggles. The letters remind the reader that participation in social movements, particularly power struggles related to class, ethnicity, na-tional origin, and gender, is a commitment that requires personal sac-rifice and difficulty. Ultimately, Huerta's letter writing provides greater insight into her public life, the UFW as a union, the Chicana/o move-ment, and social movements more broadly.

Chapter 4

MOTHERHOOD, FAMILIA, EMOTIONALITY

STRATEGIC USE OF GENDERED PUBLIC PERSONA

It is widely known that the growers do not like to face Huerta over a bargaining table. During the 1970s, they labeled her as "crazy" and walked out on her. They say she is "unprofessional"—because she shouts at them and cries easily and condemns them for decades of repression. ("A Life-Time Commitment," 1979, p. 6)

In contrast to the way in which Dolores Huerta wrote and talked about her private feelings, experiences, and identities in her letters to Chávez, as the previous chapter explores, Huerta as a public figure, and especially as she gained experience as a leader, was confident, outspoken, and unafraid in her commitment to social justice. The elements of intersectional habitus in her early life and her private relationships with her mother and people like César Chávez helped to shape her leadership style, which relied on diverse rhetorical maneuvers. Dolores Huerta was well known both within the United Farm Workers (UFW) union and to outside audiences as an outspoken advocate for not just farm workers' rights but also women's, Chicana/os', and other marginalized people's rights. Lobbyists, politicians, farm owners, and others saw her as a force to be reckoned with, and farm workers and Chicana/os were inspired by her actions.

However, not all were fans. Some called her "the Dragon Lady," "referring to her ability to speak 'with fire'" (A. Chávez, 2005, p. 248; Huerta, 2003; Foster, 1996). This term is problematic as both a gendered and racialized assessment of her rhetoric and a term often used to critique Asian and Asian American women for their outspokenness, in violation of the stereotypical expectation of the quiet, silent woman. The opening quotation of this chapter also illustrates gendered and racialized assessments, calling Huerta crazy and unprofessional. Understanding Huerta in this way implies that she was

extremely aggressive, combative, and uncompromising, rhetorical
styles that countered expectations related to stereotypical standings
of race, gender, and class. Yet her detractors negatively connoted her
rhetorical style primarily because, as a Mexican American woman, she
was expected to be reserved and apolitical. Alicia Chávez (2005) documents both how growers and politicians responded to Huerta, calling
her crazy and violent, for she often attacked and insulted those who
violated her sense of social, political, and economic justice, and how
Huerta responded to such charges: "Why do we need to be polite to
people who are making racist statements at the table, or making sexist
comments" (quoted in Chávez, 2005, p. 249)? Huerta thus called into
question the racist and sexist manner in which many reacted to her
calls for social justice.

In this chapter, I propose a different rendering of Huerta's public
persona, as Huerta employed gendered tactics of familia and emotionality that enacted her sense of identity, resistance, and strategic moves
to engage with diverse audiences. Huerta often used such tactics strategically and intentionally to disrupt traditional speaking, negotiating,
and bargaining styles; rather than use these techniques to persuade audiences, she used them to break with expectation and tradition. I contend that Huerta's style is complicated, as she drew from her own cultural experiences and intersectional habitus, but she was also able to
effectively read the rhetorical situation and capitalize on her strengths
as a speaker. In what follows, I first discuss intersectional issues and
their relationships to rhetorical styles, which frames the second section,
on how Gloria Anzaldúa's concept of haciendo caras elucidates the nuances and complicated nature of style and public personae. Using haciendo caras, I then develop two exemplars of Huerta's rhetoric: first, her
rhetorical style through emotion, and second, her use of motherhood
and familia. The chapter concludes with an exploration of what such
styles mean in relationship to haciendo caras and public personae.

Intersectionality and Rhetorical Style

Rhetorical scholars have addressed personae as a way in which rhetors
or agents employ rhetorically diverse tactics and strategies to achieve
their goals. As Doss and Jensen (2013) explain, the term "persona" first
referred to masks, such as those worn in theater in ancient Greece.

Scholars have since described first, second, third, fourth, null, and transcendent personae to explicate rhetorical options and diversity (e.g., Black, 1970; Cloud, 1999; Doss & Jensen, 2013; Morris, 2002; Wander, 1984). The transcendent persona is perhaps most complex. As Doss and Jensen (2013) contend, there are elements of mystery and identification within the transcendent persona of Dolores Huerta. They define this persona along three key points in which the speaker identifies boundary-breaking experiences, connects with the audience but also develops a sense of self that is different, and develops new visions that emerge from the transcendent persona. Other rhetorical scholars have argued that women of color are rhetorically adroit and do not easily address the public and private spheres in how they think about context and audience (Campbell, 1986, 1989, 1995; Fabj, 1993; Flores, 1996; Hayden, 2003; Holling, 2000, 2012; Japp, 1985; Palczewski, 1996; Ruiz, 1998; Shome, 1996; Tonn, 1996).

The notion of constitutive intersectionality in the context of rhetorical studies also enables an understanding of how identities are interpellated in moments of speech and embodied nonspeech acts. Hahner explains that "[c]onventions of address provide cues to both rhetor and audience as to what sort of performances and identifications are preferred. Further, the repetition of convention becomes the mechanism through which privileged bodies find comfort in familiar locales, and disadvantaged bodies discover the moving monotony of discomfort" (2012, p. 162). In many ways, Huerta navigated places of both comfort and discomfort with many kinds of audiences. Huerta's leadership can, in part, be explained by how she built connection and affective involvement with her audiences while employing strategic essentialism and embracing her own sense of identities in those particular moments. She manipulated preferred and comfortable rhetorical forms while turning uncomfortable or marginalized forms into potentially acceptable practice.

Huerta's rhetorical styles, then, move in different ways beyond traditional notions of rhetorical styles. Although Rose (1990a, 2004) has argued that Huerta's style was not typical of Mexican and Mexican American women's leadership styles in the UFW, her rhetorical practices are interesting for precisely that reason, as Huerta was able to subvert cultural traditions and expectations, and she was certainly not the only Mexican or Mexican American woman to take on such leadership roles (see also Rose, 1994, 1995). To explain Huerta's public rhetoric and to complicate gendered and racialized understandings of how people understood and responded to her, I use Gloria Anzaldúa's concept of haciendo caras (making face, making soul) to move to more nuanced readings of Huerta's persona. Even as she drew from a traditional notion of gender, she also turned it on its head. Haciendo caras, as illustrated in Huerta's life and career, is another facet of rhetorical agency. In previous chapters, I discussed one aspect of rhetorical agency as intersectional habitus, but life influences are not the only aspect of rhetorical agency, as this chapter examines. Here, I argue that haciendo caras, as demonstrated in Huerta's public persona, expands our understandings of intersectionality and personae through motherhood, familia, and emotion. Her rhetorical styles as haciendo caras illustrate how she negotiated many different constraints, audiences, contexts, and time periods.

Haciendo Caras: Rhetorical Agency through Adaptability and Embodiment

Gloria Anzaldúa (1990) employs the idea of haciendo caras to demonstrate rhetorical limitations and enabling mechanisms, even while recognizing that it is fostered through collaborative relationships and the tacit approval of such caras. First, she explains, "'[f]ace' is the surface of the body that is the most noticeably inscribed by social structures, marked with instructions on how to be *mujer, macho*, working class, Chicana" (1990, p. xv). Beyond the literal face, haciendo caras is the embodiment of identity and what that means for political struggle and activism. Elsewhere, Anzaldúa and Moraga (in their 1981 anthology, *This Bridge Called My Back*) call this "theory in the flesh," that is, the need for theories to address how "face" or "body" influence and affect our political and rhetorical stances as well as how others see and interpret both face and body. Indeed, Jacqueline Martinez (2000) contends that "we need theory to develop more powerful and sophisticated tools for engaging the fleshy rootedness of human-world existence. The challenge (and responsibility) lies in bridging the gap between those theoretical tools and our flesh, putting them concretely to the lived experiences through which it has been possible for us to speak, hear, see, feel, and do in the first place" (2000, p. 27). Theory in the flesh addresses intersectional identities and how we physically wear those identities in addition to our politics of resistance (Griffin & Chávez, 2012). As Carrillo Rowe observes, "the face is the visual site of our expression, written on our bodies as singular and shifting marker of our relations to one another and as such, the site through which we constitute our belongings" (2009, p. 7).

Building from Anzaldúa's (1987) book *Borderlands*, Mora (1993), Blackwell (2010), and Ortega (2004) have described nepantla as a place between cultures or a middle place. In this location, rhetors or agents learn a "specialized set of skills that border dwellers, or *nepantleras*, develop as a result of surviving the violence of being caught between, translating, and hybridizing multiple systems of gendered, sexual, cultural, linguistic, and economic power" (Blackwell, 2010, p. 14). Blackwell further explains that nepantla results in "strategies based on understanding how power operates in extremely restricted spaces and on adapting tactics that move in and between those confinements to open new possibilities" (p. 15). As such, the campesinas (female farm workers) in Blackwell's study negotiate this rhetorical and physical space through their own transnational subjectivities, intersectional forms of oppression, and community organizing, which lead them to positions of empowerment. Instead of allowing their marginal status to inhibit their sense of self and the rights they are entitled to, these women are able to bring themselves together to organize and employ new interpretations of gendered roles that enable their own empowerment. Haciendo caras, through nepantla, is a tactic or strategy of resistance against dominant forces that mandate prescribed and confined roles.

In addition, Anzaldúa describes haciendo caras as an ability to "'change' faces, . . . like a chameleon, to change color when the dangers are many and the options few" (p. xv). The idea of haciendo caras is also a strategic movida (move) in which one may address internal insecurities or lack of confidence, the kinds of masks, "*las máscaras*, we are compelled to wear, [which] drive a wedge between our intersubjective personhood and the *persona* we present to the world" (p. xv). As Mitsuye Yamada writes, "My mask is control / concealment / endurance / my mask is escape / from my / self" (1990, p. 114). In some ways, these masks are más/caras, or a type of "super face" that require extra work to maintain as a result of the complex and intersectional identities many women face. These caras might also function as masks that may obscure one's true feelings, insecurities, or lack of confidence. As Margaret Montoya explains, "For stigmatized groups, such as persons of color, the poor, women, gays and lesbians, assuming a mask is comparable to being 'on stage.' Being 'on stage' is frequently experienced as being acutely aware of one's words, affect, tone of voice, movements, and gestures because they seem out of sync with what one is feeling and thinking" (1995, pp. 531–532).

While all people employ caras that function as máscaras in ways that enable them to engage tactics or strategies, there is also a danger in such máscaras. As Kenji Yoshino (2006) explains, we can downplay stigmas, disabilities, race, ethnicity, sexual orientation, and gender through the act of covering, but to do so may require a sacrifice of authenticity, as "covering is work" (p. 130). That is, maintaining caras and máscaras can be a rhetorical tactic to accomplish something, but the work required to constantly engage can also be debilitating for one's sense of self. For example, Yoshino identifies four ways in which covering might be employed: "*Appearance* concerns how an individual physically presents herself to the world. *Affiliation* concerns her cultural identifications. *Activism* concerns how much she politicizes her identity. *Association* concerns her choice of fellow travelers—lovers, friends, colleagues" (2006, p. 79). As Sara Ahmed (2017) argues, women of color have to work hard to avoid being noticeable. Such acts of covering and wearing máscaras can be exhausting and exacting on one's sense of authenticity, even if rhetorically connective for different publics.

Caras, in this context, relate to what Juan Guerra calls "transcultural repositioning and nomadic consciousness." Nomadic consciousness is a reflection of our awareness of different kinds of consciousness, such as naïve, nostalgic, and critical. That is, nomadic consciousness indicates a wavering between different kinds of consciousness, such as caras as a strategic movida (a critical consciousness) or caras as concealment of self (a nostalgic consciousness or contradictory consciousness). These kinds of consciousness, then, lead to a transcultural repositioning, which

> is a rhetorical ability that members of our community often
> enact intuitively but must learn to self-consciously regulate, if
> they hope to move back and forth more productively between

and among different languages and dialects, different social classes, different cultural and artistic forms, different ways of seeing and thinking about the increasingly fluid and hybridized world emerging all around us. (Guerra, 2004, p. 16)

While Guerra contends that such transcultural repositioning is not chameleon-like, as Anzaldúa suggests, haciendo caras requires back-and-forth movements among potentially competing positions and identities. Guerra observes that such transcultural repositioning is difficult and dangerous given the risk to the self, emotionally, physically, and intellectually, as is the process of engaging in haciendo caras.

Finally, haciendo caras, in addition to involving physical faces that express emotion, subversive gestures, and masks of identity, is also the ability to transform, giving rise to "transformations that, while often brutally painful, can allow for non-binary identity, for new states of mestiza consciousness" (Lunsford, 1999, p. 44; see also Anzaldúa, 1987). To risk putting oneself out there is both difficult and dangerous but necessary for engaging in social change and advocacy as well as personal transformation. The emergence of and experimentation with different caras of resistance, identity, selfhood, activism, and so forth are part of a bigger social movement. Creative and resistive acts are embodied through Anzaldúa's caras, and as she contends, women of color are more likely to bring such tools, strategies, and movidas to the table because they have been experimenting their entire lives as they move through intersections and different worlds of identity.

Illustrating rhetorical agency through Anzaldúa's concept of haciendo caras and other concepts discussed above, such as masks, covering, and transcultural repositioning, also enables a reading through social justice and marginality. Anzaldúa reminds us that haciendo caras is not just a strategy but also a tactic that emerges from constant rhetorical negotiation of a space/place/language game in which those who are marginal seize opportunities for resistance when possible. This kind of rhetorical dexterity, as Shannon Carter (2007) calls it, demonstrates the importance of adaptability but also a critical consciousness in which sensemaking of new spaces and resistance to such spaces requires an understanding of input, tools, output, and rules of that system. As Guerra reminds us of the difficulty and danger in transcultural positioning, Carter demonstrates the challenge in maintaining this adaptability and critical consciousness so that one can engage in both strategies and tactics as appropriate or inappropriate when disruption is intended.

Haciendo Caras through Emotion and Affect

Relying on the power of pathos, Huerta manifested emotion as a rhetorical strategy through melodrama, physical expressions, and other verbal and nonverbal aspects of her public persona. Serving as a form of embodied resistance, Huerta purposefully cultivated her public persona as a negotiator and righteous resister through this use of emotion. Ahmed notes that "[e]motion is the feeling of bodily change," which functions as a precursor to embodied activism as well as the manifestation of emotional expression in the moment of such resistance (2004, p. 5). Rob DeChaine also argues that affect is the intensity of emotion, but it is rooted in our subconsciousness and unconsciousness; it acts as a "conduit between our bodies and our souls, and it represents an intersection of our bodies and the outside world" (2002, p. 86; see also Damasio, 1999; Rice, 2008). Denise Riley (2005) connects the power of affect and emotion to language, in that language can injure with lasting effect. The "affect-soaked power of language" can shape our sense of agency and identity (Riley, 2005, p. 5).

Affect and emotion have powerful effects on identities, including gender, racial, ethnic, queer, and other marginalized identities, for they function through relationality and social circulation (Ahmed, 2004; Brennan, 2004; Clough, 2007; Hardt, 2007; Riley, 2005). Several scholars have studied how the intersection of emotion and the body emerges in the performance of bodily (cultural/racial/ethnic/queer/gendered/classed) differences (K. Chávez, 2009; Cisneros, 2012; Goltz & Pérez, 2012; Muñoz, 2000; Ono, 2012). Affective excess, as José Esteban Muñoz (2000) notes, marks the appropriateness or inappropriateness of the ethnic/racialized/gendered/queer/classed body. Huerta's use of emotionality intertwined with the way in which she engaged a rhetoric of familia represents an inversion of appropriate emotion based on how growers' representatives responded to her use of emotion and familia at the bargaining table and how she employed such styles in public protest. The cross-cultural nature of Huerta's work, in terms of bargaining, negotiating, and lobbying with growers and politicians, meant that such appeals to emotion challenged traditional understandings of rhetorical appeal, particularly as the dual and conflicting stereotypes held by mainstream US Americans construed Mexican American women as passive subject as well as the emotional spitfire.[1]

In these caras of emotionality, Huerta literally distorted her face and body to reflect the powerful emotions she felt about farm worker, Chicana/o, and women's rights. These caras rhetorically functioned in three ways, through passion, disruption, and excess. First, they functioned to demonstrate her passion and lifetime commitment to justice, especially for those in marginal positions. For example, she regularly spoke of injustices that farm workers faced, as evidenced in the following statement she made before a congressional committee in 1969: "Many farm workers are members of minority groups. They are Filipino- and Mexican-Americans and black Americans. These same farm workers are on the front lines of battle in Vietnam. It is a

---

1. Many scholars have extensively documented historical and contemporary stereotypes of Latinas in mass media (see Fregoso, 2003a; Mary Beltrán's *Latina/o Stars in U.S. Eyes*, 2009; Isabel Molina Guzmán's *Dangerous Curves*, 2010; Deborah Paredez's *Selenidad*, 2009; Clara Rodríguez's *Heroes, Lovers, and Others*, 2008, as just a few examples). One stereotype is the hypersexualized "spitfire female Latina characterized by red-colored lips, bright seductive clothing, curvaceous hips and breasts, long brunette hair, and extravagant jewelry" (Molina Guzmán & Valdivia, 2004, p. 211). Clara Rodríguez (2008) documents this same stereotype in movie stars and celebrities like Dolores del Rio, Rita Hayworth, Raquel Welch, and other Latinas from earlier decades. Chicana writers have long theorized and problematized the virgen y mala mujer (bad woman) dualism. The Virgen de Guadalupe or marianismo (Virgin Mary) represents perfection in faith and in motherhood but also the one who helps the poor and oppressed (Anzaldúa, 1987; Fabj, 1993; González Martínez, 2002; López, 2002; Trujillo, 1998). On the other hand, as Bernice Rincón explains, the stereotype of "the mala mujer is assertive, rather than passive like the 'self-denying mother,' the 'waiting sweetheart,' the 'hermetic idol'" (1997, p. 26). This sense of duty is also tied to cultural loyalty, or the lack thereof, represented in Malinche, the conqueror Hernán Córtez's translator, who represents betrayal of her indigenous people in the 15th and 16th centuries (Flores-Ortiz, 1998; Ruiz, 1998). For instance, Bernadette Calafell's (2005) performance piece reminds readers of Malinche's symbolism of feelings related to inauthenticity, pochismo, selling out, shame, embarrassment, betrayal, and so forth.

cruel and ironic slap in the face to these men who have left the fields to fulfill their military obligation to find increasing amounts of non-union grapes in their mess kits" (Huerta, 1969, p. 5). A description of Huerta's negotiating style demonstrates how she employed these faces of emotion in meetings:

> In the hundreds of negotiating sessions she led between 1966 and 1971, Huerta's emotional involvement was her strength and her weakness. She shouted and cried easily. She fought with insults, tears, and individuals' testimony, believing so strongly in winning everything the workers told her they needed that she would not compromise. . . . She encouraged spontaneous political demonstrations during negotiations as the grievances were shouted out. (Baer, 1975, p. 39)

Rhetorical studies rarely mention the use of this kind of emotionality or passion, which was seemingly so effective for Dolores Huerta. These faces of emotion connected with audiences who could see Huerta's passion and commitment for her causes literally inscribed on her face—an embodied form of resistance, particularly for her supporters, such as farm workers and the UFW leadership.

Huerta's speeches also demonstrate the notion of crowd atmosphere and the contagion and stickiness of emotions (Ahmed, 2004; Brennan, 2004). Instead of emotion existing within one's mind or within one's body, Ahmed explains, "emotions are relational" and "crucial to the very constitution of the psychic and the social as objects, a process which suggests that the 'objectivity' of the psychic and social is an effect rather than a cause" (Ahmed, 2004, pp. 8, 10). Huerta always attempted to galvanize the audience emotionally through audience participation, by calling out and requiring response, such as through speaker-audience chants of "sí, se puede," creating an atmosphere of soaring emotion. As one writer observed, reflecting on a speech given to an audience of mostly Chicana/os at California State University, Chico (formerly, Chico State): "When Huerta arrived [45 minutes late], she was led on stage by a vigorous 'huelga clap,' the passionate rhythm of the strike line. The claps started slowly, with great steady power, and then crescendoed into an outpouring of applause" (Speer, April 26, 1977, p. 1). Teresa Brennan (2004) claims that such contagious emotion operates through not just the visual but also the olfactory and auditory processes of stimulation that are at work. Importantly, Brennan also argues that the creation of such affective atmosphere is cultural, as cultural aspects work for, within, and against the display and restraint of emotion. At the end of the 1977 Chico speech that included the regular gritos, vivas, and abajos, Speer notes, "The audience joined hands and chanted with her" (April 26, 1977, p. 5), again illustrating the powerful affect generated across Huerta's audiences. Huerta skillfully managed audiences of farm workers, lobbyists, growers, the general public, and specific audiences of students, health care workers, and others through the manifestation of affect (e.g., Huerta, "Stanford University," 1974; Huerta, "Keynote Address," 1974; Speer, April 19, 1977; Speer, April 26, 1977).

Yet there is also rhetorical risk in showing this kind of emotion in public, because the use of emotion or tears is not an avowed rhetorical style in mainstream US American culture and, when used, becomes unruly and unexpected. A second rhetorical function of this style, then, is that Huerta disrupted traditional rhetorical styles through her caras de "*gestos subversivos*, political subversive gestures, the piercing look that questions or challenges, the look that says, 'Don't walk all over me,' the one that says, 'Get out of my face'" (Anzaldúa, 1990, p. xv). Anzaldúa explains that caras of resistance mean "to put on a face, express feelings by distorting the face—frowning, grimacing, looking sad, glum or disapproving" (1990, p. xv). Huerta used these faces of emotionality (both consciously and unconsciously), which often left her audiences, especially growers and politicians, without response. Huerta explained why she believed this strategy worked for her: "It's hard for them—the growers—to negotiate with a woman. . . . I think it throws them. A woman can be much more tenacious than a man. Women are not as ego-involved as men are" (quoted in Sims, 1974, p. 3-B). In one speech, she also noted that it was tenacity that created an effective bargaining persona: "They [the growers] didn't like that. They didn't. I really stuck to my guns. I was really tenacious. I never swore at them or yelled at them, that's why they called me that [the Dragon Lady]. They couldn't swear at me because it wasn't a man that was doing it" (Huerta, 2003). These reactions to Huerta's speaking and negotiating styles are also typical responses to women's rhetoric, as feminists and other female rhetors were (and still are) often considered too emotional and irrational (Ahmed, 2004).

Huerta's emotional appeals often connected to audiences through her emphasis on the plight of farm workers as well as issues that directly affected audience members, such as widespread pesticide use and its dangers to consumers. Anger that emerged from the pain of witnessing the treatment of farm workers was quite common in Huerta's passionate speeches. As Sara Ahmed contends, "The response to pain, as a call for action, also requires anger; an interpretation that this pain is wrong, that it is an outrage, and that something must be done about it" (2004, p. 174). Importantly, Ahmed observes that pain and anger in response to farm worker conditions are productive when they function "as opening up the future," in which the rhetorical context is infused with energy and moves into creative action (p. 175). The UFW regularly employed such strategies to connect to consumers beyond the problems farm workers faced. The multi-appeals approach relied heavily on a pathos of pain expressed through anger, as illustrated in Huerta's 1974 keynote address to the American Public Health Association:

> We now have a return to pesticides—40,000 acres of lettuce were poisoned with Monitor 4. This lettuce were [sic] shipped to the market. In California it was sold as shredded lettuce in Safeway stores. . . . People working out there in those fields without a toilet, people working out there in those fields without any hand washing facilities, without any cold drinking water, without any kind of first aid or safety precautions. All of this has come back again. The California Rural Legal Assistance just did a spot survey of about 20 ranches in the Salinas and the Delano area, just a couple of months ago. And every single instance they found either no toilet or a dirty toilet, and you can imagine. And this is something consumers don't understand. That that lettuce, those grapes are being picked right there in that field. If there's a dirty toilet it's right next to the produce, and that produce is picked and packed in that field and shipped directly to your store. The way you see the grapes in your market, the way you see the lettuce in that market, it comes directly from the field. It doesn't go through any cleansing process. It's direct. (p. 5)

The pathetic appeal to both a sense of justice for farm workers' rights and for consumers' own safety was a repeated theme in other UFW rhetoric throughout the 1960s, 1970s, and 1980s.

The third way in which these caras of emotionality function rhetorically relates to the use of emotional excess, or melodrama. Huerta herself observed,

[A]s a woman I can cry in negotiations and they can't, you know. I can just do ALL kinds of things. . . . I can get really melodramatic and talk about the poor farm workers and their families and all that and get reeeeally mushy about it and fellas have more problems doing that. . . . I just sort of go by instinct. Once in a while I'll do something on purpose. (quoted in Sims, 1974, p. 3-B)

As one Teamster organizer said, "[S]he cries, she rolls down the tears" (Roy Mendoza in Bratt & Bensen, 2017). Huerta's conscious rhetorical use of what Nájera-Ramírez (2003) calls emotional excess connected with audiences in her passion and disavowal of rhetorical styles that rely solely on reason. As Valenzuela Arce explains, melodrama may be especially suited for addressing and expressing issues related to social justice, especially for campesinos' concerns:

Melodrama in Mexico is constructed in the interstices of urbanized rurality and its recreation in mass communication, especially cinema and later television. The *campesino* masses expelled from the countryside with the Revolution at the beginning of the twentieth century, and the subsequent exoduses associated with misery and dispossession, formed important cultural adaptations, reterritorializations, and recreations of expressive forms and of campesino ways of life in new urban contexts no less plagued by abuses and injustices. (Valenzuela Arce, 2003, p. 222)

Although Valenzuela Arce (2003) and Nájera-Ramírez (2003) discuss melodrama in mediated form in Mexico, there are parallels of emotional performance in Huerta's rhetoric, especially in her emphases on justice, reformulating expression, and conscious choice to use emotionality. Perhaps illustrating the blurred boundaries of the physical and metaphorical US-Mexico border, Huerta uses emotional excess as a way to connect with farm workers who were predominantly Mexican and Mexican American and to challenge the boundaries of acceptable behavior for Latina women.

Steven Schwarze further explains that melodrama in US American social movements relies on constituting social and political conflict, polarizing conflict, framing issues as moralistic, and creating monopathy, or a "unitary emotional identification" (Schwarze, 2006, p. 244). Features of melodrama include (1) framing personal problems as public issues, (2) polarizing people and issues, (3) characterizing an issue with a moral framework, and (4) enacting strong emotionality (Schwarze, 2006; Schwarze, Peeples, Schneider, & Bsumek, 2014). Much of Huerta's public persona and rhetorical styles embodies this kind of melodrama. Doss and Jensen argue that Huerta specifically used "boundary-breaking experiences as a form of symbolic capital" to create social change (2013, p. 3). For example, in a speech that she gave at a Chicana conference in Los Angeles, she recounted an experience with her male colleagues:

> [F]or a long time it was a joke, and I never thought about it, and they say, "Well, where's Dolores at? Well, you gotta ask her broom" [strong reaction from crowd]. . . . And all of these—I was going to say subtle, but they're not subtle! I mean, these are all things in our culture that say to us "You gotta stay in your place." And I'm going to say this, and I know that all of you are going to agree with me, but we can sit here right now, and I can run through my list of about ten strong, wonderful, fantastic, great women that I know, and almost every one of them has been messed over by somebody, or is being messed over by somebody, either their partner in life, their corporation, or their school, or whatever. I mean, they are fighting for their political and social lives and private lives and emotional lives right now because they are being messed over, so we've got to, we've got to get those weapons. . . . [W]e've got to start [showing] up ourselves. (Huerta, 1987, p. 32)

As illustrated in this speech, Huerta shared her personal experience but demonstrated how it was also a public problem, particularly that women need to address. In her language to empower women, she also demonized men who made sexist jokes or "messed" with women's lives, through a moral framework of right and wrong. Evidenced by the audience reaction, Huerta also exuded passion and emotion for the moral righteousness of her position.

Huerta's rhetorical *cara* of emotionality also embodies these elements through her passionate beliefs in justice for farm workers. Huerta inverted seemingly powerless rhetorical options, such as tears and emotional appeals, into connective rhetorical practices that may have evoked emotional reactions in her audiences, such as guilt, anger, sentimentality, and/or passion. Persistence through emotional appeal was another strategy for motivating people to action, as she explained in a 1974 speech:

> Now there's another group of people that we have to reach. And that is all of the people that aren't involved—that don't care. The people that don't want to be bothered. You probably know a lot of them. You might even have some in your own family. I even have some in my own family. Maybe some of your own friends and neighbors—and they don't want to be bothered. They want to stay out of it. So we really have to come to them with some strong words to make them work. And you have to keep after them. Don't let them off the hook. . . . You have to keep after people. And once you get them involved and you put them to work, afterwards they're going to be grateful to you, that you got them involved. When you're trying to get them in, it's kind of a nuisance and you have to agitate alot [sic]. But after we win you see, after we win the victory will not be just the farmworkers or just yourselves. That victory will belong to all of the people that helped. (Huerta, "Stanford University," 1974, pp. 3–4)

In essence, Huerta's use of caras of emotionality functioned as a kind of differential consciousness, as a "*tactical subjectivity* with the capacity to de- and recenter" dominant rhetorical styles (Sandoval, 2000, p. 59). As Anzaldúa (1990) explains: "Our strength lies in shifting perspectives, in our capacity to shift, in our 'seeing through' the membrane of the past superimposed on the present" (p. xxvii). Huerta's sometimes conscious and deliberate choice to use these faces represents her ability to read audiences, to understand social contexts, and to use unexpected measures in order to craft a space for rhetorical agency. Her use of these caras expands the use of emotion beyond the individual private sphere into the collective public sphere because her audiences, whether growers, politicians, or farm workers, reacted to and engaged with her use of emotion.

Huerta's rhetoric also relied on essentialist interpretations of emotion as a gendered tactic, since strategic essentialism can enable a performance of difference that works as resistance to and liberation of social, cultural, and political constraints (Pérez, 1998). As Huerta noted in her own beliefs about women and emotion, "[W]omen, we have the brain, the emotional capacity, the emotional strength, the instinctiveness, all right, that decision making needs, but we just gotta get ourselves into those positions of power" (Huerta, 1987, p. 29). She also employed new and reinvented practices to challenge those social norms and strategies that are enacted through structures of power. These faces and masks that Huerta used include a range of rhetorical styles, demonstrated through both physical and verbal expressions as calculated and subconscious rhetorical strategies with what might be called "cultural coalescence," or the way one can "pick, borrow, retain, and create distinctive cultural forms" even as they are constrained by gendered, racialized, linguistic, and classed systems (Ruiz, 1998, p. 50). Her use of emotion allowed the growers and lobbyists to walk out of meetings and negotiations because they did not see her as rational or reasonable. Perhaps, then, her caras or tactics of emotion resisted social expectations but also inscribed normative expectations of how women might speak and behave in political realms. José Esteban Muñoz makes two important points about creating such disidentifications through affective performance:

(1) It is not so much that the Latina/o affect performance is so excessive, but that the affective performance of normative whiteness is minimalist to the point of emotional impoverishment. . . . (2) Rather than trying to run from this stereotype, Latino as excess, it seems much more important to seize it and redirect it in the service of a liberationist politics. Such a maneuver is akin to what I have described elsewhere as a disidentification with toxic characterizations and stereotypes of US Latinos. A disidentification is neither an identification nor a counteridentification—it is a working on, with, and against a form at a simultaneous moment. (2000, p. 70)

Muñoz's point about using such affect as resistance to the submissive Latina stereotype is embodied in Huerta's rhetorical performance and her own strategic essentialism and "liberationist politics."

Her reliance on the gender essentialism of emotion is both a production of power and a reproduction of gendered, classed, and racialized social expectations. Yet, as Valdivia observes, for Latina/os to be able to participate in social movements, academic discussions, or other kinds of discourses, "bringing [the] chair to the table is not done without stress, challenge, and/or resistance. . . . [W]hile theories of social change may be palatable, the methods and struggles that these might entail are not" (Valdivia, 2008, p. 5). Valdivia suggests that approaches used in resisting dominant ideologies can be disavowed, without recognizing the difficulties in choosing strategies or caras of resistance.

Caras of Familia

Another facet of Huerta's rhetorical strategy of resistance involved building on the strength of the family, breaking boundaries between public and private to create an amalgam ethos undergirding her public persona. The tenacity of her public role derived from her strength as a mother and matriarch, which she extended to her cause as "mother" of the union, as well as constructing the union as familia, rhetorically functioning to simultaneously disrupt traditional beliefs about and embrace values of the Mexican and Mexican American familia and motherhood. Irasema Coronado explains, in her analysis of women activists in Ciudad Juárez, that many women who are drawn to social activism come to see their roles as supermadres (supermothers), "caring for and nurturing the citizenry as they would their own families . . . [drawing] upon family and cultural traditions and list[ing] 'helping others' as a major motivating force for their political activity" (2008, p. 145). Indeed, Sara Ahmed (2004) identifies the emotion of love for others as tied to maternity. Valeria Fabj (1993) has also written about marianismo in motherhood and social activism in relation to the mothers protesting the disappearances of their children in Argentina. These mothers employed innovative rhetorical strategies to question the government's role in their children's disappearances, using images and embodiment to express their motherhood as tied to political action (see also Foss & Domenici, 2001).

As Huerta was one of the very few female leaders in the UFW, she also symbolically served as the mother of the union itself, along with Helen Chávez, César Chávez's wife. However, Rose (1990a) contends that their respective roles as mothers were very different, as Helen was more of a behind-the-scenes caretaker and Dolores was outspoken and very visible in union activities, especially negotiating, bargaining, and lobbying. Family itself was important to both women, both their immediate families and their extended families, by blood and association through the union. As Margaret Rose (1994) argues, the ideas of family and home were/are often central in Mexican and Mexican American community organizing. Even as gendered roles persisted, historically, both women and men widely participated in Mexican American social and political issues (Rose, 1994), often blurring the lines between family and community. According to Flores and Holling (1999), "the concept of *la familia* [the family] among Mexican Americans serves as a means through which cultural values, attitudes, and assumptions are taught" (p. 340; see also Gangotena, 1994; Holling, 2006).

Florencia Mallon (1995) offers another perspective in her analysis of communal hegemony in Mexico and Peru. She contends that family and communal relationships should not be romanticized because of how they play out in gendered, generational, classed, and ethnic ways. Through her research in the Mexican state of Puebla, she observed that even within a patriarchal community structure, "older women with greater authority reproduced their position and privilege by making certain that younger women and men adhered to the established rules" (p. 70). The community elders constructed this sense of communal hegemony: "It is in the mutually reinforcing relationship between family and community, and in the reciprocal obligations that tied different community and family members to each other, that we find the basis for communal hegemony" (p. 73). Huerta's aspect of familia and motherhood as expanded to the union breaks down consanguineous and affinitive notions of family, for as Kath Weston (1991) argues: "In the United States, race, class, gender, ethnicity, regional origin, and context all inform differences in household organization, as well as differences in notions of family and what it means to call someone kin" (p. 28). Although Weston discusses gay and lesbian communities that extend their sense of family beyond blood relations, that is, to the families we choose, Huerta's lifestyle and rhetorical tactics also break down (and simultaneously reinforce) the construct of the nuclear, consanguineous family as well as communal hegemony.

Huerta's rhetorical style confounded the notions of genealogical family and harmony, even while such collectivity undergirded her beliefs. For example, she regularly spoke of how César and she were quite confrontational with each other:

> He and I, we get into some big, big, big arguments, you know, and [we're just] kind of like known for that. Anybody who's worked for the union will tell you that we have these big, big,

big battles, and we have to have those battles, and any time I feel instinctively that we shouldn't be doing something or doing something different and I don't fight with him about it or the rest of the board members, which are all men, then I feel guilty if something goes wrong because I kept my mouth shut, because [it's] part of our responsibility as people. (Huerta, 1987, p. 29)

While this example illustrates Huerta's value of self-expression, she embraced harmony in other ways, such as through the commitment to social justice for farm workers.

Thus, Huerta both embraced and resisted these values in the construction of her consanguineous familia (her children) and her union familia in several ways. For example, Huerta's cara of familia and motherhood was literally embodied in her persona through her pregnancies, nursing and raising her children, involving her children in UFW activities, and talking about her status as mother in interviews, speeches, and letters. For example, in the following excerpt of a 1974 speech, she talked about the importance of her children and others' children:

Now, some of you might wonder how come I have ten children, right? [Before her eleventh child was born] One of the main reasons is because I want to have my own picket line. But all kidding aside, it's really nice to be able to go to a clinic when you are pregnant with your tenth baby and not have people look at you like you are kind of crazy. Or like you don't know where they come from, or put pressure on you not to have any more children. Because after all you know, Mexicans are kind of poor people and you shouldn't have all that many kids. So that's another good thing about our clinics. Because unfortunately, that pressure not to have children translates itself in county hospitals and places where people have no power into dead babies because those babies aren't taken care of, and into very hard labor for mothers because they are trying to make it as hard on the mother as they can to have another one. And I guess I feel a little bit strongly about that because I've been in situations where I've seen children die, babies die, because somebody there thought they shouldn't have been born in the first place. (Huerta, "Keynote Address," 1974, p. 3)

The UFW's rhetorical construction of the union as familia also allowed Huerta to participate fully in union activities (Rose, 1990b, 1995; Zavella, 1987). In essence, her face of familia disrupted traditional rhetorical styles and facilitated the UFW's construction of familia as a broader concept beyond the nuclear family. Many women participated in UFW boycotts and picket lines; often as many as half of the participants were women, and boycotts across the United States were managed by families or couples rather than by individuals (Rose, 1995). Some women did manage their own boycotts, such as Dolores Huerta, Jessica Govea, and Hope López, who relied on unique strategies in which they targeted middle-class housewives through "benevolent womanhood" (Rose, 1995, p. 8, citing Lori Ginzberg).

Gangotena (2004) also discusses the importance of extended family within Mexican and Mexican American family traditions, which might include co-parenting by uncles, aunts, grandparents, and godparents (the compadrazgo [godfather/godmother] system). The family also extends to cousins and family friends, who might be referred to as compadres and comadres. The way in which Huerta often relied on the Chávez family and other union families to help support her children functioned as this large, extended family. In this sense, Gangotena's (2004) discussion on solidarity and focus on community helps explain Huerta's construction of familia, particularly in the notion of sacrifice, which was central to the UFW mission for social justice. Indeed, the union itself was deeply committed to providing farm workers with benefits related to the notion of extended familial support. In numerous speeches and testimonies, Huerta documented UFW accomplishments that focused on supporting families, such as "elimination of child labor in the fields where we have union contracts," "a medical plan that covers farm workers and their families with doctors [sic] visits, prescription care, maternity benefits," the credit union to benefit farm workers and their families, a "death benefit insurance program that covers all members and their dependents," and a "retirement village for 'worn out' farmworkers" (Huerta, "Problems in Organizing Farmworkers," n.d., pp. 1–2; Huerta, "Stanford University," 1974; Huerta, "The Importance of Union Organizing," n.d.).

Huerta was also strongly committed to the idea of consanguineous familia, as she explained: "[I]n our culture, raising kids is the most important thing you can do," and "[w]omen are getting afraid to have kids. I still believe you are supposed to conceive children" (Huerta, quoted in

Coburn, 1976, pp. 13–14). She often took her kids with her to negotiating sessions, political activities, picket lines, and boycotts. In another interview, she noted that she would drive "around Stockton with all these little babies in the car, the different diaper changes for each one." At the same time, she recognized that she didn't "feel proud of the suffering that my kids went through . . . but by the same token I know that they learned a lot in the process" (quoted in A. Chávez, 2005, p. 251).

Although she was extremely occupied with union activities throughout the childhoods of all of her children, she was also devoted to their welfare. When she began lobbying in Sacramento, for instance, she reported, "I had to do it [the lobbying], but at the same time I was too distracted to work. My husband was trying to take the kids away from me in court. I couldn't lose my children but I couldn't quit working for people who counted on me" (Baer, 1975, p. 39). The 2009 film *A Crushing Love* and the 2017 film *Dolores* document her children's experiences and responses to their mother's work, as several of them explain how difficult it was for them growing up without their mother around and living a life of their mother's imposed poverty but also how important their mother's legacy has been (Bratt & Bensen, 2017; Morales, 2009). Huerta was (and is) also immensely proud of her children (A. Chávez, 2005), as illustrated in her frequent references to their successes in articles, speeches, and conversations. She often mentioned their accomplishments, noting that her children have pursued careers in teaching, law, medicine, filmmaking, and the UFW (Huerta, 1987, 2002, 2003).

However, Huerta's traditional beliefs in having children did not prevent her from also challenging the traditional values of the Mexican American familia. For example, because she was twice divorced and never married her last partner, Richard Chávez, she rejected the social norms of the nuclear family and Catholic tradition that discouraged and prohibited divorce. After Huerta divorced, she often struggled to provide for her children, as evidenced in her letters to Chávez in chapter three in which she asked for financial support for babysitters, food, clothing, gasoline, and other living expenses (e.g., Huerta, 1962, "Just a few short lines," n.d.). Fregoso explains that "Chicana/o family ideology also draws from Anglo-American norms around heterosexuality and consanguinity, especially in its assumptions about very particular roles for women as wives, mothers, economic dependents, nurturers, and cultural transmitters" (Fregoso, 2003b, p. 77; see also

Holling, 2006; Williams, 1990; and Zavella, 1987, for further discussion). Huerta rejected the economic dependence and wife role within the nuclear family, yet she used the union (and Chávez) as a support mechanism, creating the union as her familia.

Instead of allowing her struggles in raising her children to impede her leadership role in the UFW, she sometimes used this status as an enabling mechanism. As Huerta notes in the excerpt below, she used breast-feeding strategically:

> When I had my younger children and I was still negotiating, I would take nursing breaks. So I would take my baby into the negotiations and then I would take a nursing break, and everybody would have to wait while the baby ate. Then I would come back to the table and start negotiating again. . . . I think it made employers sensitive to the fact that when we're talking about benefits and the terms of a contract, we're talking about families and we're talking about children. (quoted in Covey, 1994, p. 47)

In an interview with filmmaker Sylvia Morales, Huerta also recounted a time in which she took her daughter Camila with her to bargaining sessions:

> I had Camila with me, and so it was really interesting because whenever the United Farm Workers' attorneys were talking or I was talking, she wouldn't cry. As soon as the Teamsters' attorneys would start talking or the growers' attorneys, she would start crying. And so I would have, you know, to take her out, and I was breastfeeding her so we would have to take a nursing break and take her out and nurse her. And then we would bring her back in again and everything would go smooth as long as we were talking, but as soon as the Teamsters' attorneys started talking, or the growers' attorneys again, we would have to take another break. So one of the growers' attorneys turned to one of the Teamsters' attorneys: I think she's pinching that baby every time we start talking because that's the only time she cries. (2009)

In these examples, Huerta turned her breast-feeding body into a tool of disruption and a reminder of the very real people involved in farm work. Vicky Ruiz argues, "A tough, savvy negotiator, Huerta skillfully manipulated her positionality as a mother at the bargaining table"

(1998, p. 134). Huerta may have used her family's status as a way to control the bargaining process by forcing a break in negotiations on her own terms. Rather than allow the physical aspects of motherhood, such as breast-feeding, to constrain her ability to speak and participate in the UFW and bargaining processes, Huerta embodied resistance to dominant social expectations.

In addition to nursing some of her children during meeting and negotiation breaks, Huerta also involved her children in other union activities. When possible, she encouraged them to participate in marches and protests, and all of them were raised within the union family structure, sometimes staying with the Chávez family or other union families. Felner explains: "Rather than choose between being with her children and going to work, she brought her children to work (and, as they became adults, put them to work)" (Felner, 1998, p. 2). Her children became a part of her rhetorical cara of familia because her audiences saw how she melded her family life with her union life. In fact, some of her children were arrested and sent to jail for their participation in strikes, including one of her children who was three months old at the time (Cárdenas, 1977). Rhetorically, the presence of Huerta's children at union activities allowed audiences to see her as a family-oriented person and to remind non-farm worker audiences that children and families would be affected by policies, decisions, and contracts.

This practice of bringing along children was typical of UFW activities, as Huerta noted in another speech referencing a farm worker family and the work they did on strike and boycotts:

> [T]hey are a kind of typical kind of people that made everything happen in California. The people that had the courage to go out on strike, boycotts, taking their families with them. Going to super markets. . . . But the thing is that they're organized people who made all this happen. I would like them to stand. Se puede poner de pie, por favor [farm workers stand up, applause and cheering, chants of "sí se puede" from the audience]. . . . The whole family, it's a big family. They're typical, they're farm workers, and they're the ones who went out there and did the work. We need people just like them. (Huerta, 2013, p. 3)

As Huerta noted in a 1973 interview in *La Voz del Pueblo*, "the idea of a communal family is not new and progressive. It's really kind of old fashioned. Remember when you were little you always had your uncles, your aunts, your grandmother, and your comadres around. As a child in the Mexican culture you identified with a lot of people, not just your mother and father like they do in middle-class homes" (Huerta, 1973). This interview specifically targeted Chicana/os, so she created a sense of identification with the readers through an emphasis on similar family experiences (Doss & Jensen, 2013).

In a speech that Huerta gave to a largely Chicana audience, she recounted the importance of involving her children in her work and how that was part of her cultural heritage, to include children in all aspects of her life:

> [A]ny kind of gathering where you have people from Mexico or any Latin American country, boy, you got kids running around all over the place, right? (laughter). And I think that's very important, 'cause I remember my mother, you know, always taking me with her. . . . We signed a bill to give the [viejitos] (older farm workers) old age pensions even though they weren't citizens, right? Well, I had to take my kids with me, and so there's this picture with the governor, you know, signing it, and my two little girls are like this (laughter). And now it's such a great picture! They're so proud of that picture . . . my kids are so proud of those pictures that they had 'cause I used to drag them all over with me, and I think it's important to do that. I remember once we had the session, and my three year old was walking in and out—she was three years old then. Then she got on her little play telephone, and I said, "Oh Juanita, you're calling people to picket? "No, Mom!" She said, "They're not going to picket, they're going to leaflet!" . . . I think it's important to have childcare centers, but I also think it's important to have kids present, because they learn everything. They're little sponges! And if we exclude them, you know what I mean? . . . We should let them come in and out, because when they're coming in and out they pick up so much stuff. I mean, my children are so political and they know so much and they're so strong, you know? (Huerta, 1987, pp. 45–47)

At a 2017 showing of the documentary *Dolores* in El Paso, Huerta's son Ricky Chávez also recounted how his mother would leave the kids outside Safeway to distribute leaflets as a family activity. This approach was also a UFW rhetorical strategy, because the boycotts, pickets, and protests often involved entire families (Rose, 1990b). The familial bond thus expanded to include a much larger union family in which people worked together to support one another and their causes.

Anzaldúa (1987, 1990) argues that la mestiza must constantly look for different faces, moves, and ways of thinking to subvert dominant structures, to access places of rhetorical space and agency. Huerta used familia as a way to "read the current situation of power and self-consciously choos[e] and [adopt] the ideological stand best suited to push against its configurations" (Sandoval, 2000, p. 60). She interrupted dominant ways of thinking, as illustrated through her practices of breast-feeding during meetings and negotiation breaks. In another way, Huerta's children were often visible or referenced within the union and various articles that have been written about Huerta, demonstrating her values of familia and culture, both resisting and reinforcing traditional familia structure. Huerta embodied a cara of familia and motherhood that emphasized both her independence and her children's independence and values of social justice and her total life commitment to the union. In essence, Huerta used familia within the union to construct her own way of being and her own identity. As with her use of emotion, she invoked gender (and racial/ethnic) essentialism in resistive ways through her emphasis on the consanguineous family and the role of woman as mother. In this sense, familia was a powerful connection among and between members of Huerta's consanguineous family as well as the bigger union family.

Huerta used family and motherhood, often strategically and, because it was necessary given her childcare constraints, in ways that are both similar and different to how other scholars have conceptualized womanhood in social protest. For example, Foss and Domenici (2001) and Fabj (1993) analyzed the aforementioned mothers protesting the disappearances of their children within and by the Argentine government. Employing their roles as mothers as a way to demand answers from a government that disappeared political agitators was certainly a risky endeavor but one that worked precisely because of their motherhood status. Constructing motherhood through marianismo, these scholars argue, allowed these mothers to engage in political activism at a time when everyone was afraid because of the repressive nature of the Argentine government. Yet, like Huerta, they were labeled as crazy, insane, and bad mothers for letting their children engage in political protest in the first place. Similarly, Shanara Reid-Brinkley (2012) demonstrates how politicians such as Carol Moseley Braun employ the Good White Mother frame, relying on a narrative that demonstrates commitment to "family (which includes husband and children), caretaking, and homemaking" as well as religion and community (p. 46), contrasted with the Bad Black Mother frame, which emphasizes welfare dependency or lack of attention to the home because of work.

Huerta's rhetoric often employed the Good White Mother frame, but she was also accused of being a bad mother in that she left her kids with other people and was more committed to farm worker organizing than to her own children. Rose (1995) explains how motherhood was used within the UFW by other female leaders, as did Hope López in a message as part of the Philadelphia grape boycott of 1969–1970:

> The female farmworker is as unique as the unique industry that she works in—agriculture. She is practically born in the fields. My mother was working in the fields when I was born. . . . Childhood is spent in the fields and she pitches in as soon as she is able to understand instructions. . . . She gets married and her honeymoon is spent helping her new husband harvest the crops. She gets pregnant & spends her pregnancy in the fields. After her baby's born she doesn't have to worry about a baby sitter, that baby goes right to work with her. And the cycle starts all over again. (cited in Rose, 1995, p. 16–17)

López appealed to middle-class white mothers by emphasizing similarities in the motherhood experience while simultaneously appealing to values of the women's liberation movement at the time. These examples illustrate how the pregnant, nursing, and attending-to-children bodies of women as mothers can be used rhetorically to achieve certain ends.

However, Dana Cloud (1999) cautions against the use of the family metaphor in social movements, especially when used to construct positions of paternalism by those in power, that is, the powerful who take care of their "families," such as the mill owners and mill workers in her analysis. On a related note, Rose (1995) also contends that the UFW leadership accepted the use of maternal rhetoric but thought of appeals to feminism and women's liberation as divisive. In Huerta's case, familia became a powerful way to connect with audiences, especially Chicana/o activists and possibly mainstream US American audiences, and disrupt traditional, normative, and what are deemed appropriate rhetorical tools. Challenging these norms meant that Huerta was often criticized by growers and politicians, as well as farm worker communities, for not embracing more female-oriented tasks, such as those that Margaret Rose (1995) identifies (e.g., secretarial and hostessing work). Her approach, however, allowed her to control the rhetorical situation, giving her power not only in that moment but in negotiating contracts and garnering attention to her broader messages. On the other hand, her Catholic and cultural beliefs about having a large consanguineous family also reinforced hegemonic notions of kinship and privileged the construct of the genealogical family (see, e.g., Kath Weston [1991] for how LGBTQ communities have critiqued and reformed what family means).

Conclusion

Dolores Huerta's caras of emotionality, motherhood, and familia are not distinct and separate manifestations of her rhetorical style but rather intersecting aspects of it that build on her life experiences and work within and for the UFW. Similarly, these caras represent the intersections of how Huerta experienced race, ethnicity, class, gender, the US American educational system, language fluency, and other domains of hegemonic ideology. Furthermore, caras of emotionality are often tied to expressions related to familia and vice versa. As evidenced in her public rhetoric, Huerta often employed pathos through familia and her role as mother, as she noted in a 2006 speech about what to pass along to family: "[W]hen you die, the best thing you can leave your children, the best inheritance that you can possibly have is the love for justice and how to struggle for their rights and the rights of others. This is a very, very great inheritance we can leave our children" (Huerta, 2006, p. 3). The passion for social justice and passing that through to the next generation illustrates how the connections between emotion, familia, and motherhood cannot be separated. As a rhetorical concept, then, caras build and expand our understanding of intersectionality and its relationship to rhetorical agency.

Furthermore, such caras embody rhetorical styles through physical, facial, and bodily distortions, such as expressing pain, fear, or anger, or through physical aspects of motherhood, such as pregnancy, breast-feeding, or immediate care for a child. Again, this embodied rhetoric is gendered, racialized, and classed in how others assessed Huerta's rhetorical style, but it also represents a reappropriation of disavowed styles through strategic essentialism of familia, motherhood, and emotionality. Similarly, Emma Pérez contends that Gayatri Spivak's notion of strategic essentialism manifests as

> one who exercises political representation, or identity politics, within hegemonic structures. The strategy asserts counter-sites within dominant society. As a dynamic process, this tactic gives voices to each new marginalized social or political group, bonded temporarily at specific historical moments. . . . The process is not permanent or fixed but instead somewhat dialectical, acknowledging irreducible differences within separate *sitios y lenguas* where the resolution of differences is neither desirable nor necessary. (1998, pp. 87-88)

Chela Sandoval writes that differential consciousness "can thus be thought of as a constant reapportionment of space, of boundaries, of horizontal and vertical realignments of oppositional powers" (2000, p. 181), while Jacqueline Martinez (2000) emphasizes the importance of understanding theory through embodied and in-the-flesh lived experience.

Finally, these caras are manifestations of motivation for social activism. Irasema Coronado explains that the supermadre phenomenon may invoke feelings of "maternal instincts of caring and nurturing and providing for their families [that] transcended into the community" through pain, fear, and anger as emotionally motivating forces (2008, p. 146). Huerta has often discussed her motivation for leaving a good and stable teaching job for the Community Service Organization (CSO) in 1955 and then to start the National Farm Workers Association (NFWA) with César Chávez a few years later. She has explained that she felt she couldn't do as much to help farm workers whose children were coming to her classes without proper nutrition and clothing. Since then, she has learned what Coronado calls "gestionar" as part of her rhetorical persona:

Gestionar (to diligently pursue actions that will lead one to achieve a goal), an expression used by activists, is also the ability to discern how to work and which person to approach to achieve the desired goal. In this context, gestionar means much more: knowing how to make a demand, to whom to present the demand, and how to ask for government assistance or support. (2008, p. 151)

Huerta's passion for helping and caring for others, including her children, is demonstrated in her lifelong commitment to social justice causes and evidenced through her embodied rhetoric and her ability to gestionar, not just persistently, but passionately and with her whole being.

Chapter 5

PUBLIC PERSONA OF DIFFERENTIAL BRAVERY THROUGH COLLABORATIVE EGALITARIANISM AND COURAGEOUS OPTIMISM

The developments of the past seven months are only a slight indication of what is to come. The workers are on the rise. There will be strikes all over the state and throughout the country because Delano has shown what can be done and the workers know that they are no longer alone. [cheers from crowd] The agricultural workers are not going to remain static. . . . On behalf of the National Farm Workers Association, its officers, and its members, on behalf of all the farm workers of this state, we unconditionally demand that the governor of this state, Edmund Brown, call a special session of the legislature to enact a collective bargaining law for the farm workers of the state of California. We will be satisfied with nothing less. . . . [cheers from crowd] We will call on a general strike to let the legislators and the employers know we mean business. We will take economic pressure, strikes, boycotts to force recognition and obtain collective bargaining rights. The social and economic revolution of farm workers is well under way and will not be stopped until we receive equality. The farm workers are moving. Nothing is going to stop them. The workers are crying for organization and we are going to organize them. We may act in strange and unusual ways in our organizing, but we are willing to try new and unused methods to achieve justice for the farm workers. (Huerta, 1966, n.p.)

In 1966, farm workers organized by César Chávez, Dolores Huerta, and other United Farm Workers (UFW) leaders marched from Delano to Sacramento, California, to bring awareness to their cause. After walking more than 340 miles over a period of several weeks, the farm workers held a rally on the steps of the capitol building on April 10, 1966 (Easter Sunday). As shown in the above quotation from her speech given in front of the Sacramento capitol building, Dolores Huerta called on the California government to enact legislation, noting that the UFW would not let up until they achieved their demands and would continue to use new tactics, such as the very pilgrimage/ peregrinación to Sacramento that they had just completed.

As discussed in the previous chapter, Dolores Huerta's public persona was built around familia and emotionality. This chapter explores how these caras extended to collaboration, egalitarianism, hope, and optimism, as evidenced in the peregrinación of 1966. This sense of social justice through collaborative egalitarianism and courageous optimism stemmed in part from her own immediate family and her relationship with others, as outlined in chapters two and three. The understanding of possibility was further strengthened through the rhetorical risks she took, as well as her ongoing relationships with farm worker communities and her work as a lobbyist and boycott director. Huerta gave many speeches, most of which were not recorded or transcribed, but her speaking style embodied values of egalitarianism and optimism. The content of the speeches, as illustrated in her 1966 peregrinación speech, focused on social injustices that needed to be rectified and ways in which the UFW was working to combat those injustices, best illustrated through the gritos (cries or calls) at the end of every speech in which she employed a string of chants: viva, abajo, and sí, se puede.

This chapter thus focuses on Huerta's sense of intersectional habitus, which enabled her to have the courage, bravery, and hope to take on major social justice issues while raising her children at the time she quit her job and started working to organize farm workers in 1962 (Rose, 2001). First, I briefly explain where Huerta's values of egalitarianism and optimism came from, and then how they embody rhetorical agency, which functions through Chela Sandoval's theory of differential consciousness, building from Gloria Anzaldúa's notion of haciendo caras. I then examine two caras/faces of collaborative egalitarianism and courageous optimism that she was able to employ through differential consciousness and vision (K. Chávez, 2013; Sandoval, 2000). Ultimately, I argue, caras of collaborative egalitarianism and courageous optimism extend and build these constructs of differential consciousness and vision as a form of differential bravery.

Originating Values of Egalitarianism and Optimism

Huerta's sense that she could accomplish justice for farm workers and her fearlessness in quitting her job and supporting her children did not necessarily originate from within herself but was an ongoing process that was shaped over many years by her family, her extended family and friends, and the Chávez family, as well as others, as chapter two explains. Huerta herself has cited her middle-class upbringing and college education as key factors in becoming a central activist for the UFW. Whereas César Chávez and other Chicana/os and farm worker activists struggled with assimilation and feelings of exclusion, Huerta was comfortable in both Spanish and English, often moving rhetorically and physically between Mexican and white US American cultural traditions (Hammerback & Jensen, 1994). As Griswold del Castillo and Garcia contend (1995), "Huerta grew up in a communal atmosphere of security and self-esteem, where ethnic differences were not insuperable barriers," even though she experienced class and racial segregation in school (pp. 64–65).

Huerta's orientation toward social justice issues of all kinds was also built upon values that she learned while initially working for the Community Service Organization (CSO) and became engrained in her and the UFW's lifeworld. Fred Ross drew values from Saul Alinksy, the leader of the Industrial Areas Foundation (M. T. García, 2008); both Huerta and Chávez were inspired by values of nonviolence originating in social movements led by Mahatma Gandhi and Martin Luther King Jr. (Hammerback & Jensen, 1998). As Griswold del Castillo and Garcia (1995) observe, Alinksky's ideology influenced both Huerta and Chávez in the "basic belief that the poor must determine their own issues and that a mass organizational drive for power is basic" (p. 60). These values of self-determination and nonviolence became organizing principles for the UFW movement. Boycotts, consumer campaigns, lobbying, and negotiating with growers were grounded in this ethic of nonviolent resistance.

Notions of social justice also extended to how the UFW's leadership lived their personal lives. Huerta and Chávez both purposefully adopted a life of poverty. This vow of poverty stemmed from the influence of the Catholic Church with its emphasis on "conspicuous poverty" (Hammerback & Jensen, 1998, p. 89). As Mario García (2008) notes in his interview with her about spirituality and Catholicism, Huerta has always maintained a deep spiritual connection to and relationship with the Catholic Church. Huerta was raised as a Catholic, and despite her conflicted feelings about divorce and motherhood in relationship to the church, the Catholic vow of poverty and focus on social justice were major influences in her life. A writer in *Regeneración* pointed out that Huerta often endured conditions of poverty:

> Eighteen hour days of planning boycotts, of speaking at rallies, of negotiating, of traveling, and of seeking public support for La Causa are more common than not. Nor is the work well paid. Like all other union officials and employees, she makes a minimal salary and a bare subsistence depending upon contributions of food and clothing. In her own humorous words Huerta has said of her choice: "All of us have very exotic wardrobes. We get our clothes out of donations." (quoted in Griswold del Castillo & Garcia, 1995, p. 68)

Huerta's vow of poverty for the betterment of farm workers' lives became an embodiment of her social justice agenda and extended to her own family. She reflected on those times in a 2009 interview, noting the connection between her faith in God and her commitment to poverty:

> I didn't have money to buy my daughter Celeste shoes for her confirmation and so she had these white shoes [that] were all torn with holes on them . . . and I see Celeste coming down the aisle with her torn tennis shoes and I'm kind of flinching, and just behind her, there's several farm worker children that are coming down the aisle with torn tennis shoes and to me that was a sign. (Morales, 2009)

Huerta also noted in this interview that she "used to pray all the time that what I was doing was the right thing to do. I would ask God to give me signs" (Morales, 2009). These signs, such as the farm worker kids and Huerta's daughter wearing torn shoes, helped Huerta commit to a life of poverty in the name of promoting social justice because she felt it was the right thing to do. Living a life similar to what farm workers experienced served as a constant reminder to keep pursuing the goal of social and economic justice.

Finally, the sense of hope and optimism that Huerta and Chávez sustained throughout their years with the UFW was another major factor in their commitment to the farm worker cause. They are often described with characteristic optimism and faith in their work

(Hammerback & Jensen, 1998; Rose, 2004), taking personal risks, including financial, familial, and physical ones. Their initial act in forming the NFWA in 1962 is a good example, since they both resigned from paid positions at the CSO to start the NFWA with little guarantee of success. Margaret Rose quotes Huerta as saying, "[W]e really operated totally on faith" (2004, p. 220). Huerta often promoted the idea of doing, not thinking, and felt that the leaders of the NFWA and UFW had to be unafraid and courageous in their actions (Griswold del Castillo & Garcia, 1995). And not only did the UFW leaders have faith and optimism that change could and would happen, but they also were completely immersed in the work itself (Rose, 1990a). As Griswold del Castillo and Garcia point out, "Huerta's egalitarianism and sense of justice also seem to be taken from America's trashcan. Out of discards she has fashioned a sense of hope and leadership, a hope based on the conviction that justice and fairness are the intellectual basis for a new society" (1995, pp. 68–69). Like the caras of familia and motherhood discussed in the previous chapter, Huerta's public persona of collaborative egalitarianism and optimism required both strategic and unconscious rhetorical choices; these orientations and caras are a rendering of rhetorical agency as differential consciousness.

Differential Consciousness: Rhetorical Agency as Strength, Flexibility, and Grace

The rhetorical dexterity of haciendo caras is closely connected to a social justice and oppositional disposition that Chela Sandoval calls differential consciousness, through components of strength, flexibility, and grace:

> enough strength to confidently commit to a well-defined structure of identity for one hour, day, week, month, year; enough flexibility to self-consciously transform that identity according to the requisites of another oppositional ideological tactic if readings of power's formation require it; enough grace to recognize alliance with others committed to egalitarian social relations and race, gender, sex, class, and social justice, when these other readings of power call for alternative oppositional stands. (2000, p. 60)

Rhetorical tools such as strength, flexibility, and grace establish grounds to employ caras and to maintain a disposition focused on resistance. In essence, haciendo caras, infused with an understanding of differential consciousness, function as rhetorical styles (or practices) related to language and delivery choices and as rhetorical strategies or conscious efforts to command audiences. As Sandoval argues, differential consciousness is "a form of agency that is self-consciously mobilized in order to enlist and secure influence; the differential is thus performative" (2000, p. 58).

Critical to differential consciousness is a politics of resistance, that is, the sense of injustice we experience that invokes a call for change. Simon Critchley (2012) defines this politics of resistance as the "disappointment [that] is the response to a situated injustice or wrong that provokes the need for an ethics. The hope is that such an ethics might be able to face and face down the inequities of the present. . . . Politics is an ethical practice that arises in a situation of injustice which exerts a demand for responsibility" (pp. 88, 92). The search for such ethical practices in response to injustices is reminiscent of Jean-François Lyotard and Jean-Loup Thébaud's (1985) discussion on the universal call for justice that can be understood only in specific contexts and cases "because one is never certain that one has been just, or that one can ever be just" (p. 99), a stance that should be maintained in both humor and worry. That is, Critchley contends that worry, as a state of critical consciousness, and humor, the ability to not take ourselves too seriously, are important for defining responses to injustice at the moment of occurrence. Sandoval (2000) also outlines several tactics, such as parody, pastiche, cognitive mapping, the use of nonstandard languages (e.g., working class, caló, bricolage), and strategic essentialism, that enable agents to expand their repertoire of tactics and caras as forms of rhetorical dexterity. Raka Shome (2003) makes the important point, however, that marginalized identities are not politicized just because of positionality; rather, we need to understand how such political motivations work within contextual identities and spaces. In particular, Shome argues that spatialities and modalities of power affect relations of identity and culture: "What matters are the material relations of empowerment and disempowerment that are enabled through the production of mobility" (2003, p. 52).

The differential, according to Sandoval, also has two other meanings. The second meaning focuses on the technologies used by those in marginal standing to develop and maintain an oppositional consciousness. For example, theorists have invented new vocabularies to describe previously unnamed experiences or to better explain the nuances of such experiences. Drawing from Roland Barthes's work, Sandoval identifies inner technologies ("manipulation of one's own consciousness"), such as semiology, deconstruction, and appropriation and transformation of ideology, and outer technologies, such as engaging with the inner technologies to resist and bring about social justice (democratics) and enacting difference (differential movement) (Sandoval, 2000, p. 111). The main goal of such technologies is to "reappropriate and reapportion ideology, and in doing so, they serve to make the languages of emancipation more subtle, more rich, multiple, supple, and flexible" (p. 112). The third meaning of "differential" is located in the "workings of the 'soul'" and "a place where 'our deepest knowledges' are found" (citing Gloria Anzaldúa and Audre Lorde, p. 6). Sandoval further explains, "Differential consciousness is linked to whatever is not expressible through words. It is accessed through poetic modes of expression: gestures, music, images, sounds, words that plummet or rise through signification to find some void—some noplace—to claim their due" (p. 140). That is, the differential is a rupture or shock that inspires new ideas, identities, and hope that enable actors to continue using social movement and technologies of opposition, a kind of decolonial love that is outside of mainstream ideology, culture, and practice. Along those lines, María Lugones (2003) proposes the "streetwalker theorist," who "cultivates a multiplicity and depth of perception and connection and 'hangs out' even in well-defined institutional spaces . . . [and] cultivates an ear and a tongue for multiple lines of meaning" (p. 224). Because the streetwalker theorist hangs out in unexpected places and listens with intention, possibilities for new knowledges and multiple tools in resisting oppression can be learned.

The differential consciousness that disrupts or shocks into new ways of thinking, actions, and ideas is reflected in Aimee Carrillo Rowe's work on differential belonging. Carrillo Rowe (2009) contends that the politics of relation or belonging can invoke disruption if we maintain the kind of critical consciousness described here: "The *politics of relation* is a placing that moves a politics of location through a relational notion of the subject to create a subject who recognizes and works within the coalitional conditions that creates [sic] and might unmake her—and others" (p. 3). Relationships and belongings "constitute how we see the world, what we value, who we are (becoming)" (2005, p. 16). Differential belonging then "places oneself at the edge of one's self and learning and tipping toward the 'others' to whom you belong, or with whom you long to be—or those who are 'you'" (p. 17). While Carrillo Rowe describes and theorizes about differential belongings that transform the individual, these belongings enable us to move beyond ourselves as individuals and our own social justice interests because of the disruptions we experience in our sense of selves, which often lead to a politics of relation that extends to the politics of resistance and social movement.

In another interpretation of the differential, Karma Chávez draws on both Sandoval's and Carrillo Rowe's scholarship in her book *Queer Migration Politics*, through what she calls differential vision, which "turns back to political activism and social movement, and . . . requires conjoining orientation with belonging" (2013, p. 28). Such vision demands attention toward an orientation centered on a politics that addresses "the most vulnerable, shifting imaginaries, achieving legislative objectives, and constructing a 'gray politics'" (p. 29). Chávez also argues that "[a]lthough the idea of differential belonging could suggest that one should build strategic interpersonal alliances even across deep ideological lacunae . . . differential consciousness returns us to orienting toward those with politics that resist dominant and hegemonic systems of power. Combined, they create a differential vision" that enables coalition building (2013, p. 41).

The differential, whether it is attached to consciousness, belonging, or vision, demands a politics of justice and action. While these politics may imply a kind of utopian narrative, Chávez contends that a utopian differential vision enables new imaginaries, potentialities, and possibilities for social activism. Understanding differential consciousness, belonging, and vision, then, is part of an understanding of rhetorical agency that allows social activists to succeed in creating social change, particularly for those struggling against oppression related to class, gender, race, ethnicity, sexuality, and other marginal positions, as illustrated in Huerta's public persona (or cara) through collaborative egalitarianism and then through optimism, faith, and hope. Collaborative egalitarianism works through and within differential consciousness, while courageous optimism functions as differential vision. However, through courage, Huerta's rhetorical positionings manifest an element missing in these discussions of the differential; it is more than strength, flexibility, grace, belonging, and vision. Huerta's rhetoric illustrates a form of differential bravery that extends these understandings of differential politics, as the rest of the chapter explains.

Differential Consciousness as a Cara of Collaborative Egalitarianism

Huerta's rhetoric of social justice, as evidenced by her family's lifelong activities in the UFW (and other causes), was both collaborative and egalitarian in nature. As in the collaborative relationship Huerta had with Chávez, as documented in chapters two and three, Huerta also worked to establish a collaborative egalitarianism with her audiences, especially those made up of farm workers. For example, every speech ended with gritos that demanded audience participation. Huerta and Chávez's connection to farm workers was based on their lives of sacrifice and solidarity, as well as their own involvement in farm work. Huerta had done some farm work and capitalized on that experience to become a part of the farm worker communities in California and a union organizer, playing out both economic materialities and a vision for social hope and justice. Vicki Ruiz (1998) contends that "[s]uccessful union organization depends, in large measure, on a sense of solidarity and community among workers. Effective political and community action requires the intertwining of individual subjectivities within collective goals. Claiming public space can involve fragile alliances and enduring symbols, rooted in material realities and ethereal visions" (pp. 127–128).

In addition to enacting a lifestyle that reflected the living conditions many farm workers faced, Huerta also used language that rhetorically functioned to establish egalitarianism. For example, in a presentation at the Campesino Centers Conference, Huerta spoke about paternalistic approaches to helping farm workers:

> Part of the "agency mentality" is paternalism. Get rid of it! You need to sort out your feelings. Watch out for feeling superior to "those illiterate farm workers" or for ****** xxx [illegible] in reverse, feeling sorry for the "the poor,little [sic] farm workers." I know what I'm talking about. I used to be a schoolteacher and had to sort through my own feelings. Feeling superior or feeling

sorry for the farm workers are both wrong attitudes. We have to establish equality—service for service. We're neither more nor less than farm workers, we are equal. ("Martin Luther King Farm Workers Fund," 1976, p. 6)

Huerta's approach demonstrates her commitment to egalitarianism, a view that she fostered within the farm worker movement. She believed that farm workers had the ability to help themselves, as she noted in her 1966 peregrinación speech: "[C]onditions can be changed by only one group of people, themselves" (Huerta, 1966). She and other UFW leaders demanded great sacrifice from the farm workers, who had to pay dues to the union, participate in boycotts and pickets, and give their time to work for the union, all while working to support their families on very little income (Huerta, 1966). The demand for justice and farm workers' rights was a call not for charity but rather for egalitarianism and collaboration, for finding ways in which farm workers could help themselves. Avoiding paternalistic approaches in helping others while focusing on collaborative egalitarianism created space for both collective and individual agency.

Huerta's beliefs about paternalism meant that she constantly looked for ways to help people empower themselves through participation in the UFW movement. Chávez felt similarly on issues of self-help; they were both adamant about empowering people to help themselves rather than serving as a charity organization (Rose, 2001). The excerpt below is just one of many examples of how Huerta and the UFW called for help but differentiated that help from charity:

[W]hat I'd like to tell people that we're no longer asking anybody for charity. We're not saying to people, "Well please help the poor farmworkers." . . . Chale [no way] on that. No more of that. But we say to people now—You have a responsibility to farmworkers, because the farmworkers feed you. A farmworker puts food on your table every single day. And so you have a responsibility, so we ask you just do a very simple thing. Fast! Don't eat lettuce. Don't eat grapes. Don't drink wine. That's a very simple thing for people to do. Just don't eat those three things. I think people can do that.

Then we ask people to help picket. Well that's a little harder. Some people will say, "Well that's not my bag." Picketing is passé.

People don't do that anymore. What is picketing? Picketing is just walking, just like a peregracion [sic, peregrinación]. You know what a peregracion [sic, peregrinación] is—a pilgrimage. You're walking because you're walking for justice. And when people say to you that they don't want to walk, remind them that a farmworker has to walk thousands of miles in his lifetime to feed you, to put food on your table. And when he walks he doesn't walk straight up—he has to bend over like a hairpin when he's thinning, when he's cutting the lettuce, when he's cutting thecelery [sic], when he's picking tomatoes. He's bent over. And that's the way he's got to do it 8, 9, 10 hours when he's picking cucumbers, tell people that, and when they're picking grapes or onions a farmworker has to walk on his knees. So tell people that if we ask them to come out and join us for a couple of hours on Friday and Saturday, that's nothing compared to what a farmworker has to go through to put food on their table. He has to work out in the heat, he has to work out there in the cold. (Huerta, "Stanford University," 1974, p. 4)

UFW membership indicated a collaborative effort and belief in the movement by all those who participated by paying membership dues or joining in picket lines, boycotts, and other union activities. And those who walked on the picket lines and boycotted produce were not just farm workers; as the Stanford University speech indicates, Huerta was calling for all people to take up the UFW cause.

Her use of both Spanish and English, audience involvement, and repetitions of resistance and optimism through gritos also functioned to equalize speaker–audience roles through collaborative egalitarianism. For example, at the end of her speeches Huerta's rhetorical style called for audience involvement; almost all of Huerta's speeches ended with audience participation through gritos. By offering the audience a way to contribute, she was able to foster this sense of egalitarianism through collaboration:

All together, huh. I'll say Viva La Causa and everybody yells Viva, really, really loud, okay? Viva La Causa! Viva! Ugh, that was very weak. This is very important. This is like kind of praying together in unison you know, so it's really important. Let's try it again. Viva La Causa! Viva! Viva La Justicia! Viva! Now so Cesar can hear us in the hospital—where he's at and the growers can hear us where they're at. Viva Chavez! Viva! Okay, now we'll try Abajo. Down with Fear! Abajo! Down with Lettuce and grapes! Abajo! Down with Gallo! Abajo! You know, this really works. . . . Can we live in a world of brotherhood and peace without disease and fear and oppression? Si Se Puede, right? Okay, let's all do it together. Si Se Puede. Clapping. Si Se Puede, Si Se Puede. (Huerta, "Keynote Address," 1974)

Such audience involvement functioned to develop an egalitarian relationship with the audience by strengthening audience commitment to the cause through their participation and use of language such as "sí, se puede" and "viva justicia." The mixed use of Spanish and English, which was quite common at the conclusion of her speeches, also functioned to galvanize audiences, in that both Spanish- and non-Spanish-speaking audience members could participate. Jensen and Hammerback (2002) explain how César Chávez was able to interchange Spanish and English in such a way that the audience accepted the usage of both languages. By introducing a term or phrase (in either language, depending on the audience's language preferences, but usually in Spanish) and then translating, audiences felt comfortable in their repetitions because Huerta (and Chávez) established grounds for acceptance of this mixed use of Spanish and English. These gritos were similar to other interactive social movement rhetoric, such as the call-and-response format used during Martin Luther King Jr.'s rally in Washington, DC, where he gave the "I Have a Dream" speech (Stewart, 1997).

Huerta also recognized the rhetorical power in the repetition of "sí, se puede" (yes, we can/it can be done) and "¡viva!" (long live). Huerta's rhetoric created space for the voices of farm workers and others who were able to participate through audience involvement and the repetition of empowering gritos such as "¡Viva!," "¡Abajo!" (Down with), and "¡Sí, se puede!" (Huerta, "Keynote Address," 1974). Huerta's audience involvement guided the audience toward a politicized consciousness of social justice issues that influenced the everyday lives of farm workers. The farm workers and other supporters became a part of social resistance, part of a larger social movement for farm workers' rights, through these repetitions and reformulations of empowering language. Huerta both consciously and unconsciously reconfigured and rearticulated the rhetorical context to create resistance on her own terms rather than adapt to normative rhetorical requirements and social structures. Similarly used in other social movements, such interactions with the audience created renewed hope for change and victory for civil rights demands (Stewart, 1997). However, as Randall Lake (1983) contends in his study of the American Indian movement, other social movements have had to adapt their rhetorical practices to the specific contexts in which they addressed audiences to create effective resistance and defy expectations. Huerta used audience interaction within her immediate local context, as did César Chávez and others, in advocating on behalf of the union (Hammerback & Jensen, 1994).

In particular, the chanting of "sí, se puede" enabled Huerta to construct a persona oriented toward collaborative egalitarianism. Her rhetorical use of this cara fostered a sense of rhetorical agency for herself and others in the sense that repetitions of "sí, se puede" allowed the audience to speak, especially to speak about what each person could do. "Sí, se puede" is often translated as "yes, we can," but it can also be translated as "yes, one can," or "yes, it can be done." The first translation fosters the collaborative element of agency in that the group, "we," will work together to achieve social justice, while the second translation emphasizes the individual's sense of ability in that anyone can work toward social justice, and the third translation suggests a collective movement for change. Often when a speaker involves the audience, it functions to further enhance that speaker's sense of affirmation. That is, Huerta could hear that the audience believed what she said, so the act of persuasion is completed and confirmed through the audience's involvement. Repetition through audience-speaker chants may also reflect Mark Granovetter's (1978) threshold model of collective behavior in that individuals might have different thresholds for political involvement (e.g., strikes, protests, or riots). Perhaps audience involvement in such speeches, which essentially asks one to speak out through the social pressure of other audience members, moves individual thresholds to make collective action more likely. Other social scientists, using this same model, have described contagion of opinion (Karampoumiotis, Sreenivasan, Szymanski, & Korniss, 2015). They conclude that there is a critical number of initiators needed to create contagion. Through audience chants of "sí, se puede," "viva," "abajo," and others, this greater number of "initiators" might indicate higher levels of a motivational emotional atmosphere and thus commitment to act, whether through participation in picket lines, boycotts, or other UFW-sanctioned activities.

In addition to building audience rapport and interaction, Huerta's speeches were full of examples of injustices and calls for social activism from all kinds of people. For example, in her 1974 Stanford speech, she spoke extensively about the injustices facing farm workers:

> When we do the picketing and the leafleting we're trying to reach the growers, right? These men that are so blind with their own greed that they don't know what they're doing to innocent people. The same kind of blindness that the corporations have that create wars in other countries where they kill and mame [sic] innocent people and in this country now they also kill innocent people. We have to change them. We have an obligation to reach those men, to inform them to take their blindfolds off, so they can be conscientious people. So they can see what they are doing to innocent people. We have to do that for if we don't do it nobody else is going to do it. Those that care have to do it. . . .
>
> Now if farmworkers can do this—they have no fear in their hearts then the rest of us can do it. What we have to build on the boycott is a whole network of brotherhood. This is what we're trying to eliminate, racism, oppression. We [sic] trying to eliminate violence. But we can't do this without a lot of work and the work is very simple. It is talking to people. Talking to people and asking people to help. We should feel that it is an essential task that we have to do. That we have to go out and reach people and touch people to help. For only when we do that will farmworkers ever achieve that justice. (Huerta, "Stanford University," 1974, pp. 3, 9)

In this speech, like many others, she focused on corporate greed and getting people to act on such issues. Presumably, this speech, given at Stanford University, addressed college students, professors, and like-minded community members.

Not only did Huerta emphasize such injustices and calls for activism in community speeches, but she also extensively testified in Congress and the California Assembly on such issues. For example, testifying before a state of California committee in 1980, she talked about political action in California and called for more actions to be taken:

The ALRA accomplished this goal by 1) largely replacing the violence and insecurity that had been a hallmark of California farm labor relations for decades with a fair and orderly system of resolving agricultural labor disputes; 2) attempting to end generations of exploitation and powerlessness by guaranteeing farm workers access to the process of free collective bargaining through which US workers have traditionally escaped poverty and improved their standard of living; 3) enfranchising workers who had never before been granted the sacred right of freely choosing their own representatives through a state-supervised secret ballot election process. (Huerta, 1980)

Here, she emphasized the successes of the UFW and the Agricultural Labor Relations Act (ALRA) but later noted that there was still much need to continue and expand in these highlighted areas.

This collaborative egalitarianism rhetoric is both unique and similar to rhetorical styles of other civil rights movement leaders of both this era and others. Michelle Holling (2012), writing about Emma Tenayuca, who was best known for her role in the Pecan Shellers Strike of 1938 in San Antonio, contends that such rhetoric is dispensational, in that it "counters hegemonic positionings and/or narratives of a subjugated citizenry in an effort to secure rights (e.g., cultural or political) granted, but not honored" (2012, p. 66). Catherine Ramírez conceptualizes this kind of collaborative work, which focuses on equality of participants through the metaphor of family. While Huerta used her own family and status as mother both strategically and unconsciously, Huerta and the UFW also conceived of family more broadly than the literal consanguineous family, as discussed in the previous chapter. But as Ramírez contends, the Chicana/o movement, along with the UFW, extended the family metaphor to the nation (usually of Aztlán), or as "la familia de raza," as a way to create unity, solidarity, and a common cause for which to fight (2009, p. 113).

Similarly, Fernando Delgado argues that collaboration and a collectivist orientation, as evidenced in Huerta's rhetoric, is based on "interdependent needs, common experiences, shared in-group identities, and the unifying influence of tradition and group norms and values" (1999, p. 19). Thus, the family metaphor extends to Huerta's public persona through collaborative egalitarianism via her use of traditional values (e.g., appeals in Spanish that emphasize family, Catholicism, suffering, and penance) and her resistance to the status quo in demanding change and that the audience participate in such activism. As Doss and Jensen claim, "Huerta used both a transcendent first persona and a second persona to advance her persuasive argument, but also that the combination of these two helped her to achieve the fragile balance of mystery and normalcy that is at the core of the transcendent persona" (2013, p. 20). These shifting, chameleon personae demonstrate Huerta's rhetorical diversity and ability to adapt to many kinds of audiences, stemming from her early childhood, in which she became comfortable moving among and between different cultures and groups of people. As part of her core identity, she was deeply committed to the life of sacrifice, egalitarianism, and collaboration.

Finally, the collaborative egalitarian cara reflects a type of differential belonging that can also be a strategic shifting of identities, positionalities, and temporalities. This cara can situate one in different relations, locations, and belongings, either consciously or unconsciously:

> Differential belonging, like differential consciousness, allows us to move among different modes of belonging without feeling trapped or bound by any one in particular. The point is not to be correct, consistent, or comfortable. We need not, or cannot, be the same person everywhere—in different communities, on different occasions, at different times in our lives. . . . Many cross lines of class, national boundaries, racialized communities, places of work, the language communities that hail us, each movement rendering our becoming-other as our relational needs shift over time and across space. (Carrillo Rowe, 2008, pp. 40–41)

Such shiftings of belonging and relations are ways of dealing with marginalization and oppression as part of a strategy to resist and overcome such barriers, a learning process that enables an agent to engage with coalitions and one's self/identity to achieve activist and differential goals for the self and others.

Differential Consciousness as Courageous Optimism

Courage and optimism are interlinked concepts because each begets the other. That is, having courage often inspires optimism, and optimism precipitates courage that taking action or speaking out will lead to some positive result or benefit. Courage, bravery, optimism, hope, and faith are all concepts situated in a future orientation. As Sara Ahmed astutely observes, "[H]ope may expand the contours of bodies, as they reach towards what is possible" (2004, p. 185). A future orientation in a social or political movement is essential for people to feel invested in their actions and for rhetoric that can lead to transformation. Wearing a cara of hope, optimism, faith, and courage is also what enables someone like Huerta to believe in the self as an actor, that an individual's actions can have impact. Often, Huerta and the UFW defined action as the ability to organize others through community organizing techniques, but without courage and optimism in both the self and others, the movement likely would have failed.

However, at times, Huerta reports that she often lacked confidence and self-esteem, constantly worrying about her effectiveness and self-image (Rose, 2001). For example, in a 1975 interview, she talked about the guilt she had over her divorces and wondered why people saw her as a leader. In a letter to Chávez, Huerta requested a visit to the farm workers she had been working with, recognizing what she saw as her limitations: "You know they are quite used to me in Stockton, so I am not anything special to them. I keep telling them I'm here, that they don't need to talk to you, but somehow, they are not convinced" (Huerta, "Received," n.d.). It is this kind of self-doubt that requires courage and optimism to keep moving forward as a social activist.

To overcome these feelings of insecurity and doubt, Huerta adopted más/caras (a kind of "super" face) of courageous optimism. That is, she used her public persona to reflect courage and optimism, even if she did not always feel that way in her private thoughts and life. A más/cara of courage and hope inspired both her and her followers to believe in the UFW cause as a movement that would succeed in obtaining more rights and better living and working conditions for farm workers. This mask rhetorically functioned to enable Huerta to speak out, emphasize immediate action, and develop optimism for future change, shaped through the encouragement of and authorization by others, a collaborative effect of agency. Her acquisition of voice and ability to speak out originated from years of working as an organizer with the CSO and later with the UFW, through habitus and other factors. In Huerta's own account, she reported:

One of the greatest things I have learned in the movement is courage. We really don't have courage when we have to make tough decisions. . . . When Cesar asked me to work for the United Farmworkers Union, I was divorced, had seven children, and had been a school teacher. . . . The decision . . . took a lot of sweat. I learned to have courage. . . . Working for a cause is the baptism of fire. Being involved is good, because then you lose all types of fear. Then what really happens is you become strong. (quoted in Cárdenas, 1977)

Throughout Huerta's rhetoric, this bravery and optimism were prevalent, enabling her to overcome her private fears, insecurities, and lack of confidence. Huerta also recognized the risks associated with her confrontational, courageous rhetorical style: "Internally, you know something has to be done, and you do it. You have to make decisions, and it's sometimes difficult, but you do it anyway. You have to know in advance that you will make mistakes and not be afraid" ("A Life of Sacrifice," 1990, p. 261).

Not only did Huerta commit to difficult decisions, but she recognized the riskiness of those decisions, particularly given that she had seven children and her marriage was about to end when she and Chávez decided to start the FWA union in 1962. She recounts her experience in making such "crazy decisions":

Oh, by the way, in the meantime I had been married and divorced twice, had seven children, OK—I now have eleven (laughter)—and, you know, with my seven kids went down to help Cesar start the union. The reason I'm saying this is because I made this crazy decision, like you said, about taking risks, about, you know, going out to help farm workers, not even knowing that their union could be formed. It was just a dream that we had, and we made it a reality. You know, the first [ones that] started with Cesar and his wife Helen, who's a very private person, and myself, and Cesar's cousin Manuel. We started the union. But the thing is I've never regretted my decision. Maybe in my future life, I'll be a dancer (laughter), but I never regretted my decision, and, you know, we have just accomplished miracles, and I think I have learned a lot of lessons. (Huerta, 1987, p. 23)

This courage or bravery may have originated in Huerta's Mexican American, class, and gender identities through the adoption of más/caras. As Gloria Anzaldúa (1987) has explained, the mestiza consciousness that emerges from places of marginalization embodies this kind of courage. In addition to challenging oppression and embracing ambiguity and contradiction, the mestiza "make[s] herself vulnerable to foreign ways of seeing and thinking. She surrenders all notion of safety, of the familiar" (p. 82), the kind of differential consciousness that requires strength (Sandoval, 2000) and courage or bravery.

Courage is rooted in one's own bravery to stand up for oneself and others and to create strong networks of people who are supportive in moments of courage. This understanding of courage and optimism is reflected in Roxane Gay's (2014) book *Bad Feminist* and TED talk (2015); Cindy Griffin and Karma Chávez's (2012) section in their edited collection, "All of us are intersectional and some of us are brave" (p. 17, referring to Gloria Hull, Patricia Bell Scott, and Barbara Smith's 1982 book, *All the Women Are White, All the Blacks Are Men, But Some of Us Are Brave*); and conversations about contemporary feminism with my coauthor Valerie Renegar (2018). Bravery does not have to happen all the time, but a little bit of courage can go a long way. Bravery begets bravery, which can make lives more satisfying, coherent, enjoyable, and enriched socially, economically, culturally, and politically. As Hull and Smith (1982) argue, the process of naming experiences and taking on activist or political labels is part of bravery. Huerta's speeches, congressional testimonies, and interviews provide an aspect of witnessing the injustices that farm workers and other marginalized people face. These acts are the beginning of how social change and transformation occur. Michelle Wallace contends that "being on the bottom, we would have to do what no one else has done: we would have to fight the world" (1982, p. 12).

Courageous optimism, for Huerta, is also tied to individual and collective understandings of agency. Using one's sense of power is important in engaging others in collaborative action. As Brennan (2004) argues, the transmission of emotion and the atmosphere of the crowd and context of the situation are eminently essential for building hope. Emirbayer and Mische describe this as projective agency, which "provide[s] communicative bases for the formulation of new strategies for collective action. . ., as well as for the development of new social policies, normative ideals, or ways of organizing institutions" (1998, p. 990). Huerta refers to this projective agency as power:

The only thing you have to know is how to have power. So they would say where's our power, what power do we have? And we would say, the power is in your person. *The power is in your person.* And when you come together with other people, and you take direct action, then you can make things happen. Then you can make the changes. That's all you have to do, you have to remember you have power, but you can't do it by yourself. You gotta bring other people together with you. Taking this non-violent action. And the thing we have to understand is that if we do not make the changes if we cannot get out there and work, nobody's going to do it for us. We are the only ones that can make those changes . . . [t]he people that had the courage to go out on strike, boycotts, taking their families with them. (Huerta, 2013)

Similarly, she emphasized the notion of power in another speech:

We have a lot of work to do. And we've got to remember before we think, "Oh we're powerless, we can't do anything,"— we can do a lot. The one thing we have to remember is that all changes made in this country have been made from the bottom. It has been the people that have made the changes. (Huerta, 2006)

Elsewhere, Valerie Renegar and I (2009) have described contemporary feminist rhetoric through this modality of power and projective agency, but Huerta's call for people to recognize their own power and how that power can be contagious was inspiring for many audiences during the height of the civil rights movements.

The idea of contagious hope and courage is also present in the way Huerta (and other UFW speakers) engaged in call-and-response:

I want to say something here and I want you to repeat it, okay? I want to say who's got the power? (Someone in the audience says, "we do!") And I want you to shout it out really really loud. Like a union chant. I'm going to say who's got the power, and you're going to say we've got the power. And I'm going to say what kind of power? And you're going to say people power, right? So let's do it loud. (Shouting) Who's got the power? (We have the power!) What kind of power? (People power) Who's got the power? (We have the power!) What kind of power? (People power) Okay, so we gotta use our power. (Huerta, 2013; see also the 2017 speech for the *Dolores* documentary for the same call-and-response format regarding power)

Notably, Huerta used these chants as a way for her audience to physically and bodily claim that power through their own voices. While Ott and Aoki's discussion of "counter-imagination" focuses on popular culture (specifically, *Star Trek: The Next Generation*), their point is well taken that the possibility for imagining different realities, mediascapes, senses of identities and places, and even a general understanding of the world is critical for social, political, and economic transformations: "Counter-imagination endeavors to provide historically marginalized subjects with decoding strategies that recognize and empower their voices and identities, rather than excluding and diminishing them. It is not simply enough to be critical of appeals to collective imagination, however. . . . [W]e must encourage [students] to imagine a more just future, a future of radical possibility and opportunity" (2001, p. 410). Counter-imaginations as alternative expressions of the future may be balanced by the contingent aspects of context and circumstance, but as Valerie Renegar and I (2018) have contended, a belief in minor changes that construct more hopeful futures is a critical aspect of feminist agendas and Huerta's rhetoric.

Having the confidence to take immediate action was also part of the fearlessness that fostered Huerta's public persona. Huerta directed others to be more assertive and active in whatever cause they might support, a principle in which she strongly believed. In one speech, she emphasized immediate action rather than waiting for others to make decisions:

We' [sic] can't really wait for legislation. You know there's a lot of things that we can do right away. I think that the one thing that we've learned in our union is that you don't wait. You just get out and you starting doing things. And you do things in such a way that you really help people to lay the foundations that you need. (Huerta, "Keynote Address," 1974)

Her emphasis on the need for action demonstrated her confidence in the UFW. According to Huerta, action at all levels, ranging from the individual to the entire structure of government and society, was useful.

Huerta also drew heavily from her religious upbringing and socialization through the Catholic Church, which reflects another side of optimism through both religious and nonreligious aspects of faith. She reported:

> I always say when people ask me where did you get your values from, I say I got them from religion. Especially in the Southwest where people are very devoted to St. Francis Xavier, to again follow the same values as St. Francis of Assisi about helping others and doing good for other people and not expecting gratification or rewards for what they do; if you see someone in need you should help them, don't wait to be asked. All those core values I did get them from religion. (Huerta, interview in M. T. García, 2008, p. 332)

She was also a believer in many of the UFW's rhetorical tools that were rooted in Catholic traditions, such as fasting, praying the rosary to the Virgen de Guadalupe, taking communion, practicing nonviolence (also related to Gandhi's work), and attending mass.

However, Huerta also had a tenuous relationship with the church as an institution because of its response to sex scandals and stance on issues like abortion, women's roles in society, and gay rights: "It's painful to go to Mass sometimes. The priest rants and raves about gay marriage and about abortion, but not one word about farm workers around here not being paid for their work because they're undocumented, or social justice issues" (Huerta, interview in García, 2008, p. 341). In response to a question about faith as inspiration, Huerta said, "Because you have so many setbacks in what you're doing" (p. 345). Hammerback and Jensen (1994) and other scholars of the UFW have evidenced the central use of religious symbols and images; for Huerta and Chávez as well as most activists in the UFW, religion and faith were key components of their rhetorical inspiration to their followers and themselves (see also M. T. García, 2007, 2008).

Liberation theology was also influential in Huerta and Chávez's thinking, at least in how it was introduced to them through the Catholic

Church in their communities. This philosophy, which emerged from Latin American Catholicism in the 1960s and 1970s, focused on fighting poverty and promoting political, economic, and social justice (M. T. García, 2007; Stephen, 1997). Specifically, many liberation theologists were concerned with workers' rights, participating in strikes and picket lines (Stephen, 1997), much like those in the farm worker unionization movement. And similarly, Mario García (2007, 2008) contends that abuelita (grandmother) theology was influential in both Huerta's and Chávez's lives, and thus the union itself. García (2007) defines these family-based religious teachings as "saying the rosary at home, teaching the Bible, parental blessings, and a variety of other religious forms of education offered by grandmothers and mothers to their children" (p. 25). Although Huerta has noted that she did not really know her grandmother, as she passed away when Huerta's mother was a young child, Huerta was very influenced by her mother's teachings, both religious and otherwise. Quoting her mother, Huerta said, "When you see that somebody needs something, don't wait to be asked. If you see somebody who needs something, you do it. Second thing: You don't talk about what you did. Once you talk about what you did you take the grace of God away from that act. And you never take money for anything. When you do something for somebody don't ever accept any money, because, again, that takes away the grace of God" (M. T. García, 2008, p. 304).

In sum, Huerta's rhetoric of courageousness fostered a sense of optimism and vice versa. Faith was also central to her optimistic persona, as Huerta noted: "We can make the changes as long as we have faith in ourselves" (Huerta, 2006). Faith, confidence, and optimism function rhetorically to inspire audiences (and speakers) to believe that change can and will occur. Rather than allow normative thinking to function as a rhetorical constraint, Huerta's commitment to optimism reflects a future orientation that enables new possibilities and alternatives (Emirbayer & Mische, 1998) in collaborative and collective ways. Richard Rorty (1989) contends that "[t]o retain social hope, members of such a society need to be able to tell themselves a story about how things might get better, and to see no insuperable obstacles to this story's coming true" (p. 86). Through Huerta's public persona, establishing that sense of social hope was essential for the survival of the movement. The examples of self-sacrifice, optimism, and respect that

UFW leaders had for the farm workers demonstrated that she and others really believed that they could succeed, even at times when they doubted themselves. Rorty also maintains that "[w]hat binds societies together are common vocabularies and common hopes. The vocabularies are, typically, parasitic on the hopes—in the sense that the principal function of the vocabularies is to tell stories about future outcomes which compensate for present sacrifices" (p. 86). Through the UFW central narrative of justice for farm workers emerged a sense of hope that change could happen. Huerta was instrumental in using this narrative to connect with audiences, both farm workers and non-farm workers alike.

However, Sara Ahmed also problematizes the emotion of hope. Specifically, she contends that "the politics of hope may be frustrated precisely by its over-estimation of the individual will; as if the future were dependent upon whether or not I felt it to be possible" (2004, p. 185). That is, hope is necessary for one to develop a future and action-taking orientation, but such hope does not necessarily produce results. In fact, Ahmed continues, "hope can function as a stubbornness . . . which may actually foreclose transformation insofar as it maintains an investment in something that has already been lost. . . . *The attachment then gets in the way of a process of moving on*" (2004, p. 185, citing Anna Potamianou's work; emphasis in original). In other words, in a social movement, hope cannot be the object of the social movement. Ahmed concludes by noting that "[s]olidarity does not assume that our struggles are the same struggles, or that our pain is the same pain, or that our hope is for the same future. Solidarity involves commitment, and work, as well as the recognition that even if we do not have the same feelings, or the same lives, or the same bodies, we do live on common ground" (p. 189).

Chela Sandoval's differential consciousness might provide the middle ground in that it "joins together the possible with what is" (2000, p. 180). Similarly, Richard Rorty (1989) contends that solidarity is rooted in such common ground and the recognition of the pain and suffering of others. In this sense, then, Huerta's rhetoric was incredibly effective in bringing hope and inspiration to all kinds of people, especially in the 1960s and 1970s. Hope and optimism in differential politics are best when possibilities for transformation exist but are rooted in the material realities of the here and now. As the

UFW movement continued into the late 1970s, 1980s, and 1990s, problems emerged that eroded this sense of hope and solidarity, as is explored in the final chapter.

Conclusion

Dolores Huerta was clearly a dynamic speaker capable of engaging multiple audiences simultaneously and across contexts. The UFW cause resonated with many at the time because of the broader civil rights movements but also because farm workers were (and still are) one of the most marginalized and oppressed groups in the United States. Huerta was able to use differential consciousness and bravery as caras of collaborative egalitarianism and courageous optimism to draw all kinds of people into la causa, from housewives who boycotted grapes and other kinds of produce to politicians at the highest levels, such as Robert Kennedy, who was a big supporter of the farm workers before his assassination in 1968. In fact, Huerta happened to be at his side moments before his assassination (M. T. García, 2008). Her role in the public sphere and as an advocate for all kinds of social justice issues has led Huerta to become a Chicana icon, although she is still unknown to many because Chávez received much more press attention and media coverage. Her brand of fiery courage, even amid her self-doubts and nontraditional rhetorical appeals of emotion and motherhood (as discussed in the previous chapter), was certainly unusual at the time, but it helped her stand out and draw attention to her messages. Vicki Ruiz (1998) describes this type of courageous woman in the Chicana/o movement as "La Adelita," the soldadera (soldier) of the Mexican Revolution, different from those in the women's liberation movement and other feminist activists. That is, the soldadera was courageous in her fight for the cause but also feminine and respectful, embodying her role as symbolic mother (Ruiz, 1998), both similar to and different from Huerta's public persona.

In addition to deploying this soldadera positioning, Huerta was able to read audiences and contexts effectively, demonstrating what Juan Guerra (2004) calls "transcultural repositioning," or how one engages with differential consciousness as critique, strategy, or concealment that allows for moving within and among different groups, contexts, and languages in a society. It is a type of hybrid identity that engages fluidity of self with audience, context, and space. As Guerra contends, this type of fluid movement is challenging not only in that it is difficult to always be reading and adapting to a rhetorical situation, but also in terms of how one employs and understands identities of both self and other. So in some ways, Huerta enacted a soldadera persona, but in other ways, she moved beyond and outside of the soldadera and other cultural/social expectations for Chicana activists of her generation. As demonstrated throughout this chapter, she did not adhere to these social norms if she felt that she could take on other types of personae. Doss and Jensen argue that Huerta used a shifting transcendent persona through a mestiza consciousness in which she "framed each situation as a recruitment opportunity and each audience as one willing to join her cause. . . . In the same breath, it seemed, Huerta could argue that one must be poor in order to aid the impoverished and, then, that middle-class efforts to aid the poor were vital to the union's success" (2013, p. 21).

This chapter also highlights the tensions, problems, and challenges in writing about Huerta as a union organizer, Chicana activist, and feminist inspiration. As Vicki Ruiz contends, "It is easier to celebrate the ways in which Mexican women have exercised control over their work lives than to examine the costs involved" (1998, p. 136); "neither family, neighborhood, the ethnic/racial community, nor union membership guarantees a comfortable 'community'" (p. 137, citing Patricia Zavella, 1987). Despite the success of the UFW and other labor unions, Ruiz notes that even into "the 1980s and 1990s, the transformation of women's work networks into effective union representation seems more elusive than ever" (p. 137). Mexican and Mexican American women also claimed public space for themselves in many other kinds of ways, including mutualista organizations and within the Catholic Church, for example. Again, Ruiz observes, "Mexicana/Mexican American/ Chicana activists, with determination, creativity, acumen, and dignity, have strived to exercise some control over their lives in relation to material realities and individual subjectivities as forged within both the spatial and affinitive bonds of community" (1998, p. 146).

Huerta's expressions and embodiment of caras of collaborative egalitarianism and courageous optimism also draw attention to her own lived experiences and material and social conditions. Repeatedly, she drew from her own life experiences, which were both similar to and different from those of California farm workers. She used her own experiences strategically to connect with specific audiences. For example, her 1987 speech at the University of California, Los Angeles, focused on sexism, feminism, and Chicanisma because her audience largely comprised Chicanas. Her 1974 Stanford University speech, in which she described her own start with the CSO and the UFW, addressed the importance of community organizing. Similarly, while her 1974 speech to the American Public Health Association centered on health issues and care for farm workers, she also connected the speech to her own health issues when she talked about delivering her tenth child using the services provided by doctors from the UFW medical clinic. Her interviews with journalists and others included many personal details, often because Huerta recognized that her life experience was not unique and that many could relate to and learn from her experiences as a mother, community organizer, and Chicana and farm worker activist, as well as the many other roles she held, both informally and formally (see, e.g., Huerta's 1973 interview with *La Voz del Pueblo*). As Doss and Jensen (2013) argue, in public speaking events and interviews, Huerta relied on her boundary-breaking experiences in which she emphasized courage, egalitarianism, and hope through collective efforts; she recognized that individuals do not succeed on their own but require the support and activism of entire communities to achieve social, cultural, economic, and political justice.

Such life experiences are also connected to how she was able to become a leader, for example, through intersectional habitus. The differential consciousness and emergence of courage, optimism, and egalitarianism originate in family life and extend to one's social networks moving through life. The networks and support groups behind the face of leadership of any social movement are essential for that movement's success, as Huerta's rhetoric shows. She relied on key support people throughout her life to foster her sense of confidence, courage, and bravery that were essential for taking fearless actions. Her social justice–infused upbringing played a role, along with what she saw and experienced in her own community. These are the elements that enable a sense of bravery and the courage to take on challenging social justice issues. To return to Granovetter's threshold model, many people who take action in a protest or strike do so because others participated first. Those who lead such activities may have a lower threshold (or a stronger sense of courage) than those who follow. Granovetter illustrates this point by noting that "[w]orkers deciding whether to

strike will attend carefully to how many others have already committed themselves, since the cost of being one of a small number of strikers is high, especially in a vulnerable employment situation" (1978, p.
1423). Huerta and Chávez both had to convince many farm workers
that striking was within their best interests; they used their own courage to inspire a generation of farm workers to take action that led to
major UFW victories in the fields, in the California State Assembly,
in the national and international boycott campaigns, and in the US
Congress. Huerta's enactment of differential bravery was essential not
only for her own self but for the contagion of her bravery and optimism,
which extended to an entire social movement.

In short, Huerta's sense of habitus created a lifelong framework for
understanding social justice issues with an orientation toward differential bravery. That is, Huerta's rhetoric critiqued dominant narratives
and called for civil rights for farm workers, Chicana/os, Mexicana/os,
and Mexican American communities, among others. Her optimism that
action could address and potentially solve such problems allowed for
her ongoing commitment to farm workers, even in the face of her own
poverty. Her commitment to egalitarianism and collaborative action
also meant that she understood, despite her own personal strengths,
that social change could not be accomplished alone. Enmeshing herself in communities, as did other farm worker leaders, such as Chávez,
Gilbert Padilla, and Larry Itliong, was critically important for connecting with these audiences. Marshall Ganz (2009), for instance, claims
that many other farm worker organizing attempts failed because
leaders came from outside of those communities. Huerta's differential bravery and ability to move among and within all kinds of groups,
narratives, and structures, adapting to each rhetorical situation, context, and audience, reflect rhetorical maneuvers that are hard to come
by. Yet Huerta subverted social expectations and cultural norms to become a well-known and outspoken advocate for those in marginal positions of US American society. She represents a unique rhetorical figure
and icon of the 20th and 21st centuries' social movements.

Chapter 6

DOLORES HUERTA, ICONICITY, AND SOCIAL MOVEMENTS

Dolores Huerta's long history with social justice causes is well documented in numerous accounts, including her own, even as she has been obfuscated within official and academic histories in comparison to Chávez. Her rhetorical tactics and strategies confounded social norms and expectations, which inspired many, but she also received a fair share of criticism. Most of this book has framed Huerta positively and has sought to understand how she was able to craft private and public personae. I deeply respect and admire Huerta—she is one of my idols. Yet no person, iconic or otherwise, is without faults. The first part of this chapter details a range of criticisms that mostly target Chávez and the United Farm Workers (UFW) but, by association, also include Huerta. These critiques reveal the inner workings and alleged problems of the UFW's leadership, providing insight into the decline of the UFW as a union and activist organization. Such accounts also complicate Huerta's public rhetorical work and iconic status but, at the same time, demonstrate her outspoken persona and ability to stand up for herself and what she believed in. Some of these criticisms are gendered, classed, and racialized assessments of her public persona and private life, while others might be considered to reflect aspects of both positive and negative human qualities, humanizing Huerta as a person, mother, and activist.

This chapter also emphasizes how social movements and other contextual facets illustrate how rhetorical agency functions beyond the individual agent. Specifically, this chapter explores how Huerta's rhetoric contributes to more refined understandings of iconic leaders, social movements, and intersectional approaches to social justice that focus on marginalization affecting all kinds of people. In addition, this chapter explains how this study of Dolores Huerta's rhetoric, through the lens of rhetorical agency as intersectional habitus, haciendo caras (making faces), differential consciousness and bravery, and the negotiation of gendered, racial, and classed constraints, makes important contributions to both rhetorical studies and the histories of Huerta, the UFW, and Chicana/o social movements. Huerta's rhetoric offers a reframing and expanded understanding of rhetorical agency through her individual and social movement rhetorical practices as well as her relationships with family, Chávez and others, religion, and spirituality.

Complicating Iconicity in Social Movements: Critiques of Huerta and the UFW

While Huerta and Chávez became social justice and Chicana/o/x icons, their lives were certainly not perfect, even as their iconic statuses demanded such perfection. Huerta has mostly been widely admired and praised for her civil rights leadership and work with the UFW. However, historians and journalists have revealed other sides of the purported UFW success. Miriam Pawel (2009, 2014), Matt Garcia (2012), Frank Bardacke (2012), and Marshall Ganz (2009) have published histories that take a more critical look at the UFW in the 1970s and beyond. Most of this scholarship focuses on Chávez's leadership and paranoia, arguing that it led to bad decision-making, possible financial malfeasance, and purges of high-quality and committed people from the union. The latter, in part, resulted from an activity called "The Game," in which UFW leaders, members, and volunteers gathered to air their grievances through personal and professional attacks on one another. As Miriam Pawel describes it, "[a] dozen players would gang up on each other, 'indicting' a participant for bad behavior by hurling abusive and often profane invective" (2006a, para. 2). The Game created a lot of tension and frustrations within the UFW leadership, causing irreparable rifts, according to Pawel, Garcia, Ganz, and Bardacke. Chávez became increasingly paranoid, often accusing UFW volunteers, employees, and leaders alike of attempting to overthrow him. He would then expel them from UFW headquarters. Furthermore, during the late 1970s, contracts declined significantly, as did the success of UFW boycotts. Even though Chávez is considered the instigator of most of these problems, Huerta, as his key advisor and cofounder, may have also contributed to these difficulties, as did the fights that they had with each other and others. Publicly, she defended Chávez's decisions and actions, as noted in Pawel's four part *Los Angeles Times* series: "Huerta said it was a time when security had become a major concern in the loose-knit organization, after Chavez received death threats. 'If Cesar was a little paranoid, there's a reason for it'" (2006a, para. 27). Huerta's response may also indicate that scrutiny from a number of people and organizations was a key reason for Chávez's concern about loyalty, a legitimate worry that may have led to paranoia. Law enforcement organizations were often surveilling UFW leaders, and negotiation conflicts with the Teamsters over contracts were frequent and sometimes violent.

Huerta was also accused of being ineffective as a negotiator from within the organization, even though she has been widely lauded for her negotiating work in histories, newspaper and magazine articles, and other UFW accounts of the 1960s and 1970s. When Huerta was serving as a lead negotiator on talks with two major growing companies, Freshpict and D'Arrigo, several of those involved on the UFW side contended that she had "mismanaged the negotiations—to put it mildly" (Monsignor George Higgins, quoted in Pawel, 2014, p. 220). Apparently, some of the dissatisfaction was due to the controversy of Huerta's unwed, pregnant status and the affair that she was having with Richard Chávez (César's brother), who was married at the time. Pawel's observation that Huerta was a poor negotiator in this one particular case, followed by her discussion of Huerta's affair, suggests that perhaps the real issue was the affair and her subsequent pregnancy. As Pawel writes, "Kircher [Bill, director of organizing for AFL-CIO] was perturbed about Huerta's involvement for another reason. He had found out she was six months pregnant. An unwed pregnant woman as the lead negotiator and key figure in the union was a major crisis, Kircher told Cohen [Jerry, UFW lawyer]" (2014, p. 220). The mismanagement of negotiations is certainly a gendered assessment of Huerta's work, as she was scrutinized for her pregnancy resulting from the affair, although some of the criticism could have been a valid evaluation of interpersonal skills or a lack of time to complete the negotiations effectively. Such perceptions matter in terms of negotiation and the visibility of Huerta's public UFW roles, but they also demonstrate how women were judged differently from their male counterparts. Notably, César Chávez is also reported to have had at least one affair while married to Helen Chávez, but those marital infidelities seemed to have little impact on public veneration for César Chávez (Garcia, 2012).

Huerta and César Chávez also fought viciously at times and yet somehow managed to continue a very close and supportive relationship. As Pawel reports: "They had been sparring partners since the earliest days of the union, but the fights had grown more personal and more intense. . . . Chavez could count on Huerta's loyalty; he was confident she would not leave, no matter how much abuse he heaped upon her" (2014, p. 408). Chávez was sometimes verbally hostile with Huerta, as illustrated in the following extended exchange at a board meeting in 1979, when Huerta questioned why she had been taken out of her lobbyist role in Sacramento:

> "You talk to Richard [César's brother] and find out why you were taken off," Chavez retorted. "Don't blame me. I had nothing to do with it."
>
> "I am blaming you!" said Huerta, seven months pregnant with the couple's fourth child [referring to Richard Chávez, her partner].
>
> "Look, Richard wants you to stay home, you're going to have a baby, and goddamn it that's why I did it!" Cesar said, angry and patronizing at once. "I did it because he wanted me to do it. He was going out of his mind there in Delano." . . .
>
> [Later] Chavez exploded at Huerta for failing to turn in a few hundred dollars' worth of receipts, an omission she disputed.
>
> "Don't you fucking lie! Why do you lie?" Chavez yelled at her. He questioned his brother about a missing receipt, and Richard joined the fray: "I'm fucking sick and tired of being harassed!"
>
> "You're upset because she's screaming," Cesar taunted Richard, before turning back to Huerta: "You're the goddamn stupidest bitch I've seen in my whole life! . . . You're crazy. I can't deal with you on business. . . . I don't want you on the board."
>
> "You have my resignation," Huerta said as she walked out. (Pawel, 2014, pp. 408–409)

On the one hand, this exchange illustrates a very contentious and volatile relationship that is potentially deeply problematic given the kind of language Chávez used in addressing Huerta. On the other hand, it is possible that because of their very close relationship, they fought like this regularly and were able to forget and move on, as might brothers and sisters after a fight. However this exchange is interpreted, it suggests a close and intense relationship that was formed and sustained throughout many years of hard work and the duress of social justice organizing.

Garcia (2012) contends that Chávez also pitted board members, such as Marshall Ganz and Dolores Huerta, against one another, as illustrated in recorded tapes of executive board meetings (e.g., June–July 1977 meeting), during which "The Game" was played. For example, Garcia reports:

> Huerta resented the close relationship between Chavez and Ganz and regarded Ganz as a "spoiled brat" and "Cesar's little boy." . . . Virtually everyone had conflicts with Dolores Huerta, whose esteem in the union had diminished since the early 1970s. Her tendency to pick fights with younger staff had earned her the ire of many volunteers, especially those in the Huelga School, an educational program for the children of farm workers in Delano funded by the Migrant Ministry, whom she suspected of counterorganizing. "None of them can fuck me up with the members," she told the board in a fit of insecurity, "because my roots go back many years." (p. 233)

Chávez also used harsh and strong language, as Garcia again reports: "At board meetings, however, Chavez openly used (and abused) Huerta as either his one-woman cheering section or a punching bag, depending on the circumstances. His dependence on her sycophancy and his tendency to make her the butt of his jokes did little to improve her confidence at a time when she most needed it" (p. 233). The description of these exchanges is framed negatively, which may or may not have been an accurate assessment of Huerta's confidence and relationship with others. In particular, the use of the phrases "in a fit of insecurity" and "did little to improve her confidence" assesses Huerta's psychological mind at the time, when Garcia could not have known if she felt insecure or confident.

Several accounts report that UFW leaders verbally fought with one another, resulting in shouting matches; berating staff, volunteers, and one another; and using prolific profanity. The passage below is quite telling about how relationships were unraveling among the board members and provides new insight into the characters of Chávez and Huerta. Constantly worried about people trying to sabotage the union and Chávez's leadership, Huerta made the following statement at the 1977 board meeting:

"If anyone tells me anything about Cesar right now, man, I got my antenna up! Before I'd just listen to it. . . . From now on, I've got a whole goddamn different attitude. If somebody starts giving me a bad time, man, I'm going to start noticing. Before I thought it was because I wasn't popular, that people didn't like me. But now I know that's not it at all. It's that people are trying to fuck me and they *are* fucking me!" Huerta's emotional tirade revealed more about her deteriorated state of mind than it did the existence of a well-planned conspiracy against the union during the summer of 1977. When [Jim] Drake and [Jessica] Govea challenged the facts of her stories, she shot back angrily, "If someone fucks me, they assume it is my fault." She complained, "I can't go to one person on this board to defend me." (Garcia, 2012, p. 243, emphasis in original)

In another exchange, Chris Hartmire, one of Chávez's supporters, challenged Huerta on the firing of Shelley Spiegel, a teacher at the UFW Huelga [Strike] School: "'You're so emotionally involved with the attack on you at Delano,' [Hartmire] told her, '[that] you are out to get certain people, even if you have to exaggerate and lie.' The accusation stung Huerta, who angrily threatened Hartmire, 'Where I come from, we kill people for calling someone a liar'" (Garcia, 2012, p. 245). Although these examples do not paint a positive image of Huerta, they do illustrate that she was not afraid to speak out or to defend herself from attacks.

Some of these reports are curious, such as Matt Garcia's (2012) interpretation of Huerta's words, which he claims reveal insecurities or lack of confidence. From the UFW's tape-recorded meetings, tone and voice can reveal a lot, but it seems difficult to know exactly what Huerta was thinking during these meetings, even with the additional vocal aspect of Huerta's words. References to resentments, picking fights, "deteriorated state of mind," "insecurity now consuming her," "Huerta's temper tantrums," and "Huerta's fits of insecurity and explosive anger" (pp. 237–238, 243, 266) reflect unfair assessments. That is, Garcia could not have known if she was speaking from a place of insecurity or resentment or what her state of mind was at the time. Furthermore, these excerpts are taken out of historical context, and it can be problematic to interpret words among people who know each other very well. Use of profanity, for example, seems harsh on the page or in any another context, but may not have sounded as threatening

among the board members, as they were all cursing and knew one another very well. On the other hand, these exchanges were part of a very
serious several-days-long meeting with a lot of attacks, threats, and
verbal spars that included Gilbert Padilla's resignation from his position as a board member, indicating that there were troubled relations
on the executive board.

Another relevant and important criticism of the UFW (including
Chávez's and Huerta's leadership) involved how the organization targeted braceros and undocumented immigrants who worked in the
fields. In essence, the UFW was charged with harming workers and
families of Mexican and Filipino backgrounds, who were just like the
workers they were trying to protect, except without legal documentation. Garcia (2012) details how the UFW reported many undocumented immigrants to the Immigration and Naturalization Service
(INS; now called Immigration and Customs Enforcement [ICE]) as
a way to get them out of the fields. The UFW rationale was that these
workers, first the braceros (until 1964–1965, when the bracero program ended) and then undocumented immigrants, worked as scabs
when UFW workers were on strike. The growers were able to exploit
scab workers while making the success of strikes much more difficult.
To be fair, however, this same problem had arisen much earlier during
union organizing attempts and was a major criticism of the bracero
program, in which the US government, in collaboration with big growers, imported cheap labor from Mexico at the expense of workers already living in the United States.

There are more such examples of criticisms of Huerta, Chávez, and
the UFW as the organization changed tactics and lost influence, especially after Chávez's death in 1993. Miriam Pawel, an investigative
journalist for the *Los Angeles Times* (in 2006), wrote a lengthy, four-
part series on the evolving nature of the UFW and how it has become
an organization that is more about the image of helping farm workers
than the actual work of union organizing:

Chavez's heirs run a web of tax-exempt organizations that
exploit his legacy and invoke the harsh lives of farmworkers to
raise millions of dollars in public and private money. The money
does little to improve the lives of California farmworkers, who
still struggle with the most basic health and housing needs and
try to get by on seasonal, minimum-wage jobs. Most of the funds
go to burnish the Chavez image and expand the family business,

a multimillion-dollar enterprise with an annual payroll of $12 million that includes a dozen Chavez relatives. (2006b)

The UFW has evolved into a different organization, one that does not always live up to its legacy or activists' expectations, although the UFW has refuted these accounts. Farm worker conditions are little better today than they were in the 1950s and early 1960s, when Huerta and Chávez cofounded the union to help farm workers (National Farm Worker Ministry, 2016). Although achievements have been made, backslides have also returned too many farm workers to living and working conditions similar to those in the pre-union years. Many 21st-century field workers are undocumented, meaning they have few legal protections. Pawel maintains that the UFW has a great deal of money and yet is not spending it to help organize farm workers or for benefits such as the health care and pension plans that were developed in the 1960s (Pawel, 2006b, 2006c).

Other writers and researchers have similarly noted that one of the major strengths of the union and leaders like Huerta and Chávez was that they gave hope, inspiration, and motivation for social change. Around the 1980s (or arguably, as early as 1973), as the union's power and image fell into decline, that sense of hope and motivation was somewhat lost. Chávez's 1993 death was a major blow to the organization; a leadership vacuum occurred around this time. Huerta was the obvious successor, but the board did not select her to take on the role of president, which hurt her deeply according to her friend, artist and activist Barbara Carrasco (Bratt & Bensen, 2017). Chávez's son-in-law Arturo Rodríguez assumed the presidency of the union, but it has really never regained the prestige and effectiveness it had under Chávez's leadership. Unfortunately, many organizations that rely on a single, charismatic leader for action have fallen into decline with the loss of that leader. Once that leader resigns, retires, passes away, or is removed, the organization loses its purpose, motivation, effectiveness, and audience responsiveness. In many ways, this decline is exactly what happened to the UFW, even though Huerta was still a powerful leader in the organization (Bardacke, 2012; Garcia, 2012; Ganz, 2009; Pawel, 2014).

In 2002, shortly after Dolores Huerta retired from the UFW, she started the Dolores Huerta Foundation, where she serves as president of the board of directors. The goal of the foundation is to organize communities to achieve social justice. Huerta has also been an active political organizer and speaker, particularly focusing on getting more Latinas involved in politics and running for office. In 2012, Huerta received the Presidential Medal of Freedom, the highest civilian award given by the president, recognizing contributions to world peace or other significant activities. In her acceptance speech, she said:

> The freedom of association means that people can come together in organization to fight for solutions to the problems they confront in their communities. The great social justice changes in our country have happened when people came together, organized, and took direct action. It is this right that sustains and nurtures our democracy today. The civil rights movement, the labor movement, the women's movement, and the equality movement for our LGBT brothers and sisters are all manifestations of these rights. (Huerta, 2012)

This statement demonstrates Huerta's lifelong commitment to social justice, community organizing, and social movements. She has done much to advance civil rights in the United States and elsewhere in the world, even if not always perfectly.

However, Huerta is not without contemporary controversy in other ways. For example, during the 2016 Democratic Caucus in Nevada, Huerta tweeted, "I offered to translate & Bernie [Sanders] supporters chanted English only! We fought too long & hard to be silenced Si se puede!" (@DoloresHuerta, February 20, 2016). Some accounts indicate that she misrepresented what happened, that Sanders's supporters were only calling for neutral moderators when Huerta was clearly a Hillary Clinton supporter (Frydl, 2016). Others say that she was booed and hissed at for her efforts to translate at the caucus, thus demonstrating discriminatory practices by Sanders's supporters (Marcotte, 2016). The actress America Ferrera also tweeted about this issue in defense of Huerta, while other actresses, notably Gaby Hoffman and Susan Sarandon, indicated that they were present and no such chanting of "English only" occurred. Later, Rosario Dawson, the actress who played Dolores Huerta in the 2014 film *César Chávez* and was a cofounder of Voto Latino, accused Huerta of misrepresenting Sanders's positions on immigration and other Latina/o issues (Dawson, 2016).

Regardless of what happened at the Nevada caucus or Huerta's political support of Hillary Clinton, her outspokenness, political involvement, and support of social justice continues, sometimes with controversy and criticism, as is the case with most public figures. A 2017 documentary film has highlighted her contributions to the UFW and civil rights movements (Bratt & Bensen, 2017). As a result of the film, Huerta has received increased press coverage and attention, such as her interview with María Godoy (2017). In this interview for Texas Public Radio, Godoy asked Huerta about her activism and her relationship with her children. Huerta responded by saying:

> I think that's something that all mothers have to deal with, especially single mothers. We work and we have to leave the kids behind. And I think that's one of the reasons that we, not only as women but as families, we have to advocate for early childhood education for all of our children. To make sure that they're taken care of but also educated in the process. Because we do need women in civic life. We do need women to run for office, to be in political office. We need a feminist to be at the table when decisions are being made so that the right decisions will be made. But you know, actually, in the farmworkers union—and the film doesn't really show this—we always had a daycare for children. Because when we did this strike, and especially when all of the people went on the march to Sacramento, the women had to take over the picket lines.

Even into the 21st century, Huerta has still had to defend the decisions she made years ago about working and motherhood. Yet her statement indicates that she still believes she made the right choices and that women need to be involved in politics, community organizing, and social activism. Her continued political and social activism is a mark of how she remains a powerful Latina leader and icon for Chicanx, Latinx, women, and many others in US American society.

Iconic Leaders and Social Movements

Huerta is a popular figure among Chicanx/a/os and others focused on social justice issues. Huerta's rhetorical legacy has transformed her into a Chicana/Latina and social movement icon. As the union declined in effectiveness and popularity in mainstream activist cultures in the 1980s and 1990s, the UFW leadership capitalized on the nostalgia for

the UFW and Chicana/o movements of the 1960s. Although Chicana/
os were still largely marginalized within the larger US American context, their growing power in politics, education, and middle-class status led to their continued support of the UFW and Chávez as its leader
until his passing in 1993. In the 1980s, the union started to rely more
heavily on donations and public-speaking tours, rather than membership dues, to support its activities and to prevent the union from bank-
ruptcy (Pawel, 2014). The union, while in decline in terms of power
and influence in farm worker organizing, still had cachet due to its
iconic leaders, who inspired those involved in the social movements of
the 1960s and 1970s. As these social movement leaders became iconic,
the movement itself was also starting to lose its original sense of purpose. Relying on the lore of the union in the 1960s, the movement still
represents a certain ideology and community organizing approach to
address injustice to this day.

UFW icons are tied to certain signs, or ideographs, embodied in
the historical successes of the union, namely, negotiating contracts,
striking, and boycotting. The ideograph as defined by McGee (1980b)
is tied to contextual discourses that operate "as agents of political consciousness" and articulations of intentions through specific practices
(p. 7). Darrel Enck-Wanzer further explains the connection of the ideograph to social imaginaries:

> Understood as the verbal, visual, and embodied symbolic reper-
> toire that is defined by (and defines) the social imaginary, ideo-
> graphs facilitate ideologically, historically, and doctrinally con-
> strained modes of stranger relationality, thus constituting social
> imaginaries and sociopolitical subjectivity. (2012, p. 16)

The iconicity of Huerta and Chávez, then, is deeply connected to the
ideographs of the UFW, such as unions, farm workers' rights, Chicana/o
rights, and nonviolence contextualized within the civil rights movements of the 1960s and 1970s.

However, iconicity is rooted in the action of the past rather than
oriented toward the future. When a social movement leader becomes
an icon based on past performance and legacy, such a leader no longer
needs to prove his or her value to the movement, since that worth has
already been established and recognized internally with constituents

and externally to the general public. Such icons, like Huerta or Chávez, can employ the social, cultural, political, and economic capital that emerges from iconicity without the same kind of expectation that once existed within the hopefulness and optimism of the movement at its stages of inception. Icons thus reiterate their own capital by the very virtue of being icons. The icon as ideograph means loss of control over symbolic action that emerges as new leaders become prominent within a movement. Suzanne Daughton (1995) notes that "[i]conicity guides audiences stylistically, implicitly, and ethymematically, inviting them to make connections on their own" and "*illustrates itself,* embodying its own meaning metaphorically, just as a rhetor using enactment can *embody* her or his meaning literally" (pp. 24, 27, emphasis in original). The UFW, along with Huerta and Chávez, came to represent workers' rights and justice through nonviolence, which carried forward even when the union's leadership wanted to move beyond such ideals to accomplish other goals through other means. Daughton further explains that iconicity lasts long beyond the agent him/herself, functioning most powerfully as a subconscious metaphor or stand-in for such principles. The UFW is a far different organization in the 21st century, but it is able to draw on the iconicity of Huerta, Chávez, and other UFW leaders and images.

As movement leaders become icons for social justice, their movements may also develop internal conflicts. Iconicity develops a sense of permanence for its publics, and that so-called stability of the icon becomes established, whereas many movement participants, especially those of the 1960s and 1970s, were drawn to a movement because of its antiestablishment rhetoric. As Charles Stewart (1997) explains in his analysis of Stokely Carmichael's leadership of the Student Nonviolent Coordinating Committee (SNCC), new generations of movement activists may want to continue to draw on the antiestablishment rhetoric of the movement's initiation, whereas the more established leaders of movements often have different leadership goals. Established leaders may become comfortable in their fight for social justice from a reform or moderate approach, concluding that working within the system is the only viable solution to create social change: "The resulting internal conflict is intended to perfect the movement through purges of the movement's failed leadership, organizations, strategies, and principles" (Stewart, 1997, p. 430). In the 1970s, Chávez's purges were the result of internal conflict, distrust, and paranoia, yet both Huerta and Chávez's iconic status was essential for maintaining UFW organizational identity.

One of the UFW's greatest challenges was that it started as a movement intended to establish a union for farm workers' rights. As the union and the movement evolved, Chávez and other union leaders, like Huerta, came to see the union as a bigger movement and started to move beyond its focus on union organizing and collective bargaining. In essence, they saw the movement becoming much bigger in terms of its goals, purposes, and objectives; it moved beyond the union's original activities of collecting members, negotiating contracts, and organizing produce boycotts. Scholars of the UFW have well documented activist dissatisfaction with the UFW leadership in the late 1970s, but perhaps such dissatisfaction was more a result of the internal conflict of old and new union goals, differing views on the function of the union, and the pursuit of greater social justice not just for farm workers but for all Chicanx/a/os and other marginalized groups. Iconicity within social movements illustrates the appropriation of past-present-future meanings. As Just and Berg argue, the plasticity of agency-meaning suggests that iconicity within social movements would be constantly changing and in flux: "[A]gency-meaning relationships are, we believe, *dialogical*, in constant, open-ended exchange among themselves, and *disastrous*, susceptible to breakdowns, blow-ups, and new beginnings" (2016, p. 44, emphasis in original). In other words, the iconicity of Huerta, Chávez, and the UFW became meanings beyond what these leaders respectively intended. In part, Huerta's iconic status has inspired generations of Chicanx/a/os to seize rhetorically agentic moments and become agents for themselves and their communities. They have built on her leadership and the UFW movement to adopt their own instances of differential bravery.

While contemporary activists may see Huerta and Chávez's iconic status as represented in the fixed place of the first strike of 1965 and the grape boycotts that followed, the two leaders invoke, as icons, an emotionality that symbolizes much more than farm workers' rights and the movement itself. As Caitlin Bruce (2015) writes,

> [Icons] are slippery, mutating, and circulating visual objects that are continually decontextualized and re-contextualized according to the aims to which they are bent. . . . Icons move in

the dual sense of the word: They circulate, generating a kind of public sphere that works through spectacle and display, and they mobilize public emotions. (p. 48)

She further argues that icons are "affect generators" because they intensify meaning and attachment to what they represent. These icons continue to circulate in mimetic and magnetic fashion, evolving affectively as meanings become larger than the actual lives, actions, and words of Huerta and Chávez and inspire other moments of rhetorical agency.

The UFW and Chicana/o movements were distinct because they focused on different issues, but due to their overlapping audiences of Mexicans and Mexican Americans, many audiences have come to equate the two movements. César Chávez, Dolores Huerta, and Luis Valdez (of the Teatro Campesino) are often considered icons of both movements. Other key Chicana/o movement leaders, like Reies Tijerina, Sal Castro, Rodolfo "Corky" Gonzáles, and José Ángel Gutiérrez, also became iconic figures, but mostly for Chicana/o audiences. Chávez and the farm worker cause were more widely known across the United States, in part because of publicity like Chávez's cover on *Time* magazine in 1969. John Hammerback and Richard Jensen (1980, 1994; Jensen & Hammerback, 2002) and Fernando Delgado (1995) have well documented the rhetorical legacies of these leaders and how their approaches differed. As Delgado argues, "Resulting from material deprivation and injustice, the Chicano movement developed and sustained itself through the articulation of culturally appropriate and constitutive ideographs," namely, terms like "Chicano," "La Raza," and "Aztlán" (1995, p. 448). The farm worker movement, on the other hand, focused on injustices through other rhetorical means, such as drawing inspiration from Catholic and Mexican cultural traditions to connect with farm worker audiences. The Chicana/o movement activists often advocated for separation from the state, whereas the farm worker movement leaders worked within the state (Delgado, 1995). Yet the movements were often inspired by each other, as well as other civil rights activism of the time. In addition, the iconic status of leaders like Huerta has led to evolving meanings and identities of who they are now and who they were then. For many Mexicans and Mexican Americans, these movements were essential for identity development, consciousness raising, and addressing social justice issues within their communities. Leaders like Huerta and Chávez, through their protest strategies and vision of the future, helped shape Mexican American and Chicanx/a/o identities for generations, with a lasting legacy that continues today. Not only did Huerta and Chávez inspire Chicanx/a/o and Latinx/a/o audiences, but they expanded their reach to many other civil rights issues, as the next section details.

Intersectional Approaches to Social Justice

One of the major challenges of social movements lies in how they often focus on singular issues, such as voting rights, farm worker rights, racism, sexism, homophobia, and so forth. While the UFW's leaders have been criticized for some of their approaches related to undocumented workers, the braceros, and problematic, language used to refer to various social and cultural groups, many UFW leaders, including Huerta, expanded their sense of social justice far beyond farm workers' rights. In fact, as Phaedra Pezzullo (2003) argues, reducing a movement to a single cause is problematic as many movements and leaders were/are aware of intersecting aspects of oppression and have fought for social justice across a number of causes. Karma Chávez (2011) rightly notes that coalition building among like-minded groups is an important aspect of achieving justice for marginalized peoples. She suggests that what brings people together to address social justice issues is not the single issue itself but rather the intersectional aspects of marginalization and injustice; activists can be both self- and other-directed in terms of what they hope to accomplish within social movement rhetoric. Through enclaves, groups can find protective spaces for internal conversations that build confidence and enable public action (Chávez, 2011; Squires, 2002). Karma Chávez's (2013) study of coalitional possibilities, or how political groups can work together, is echoed in Huerta's rhetoric, particularly in how Huerta and other UFW leaders were very much interested in other social justice issues. These coalitional concepts illustrate how Huerta's rhetoric came to embrace mainstream and radical tactics that addressed religion, women's rights, LGBTQ rights, environmental justice, and alternative government frameworks, such as Hugo Chávez's (former president of Venezuela, no relation to César Chávez) arguably failed socialist experiments in Venezuela.

A major theme in Huerta's and the UFW's rhetoric involved the Catholic Church and the sense of faith that UFW leaders and followers developed through their religious beliefs and practices. Catholic and Christian belief was a daily part of their lives, and church and religious organizations widely participated in organizing efforts and improving the lives of farm workers. Notably, Chris Hartmire and the California Migrant Ministry were major influences for UFW leaders as well as key allies in the UFW movement. Catholic leaders, such as Roger Mahoney, who was a bishop in California during this era, were also very influential. The UFW's widely used rhetorical tactics, such as pilgrimages, fasts, imagery, and icons, were rooted in Catholicism. Lake (1983), in his analysis of American Indian rhetoric, suggests that for internal audiences, religion or spirituality can function as alternative agency, which he calls "Power." That is, the internal audience (in this case, farm workers) draws Power from the belief in supernatural forces: "When viewed as a rhetorical resource, Power adds to language a consummatory capacity. Because one can acquire Power for one's own use and learn from it how to live, Power is, epistemologically, a source of knowledge which is experienced" (1983, p. 136). In terms of politics and social activism both internally and externally to the movement, the coalition building between the UFW and the Catholic Church was an extremely powerful force. However, Huerta had a complicated relationship with Catholicism because of her divorces and role as a single mother. As she reported in an interview, she noted that Father McCullough, whom she knew so well that she named one of her children after him, said to her, "Well, you really should stay home with your children, this is not a good place for women" (M. T. García, 2008, p. 335). At times, she found the gendered values of Catholicism to be problematic, even though she was also deeply influenced by her Catholicism throughout her life (M. T. García, 2008).

Partly as a result of Huerta's tenuous but important relationship with Catholicism, she eventually came to embrace feminism and the women's movement. Using her physical body and motherhood as a form of enactment, she represented intersectional identities, causes, and politics as well as the complications in doing so. Various scholars have contended that embodied politics can be effective through spectacle and/or empowerment (e.g., Daughton, 1995; Faber McAlister, 2015; Fabj, 1993; Foss & Domenici, 2001). Examples of such intersectional and embodied social justice approaches are ubiquitous in Huerta's speeches, embodied acts, and leadership practices. In a 2006 speech, for example, she touched on a number of important issues ranging from politics to education to feminism to Hugo Chávez to the status of undocumented immigrants. Huerta had claimed that at first she did not identify as a feminist, but through her work in New York City on the grape boycott, she came to know Gloria Steinem and other important leaders of women's movements and organizations, which shifted her social justice causes to include sexism, feminism, and homophobia. Huerta's words about being Catholic and a mother resonate within these intersectional identities:

> Well, you know, I am the Catholic mother of eleven children. Does that mean every woman out here wants to have eleven children? Sometimes when I ask that question, I'll have some guy in the back of the room raise his hand. I chose to have eleven children, but does that mean that every woman wants to have eleven children? No. That is a privacy issue. What we do with our bodies as women is our privacy issue. Let's attack the gays and the lesbians. They're a good group to attack. That should be the big issue. Gay marriage that's a big issue. Come to think about it, if Thelma and Louise get married, does that affect your paycheck? Does that affect any part of your life? Those are privacy, Constitutional issues. Benito Juárez[,] we just celebrate his birthday a few days ago—what was the great saying that he said? "Respeto al derecho ajeno es la paz"—respecting other people's rights is peace. How many children a woman chooses to have, who one chooses to live with and marry—that is your constitutional right. (Huerta, 2006)

In this speech and many others, Huerta illustrates the intersectional and embodied aspects of motherhood, religion, feminism, LGBTQ rights, and people's rights in general.

Although Huerta has been charged with making homophobic remarks (cited in Garcia, 2012), her memory of her activism on gay rights is one of support. For example, in an interview, she recalled:

> I remember a hearing in San Francisco in the 70s or early 80s on the issue of discrimination against gays and lesbians. When I arrived to testify, no one had any idea what I was going to say and they were nervous. When I testified and said it was wrong to discriminate against people because of their sexual orientation, the opposition forces were shocked. It was something I

felt strongly about—so much so, that I went on my own to that hearing. (M. T. García, 2008, p. 323)

Her memory may have been different from at least some of her practices, but even in contemporary activism, coalition building is difficult, as Karma Chávez documents in her book *Queer Migration Politics*. Chávez's analysis of how queer rights and undocumented immigrants' rights groups worked together illustrates perfectly the challenges and imperfections of such coalition building.

The union, along with Huerta and other UFW leaders, also focused on connections to environmental movements, such as the significant health problems associated with the toxic chemicals and pesticides used in the fields. In the 1960s, the union regularly documented pesticide application, resulting health concerns, and injuries to farm workers (e.g., "Farm union vows pesticide fight," 1969). A union-produced video featuring Mike Farrell of *M*A*S*H* fame as the narrator documented the problems farm workers faced in the fields as well as the toxic and lasting effects of such chemicals on the food that white, middle-class consumers were eating. The union also started distributing a magazine, *Food and Justice*, to connect environmental concerns with farm workers' rights (Pawel, 2014). As early as 1974, Huerta was talking about pesticide use that required greater protections for farm workers:

> When we talk about getting a union for farmworkers, we're not just talking about getting more money. We're talking about stoping [sic] this kind of harm, this kind of mutilation, this kind of death, this kind of exploitation. You know, these people don't have protection from these kinds of accidents when they go to the fields. They don't have the protection from pesticides, they don't have protection form these types of people that take them to work. (Huerta, "Stanford University," 1974, p. 7)

While in this speech Huerta considered the use of pesticides as a farm worker health problem, the union's later rhetoric on connecting environmental concerns with health issues proved effective and helped leaders like Huerta to think beyond basic rights for farm workers. The 2017 film *Dolores* also explains how the UFW was more than just a labor union; it was a social movement that included many social justice issues. In fact, historian and author Randy Shaw argues that it was the farm workers union that started the movement on environmental justice (Bratt & Bensen, 2017). The 21st-century UFW has also extensively focused on farm worker health and environmental problems, as in their call for a suspension of the pesticide chlorpyrifos. Working with a number of environmental, labor, and health groups and the Environmental Protection Agency, the UFW continues to seek environmental and social justice for farm workers today (UFW, 2016).

Although the union has been criticized for its position on undocumented immigrants, Huerta has held a more complicated position on immigration reform, particularly in the 21st century. Her thinking may have evolved on the subject, and/or critiques of the UFW's anti-immigrant rhetoric could have been misconstrued, as the issue of undocumented immigrants filling positions as scabs is much more complicated than simply being for or against undocumented immigration. For example, during the immigrants' rights marches of 2006, she spoke extensively on the need to provide greater support for undocumented immigrants. However, in a 2014 interview on immigration, Huerta talked about the importance of support for undocumented immigrants but also of having patience to wait on the legislative process to create reform: "We have to look at the big picture and don't get caught up in saying we want it now. . . . We've been waiting—we are a community that can wait. And we have to have faith in our president, because the Republicans have shown their hand. We know what they want to do" (quoted in Nevarez, 2014). Some criticized President Obama's delays on immigration reform and, by extension, Huerta's position on waiting until post-2014 elections and for supporting Obama and the Democratic party over undocumented immigrants (NBC News, 2014). These limited examples of Huerta's stance on feminism, women, homophobia, LGBTQ rights, and the environment are only a few that expand her positioning on social justice and demonstrate the evolution of her critical work in thinking beyond farm workers' rights. In addition, these examples illustrate the complicated nature of social movements as they address injustices as intersectional manifestations of oppression. While these systems of domination are interconnected and require action from all fronts, that work is also very difficult, even among coalitions. Social movement activists like Huerta seek to understand the interstices where collaborative work is possible so that effective coalition building can work to reduce such social injustice at all levels.

Conclusion

Huerta's iconic status as a civil rights leader on many issues, from farm workers' and Chicana/o/x rights to feminism to environmentalism to LGBTQ rights, illustrates the cultural, political, and social impact that she has had. While some controversies have arisen, she remains one of the most important social justice advocates of the 20th and 21st centuries on issues of race, class, work and labor, environment, and gender. She is an idol to many, particularly Chicanas. In the times that I have seen Huerta interact with audiences in California, Las Cruces, New Mexico, and El Paso, Texas, I have witnessed what she means to those who hear her speak. Audiences cheer for her and shout UFW slogans in her presence. I have seen people cry in admiration and respect for what she has accomplished. She is revered like a pop music icon for those who know and have been inspired by her work. Her rhetorical legacy represents social justice for all, far beyond, and including, farm workers' rights. The 2017 documentary film and Mario García's (2008) reader mark her contributions more fully to the farm worker cause and the social movements of the 1960s and beyond. Huerta remains an important figure in US history and social justice causes.

EPILOGUE

Re-Visioning Rhetorical Agency

Above and beyond the few negative criticisms of Huerta highlighted in the previous chapter, she has been able to establish herself as a social movement icon who has fought tirelessly on a number of social justice issues in intersectional form. Overcoming such criticisms and continuing her lifelong quest for social justice are aspects of how Huerta embodies a sense of rhetorical agency. Through Huerta's rhetoric and the theoretical works of Pierre Bourdieu, Gloria Anzaldúa, Chela Sandoval, among others, rhetorical agency can be understood as a process in which an agent negotiates past and present individual and societal dispositions (Bourdieu's habitus) that constrain, limit, or facilitate one's ability to create rhetorical space that enables social activism. Huerta's early life shaped her public personae, which in turn became iconic and central to the farm worker social movement and the United Farm Workers (UFW) as a union. Rhetorical agency, then, can be understood, using Huerta as an exemplar, through intersectional habitus and influential relationships with people, contexts, and audiences, public personas that employ caras of intersectional identities and differential bravery, and even the emergence of iconicity within social movements. This project emphasizes the significance of intersectional habitus and how the negotiation of gendered, classed, racialized, and linguistic practices and institutions can influence, constrain, and enable agents as they become public figures and icons.

Tactics and strategies, such as caras and differential bravery, are learned through intersectional habitus as well as incremental successes. A little bit of success in courageous actions and statements fosters more attempts to be brave. Just and Berg (2016) argue that the plasticity of rhetorical agency demonstrates the back-and-forth between rhetor and audience, rhetor and context, and rhetor and self:

> As such, the notion of plasticity denotes the human subject's most basic ability to give form to its encounters with the world, but also the ways in which these encounters are formative of the human subject and, finally, how the encounters may become explosive, destructive of both the subject and the world. (p. 38)

Intersectional habitus as one facet of context, audience, and self illustrates how plasticity functions in rhetorical agency, as do spatio-temporal configurations, particularly in the ways in which rhetorical events or icons can take on new meanings in other contexts, spaces, and times. In addition, as Just and Berg emphasize, such new meanings can be both formative and destructive, as seen in how the UFW evolved over time. Erin Rand (2008) similarly concludes that "[a]gency, then, emerges not as the ability to create intentionally a certain set of effects, but as a process made possible by the very undecidability or riskiness of those effects" (p. 312). For Rand, communicative agency is rooted in the idea that unpredictability is productive and "provocatively queer," by which she means that the violation of decorum and the circulation of the text beyond the agent are facets of queerness/difference (p. 298). Engaging in the provocatively queer, or in the case of Huerta, the caras and tactical maneuverings of her public persona, is a manifestation of differential bravery; it takes courage and risk to always exist and act within the margins of social norms.

Some rhetorical scholars have suggested that rhetorical agency also includes creative, inventive, collaborative, and resistive elements (Campbell, 2005; Enck-Wanzer, 2006; Holling, 2000). Using theories of haciendo caras and differential bravery also more fully explicates and expands Huerta's emphasis on flexibility, hope and optimism, resistance, and transformation of self and others and the ways in which she uses these tactics to negotiate intersectional identities related to gender, race, ethnicity, class, and national origin through linguistic and embodied strategic choices. Rhetorical agency, in Huerta's rhetoric, is marked by flexibility (Sandoval, 2000) or, as Bernadette Calafell contends, "the power of the shapeshifter and the power of Chicanas as translators . . . wearing different masks at different times"

(2007, p. 57, citing Sarah Amira de la Garza). Suzanne Daughton (1995) explains that female rhetors (and other marginalized peoples) represent complex positionalities that require rhetorical flexibility. Empowerment comes through using one's own voice to speak, a kind of embodied enactment.

Although rhetorical scholars have argued that creativity, invention, craft, and form are facets of rhetorical agency, Huerta's rhetoric illustrates to a fuller extent why flexibility, malleability, and bravery enable one to experiment, adapt, and resist dominant and normative rhetorical structures, especially for Chicanas and Latinas. Huerta relied on a mestiza consciousness that "required (and enabled) her to shift her persona to simultaneously incorporate and break through the cultural faces or masks audience members expected of her" (Doss & Jensen, 2013, pp. 2–3). That is, creativity in invention, style, and form is expanded through the rhetor's ability to be differentially brave and flexible while speaking or in the process of invention. Huerta's use of multiple caras illustrates her rhetorical movidas. It is the constant rhetorical adaptations in haciendo caras, of using available means to negotiate rhetorical barriers related to race, ethnicity, gender, class, and religion, that fostered her sense of habitus and rhetorical agency. Huerta had to adapt through a "process of taking and using whatever [was] necessary and available in order to negotiate, confront, or speak to power— and then moving on to new forms, expressions, and ethos when necessary—[as] a method for survival" (Sandoval, 2000, p. 28). She used caras to adapt to in-group and out-group audiences, negotiating dominant ideologies, power, and material conditions as suited her needs and contexts. In particular, her differential consciousness, belonging, vision, and bravery were key aspects of how she was able to navigate such constraints.

Huerta's caras of optimism and hope are also overarching currents within her rhetoric, an element of rhetorical agency little attended to by rhetorical scholars. Each of these caras, collaborative egalitarianism and courageous optimism, employ optimistic and future orientations. Emirbayer and Mische, among others, have discussed the importance of the past, present, and future in the study of agency, particularly in how a future orientation lays the groundwork for hope. Other scholars have similarly argued that agency is performative and accumulated in experiences, reflecting a past orientation that emerges into a present/ future orientation (Enck-Wanzer, 2011; West, 2008). Although a future orientation does not always suggest social change or optimism (e.g., apocalyptic rhetoric; see Sowards, 2006), Huerta's rhetoric does illustrate specific examples in her orientation toward envisioning a better future. Individuals might have the right material and social conditions to create a discursive space, but without a hopeful and optimistic vision for the future, that person may not seize the available opportunities or attempt to negotiate rhetorical situations. Huerta and the UFW's "¡Sí, se puede!" are important and significant examples of their hopeful optimism. "Yes, we/one can" or "it can be done" imbues a powerful sense of agency with future orientation, one that is optimistic and hopeful for changing social conditions. Sara Ahmed (2004) discusses how anger can beget creativity and productivity in social justice movements that contribute to the requisite sense of hope. And yet, as she contends, hope does not necessarily lead to material change and can get in the way of transformation. The UFW's hopeful rhetoric of the 1960s seemingly turned to paranoia and anxiety in the 1970s, but it was that initial hopefulness, forged by Huerta and the UFW, that enabled productive change to occur and led to her iconic status that has inspired generations of Chicanx and Latinx activists.

Furthermore, Huerta's rhetoric illustrates the importance of the resistive nature of agency, providing concrete examples that illustrate the resistive element that Chicanas and Latinas often employ to navigate the matrices of gender, race, and class constraints. In essence, Huerta used caras of fearlessness and public resistance, simultaneously utilizing expected and unexpected rhetorical styles. That is, traditional and gendered audience assumptions might expect women to be both motherly and emotional, yet Huerta used motherhood and emotion in unexpected ways to disrupt dominant ways of thinking. As Sandoval explains, "[T]he citizen-subject can learn to identify, develop, and control the means of ideology, that is, marshal the knowledge necessary to 'break with ideology' while at the same time *also* speaking in, and from within, ideology" (2000, p. 43). Although Huerta resisted dominant rhetorical styles, she did deploy those strategies when appropriate and/or useful. Navigating between and among these choices requires care and attention to audience, context, and timing (e.g., kairos). As Darrel Enck-Wanzer (2012) notes in his study of the Young Lords, resisting dominant structures is difficult, requiring finesse and constant vigilance toward decolonial imaginaries to enact collective agency. Perhaps more importantly, rhetorical agency in Huerta's case embodies transformation for both self and other. Holling (2000) and Enck-Wanzer (2006, 2012) illustrate how agency functions constitutively in Chicana feminism and the Young Lords' social movement, respectively. Holling (2000) and Flores (1996) examine identity construction in Chicana feminist rhetoric, specifically in the process of self-naming and self-labeling, while Enck-Wanzer's work explores the consciousness raising aspects of the Young Lords Organization's 1969 garbage and church offensives. Enck-Wanzer argues that the Young Lords engaged in intersectional rhetoric, mixing rhetorical forms such as the body, the visual, and the spoken word. Such rhetorical choices enable agencies that resist colonial practices and help constitute individual and collective identities. Enck-Wanzer also cautions that resistance rhetoric "should not be reduced to an instrumentality; doing so risks overlooking the constitutive effects of their performance" (2006, p. 181). Through such constitution, rhetorical agency becomes collective.

Huerta's rhetoric illustrates two important additional functions. First, Huerta used the masking function of haciendo caras to enact courage through más/caras, that is, a face of confidence that had the effect of diminishing her self-doubt and constituted a rhetorical attitude of empowerment. Second, Huerta was able to transform, empower, and constitute herself and her audiences through the repetition of key phrases that were simultaneously hopeful, optimistic, and resistive. In the process of speaking out, Huerta also created spaces for audience transformation through rhetorical collaborations, courage, and egalitarianism. Enck-Wanzer suggests that such an "intersection of images, words, and actions from an entire community of individuals formally mimics an articulation of collective agency that finds strength in the articulation of a 'people' rather than any particular person" (2006, p. 191). Ultimately, rhetorical agency, through haciendo caras and differential bravery, was transformative for both Huerta and her audiences.

Conclusion: Huerta's Rhetorical Constraints

While Dolores Huerta is one of the most recognizable Latina and Chicana icons, leaders, and rhetors, she has never been as famous as César Chávez and other Latino and Chicano activists, politicians, and civic leaders. Her sense of rhetorical agency, cultivated within the UFW movement and with the support of Chávez, her family, and many others, helps explain how she became the powerful leader of a major civil rights movement and union. Arguably, no other Latina or Chicana civil rights leader has been able to achieve such visibility. Most US Americans have heard of César Chávez and the UFW, but far fewer recognize Huerta's name. Chávez was the most prominent and visible leader of the UFW, but many rhetorical and material constraints prevented Huerta from taking that role herself. Gender, class, motherhood, race, ethnicity, and education might all be considered both enabling and constraining factors of Huerta's rhetorical agency. As Suzanne Daughton (1995) observes, privilege is complicated; Susana Martínez Guillem (2017) might call this "precarious privilege." With a very supportive mother and grandfather, Huerta grew up as a US American citizen in a lower- to middle-class family. She had access to education and some material resources that allowed her to participate in extracurricular activities and, later, attend college, enabling her to cross back and forth between white Anglo and Chicana/o and Mexican American worlds with ease. As an adult, she had the support of her family, Chávez, and others, which shaped a facilitating and intersectional habitus that authorized and empowered her to speak and participate in a wide range of civil rights activities.

However, she came from an economic background that was lower or lower-middle class. She was married and divorced twice at a time when divorce was still a social and cultural taboo. She had eleven children over the span of twenty years. Even with a large support network, she faced significant financial and material obstacles that may have prevented her from taking on greater leadership and organizing roles. As the letters that she wrote to Chávez discussed in chapter three illustrate, she was often struggling to find childcare and places for her children to stay, worrying about her finances, and trying to figure out how to attend house meetings and participate in other union activities. She took on many parental duties that Chávez did not. Even as she used her motherhood in strategic, disruptive, and embodied ways, she also managed the difficulties of mothering. Breast-feeding an infant during a break of a major negotiating event was no easy task, nor was making sure her children were properly clothed, fed, sheltered, and schooled, particularly when living on the low income allocated by the UFW to support those, like Huerta, who worked mostly as volunteers. Huerta's fearlessness was a cara, or mask, that generated a sense of audacity; after all, courage begets courage, as the idea of differential bravery suggests. But she recognized her insecurities, documenting how farm workers and other audiences sometimes (perhaps often) responded to her organizing and negotiating tactics. Matt Garcia and Miriam Pawel describe several instances in how her effectiveness as a negotiator was evaluated negatively, possibly because she was pregnant, unwed, and/ or having an affair. Her male counterparts were not similarly judged as ineffective, even though they also had families and affairs.

Beyond motherhood and marital status, Huerta also faced rhetorical obstacles related to race, ethnicity, and Spanish-language use. For example, offering to translate from English to Spanish as recently as the 2016 presidential election generated significant controversy for various reasons. In addition to Huerta's familial and social network habitus, she also engaged a linguistic habitus, "which includes accents, intonations, and articulatory styles that reflect particular class or speech communities" (C. Chávez, 2015, p. 10). Christopher Chávez further explains that

> [o]ften, those who speak minority languages must make an effort to adapt their linguistic expressions to the demands of the formal markets. As a result of the incongruency between a linguistic habitus and a field, their speech is often accompanied by anxiety, tension, and hypercorrection. (2015, p. 10)

This linguistic capital is one of many language challenges that Huerta and other Spanish-speaking UFW leaders and organizers faced. Especially when speaking to mixed audiences and contexts, Huerta knew how to use Spanish and English strategically through her rhetorical flexibility, but it was a great challenge to always negotiate these circumstances effectively. Fluency in Spanish and English is a matter not just of translation but also of how to use each language to identify and connect with audience members. Huerta's ability to simultaneously think and speak in both Spanish and English created a sense of solidarity with others who could do the same and a connection with those who spoke only one language or the other. Huerta's rhetoric, in which she uses both English and Spanish, represents the fluid and moving nature of linguistic capital and demonstrates the need to move beyond the rigid binary expectations of Spanish- and English-language fluency. In the 21st century, as US American attitudes are arguably more tolerant of bilingual speakers, Huerta's language fluencies illustrate yet another aspect of rhetorical agency that both enabled and constrained her.

The material conditions of Huerta's life and spatiotemporal context suggest that Huerta was rhetorically limited even as she was also agential. In the spirit of scholars' calls for rhetorical work to address such materiality (e.g., Cloud, 1994; Cox & Foust, 2009; Enck-Wanzer, 2012; Greene, 1998, 2004; Lechuga, 2017; Shome, 2003), it is important to recognize that despite her leadership roles, Huerta was also constrained by intersectional factors of race, ethnicity, language, class, labor, motherhood, and gender. Specifically, Dana Cloud (1994) argues that

> an emphasis on the individual human agent should not obscure the ideological power of dominant economic and political interests in structuring, framing, and setting the limits for rhetorical action. One way for the materialist to acknowledge human action is to conceive of rhetorical acts as strategic deployments of symbolic resources within an ideological frame . . . we ought not sacrifice the notions of practical truth, bodily reality, and material oppression to the tendency to render all of experience discursive, as if no one went hungry or died in war. (pp. 158–159)

Huerta's body, which is raced, classed, and gendered in material ways, is the bodily reality that Cloud writes about; audience reactions that employed stereotypes of Latina/Chicanas impeded the impact of her message. Her diminutive stature, along with skin color, eye color, hair color, clothing, shoes, hats, makeup, language, accent, multiple pregnancies, and other bodily markers influenced how audiences perceived her. Lechuga (2017) also emphasizes this role of optics and visibility of material circumstances, which influence rhetorical action in context as well as audience responses to that visibility. In addition, Huerta and her children had to eat and have a place to live; Huerta's letters to Chávez (in chapter three) are full of those constraints and the negotiations of those constraints, how she was going to feed, shelter, clothe, and school her children as well as herself.

Understanding rhetorical agency within the context of material constraints and habitus is essential for building theory around this concept. Taking Huerta as an individual and situating her within the civil rights movements of the 1960s illustrates how her rhetorical constraints were social manifestations of an intersectional habitus that shaped collective and individual agency for the UFW and Huerta. Greene (2004) challenges scholars to re-envision rhetorical agency within that context:

> The analytical advantage of such a re-specification is that we can begin to imagine how rhetorical agency as communicative labor can be abstracted and captured to perform gendered, nationalized, and raced work—forms of work and labor that can create class structures and class forms, and can distribute bodies along the international division of labor. In other words, by focusing on communicative labor we can understand how communication makes possible the invention of class. . . . As such, rhetorical agency, in all its communicative dimensions, is at once an instrument, object, and medium for harnessing social cooperation and coordination as the life-affirming value of communicative labor. (pp. 202, 203–204)

Viewing rhetorical agency as a theoretical concept requires a consideration of materiality and material consequences. Huerta was most certainly constrained by such circumstances, even as she found inventive ways to resist normative structures through habitus and her own sense of self.

Furthermore, growers (and others) attempted to discipline Huerta's outspokenness and/or the unruliness of her life by calling her crazy and emotional and lacking in civility. Lozano-Reich and Cloud explain why the emphasis on civility is so problematic, especially as an assessment of gender, race, ethnicity, and otherness:

> [Scholars] claim that civility fosters democracy. While voting is indeed civil, radical social change has not occurred in voting booths, but results, instead, from democratic grassroots tactics. Protestors inherently do not operate within the realm of decorum. Indeed, political confrontations up to and including violence have been perennial resources in struggles for justice (Kirkpatrick, 2008). The civility standard is detrimental to this project. When measured by standards of civility, protesters are

framed as wild and riotous by dominant media, rendering their
struggles illegitimate (Gitlin, 2003). (2009, p. 224)

As rhetorical agents using motherhood to engage in social protest,
mothers have challenged the meaning of civility in discourse and protest
(Fabj, 1993; Foss & Domenici, 2001). Cox and Foust (2009) note that
the body is both "symbolic and extrasymbolic" as one moves through
material discourses and realities (p. 616). Huerta called attention to her
status as mother and engaged in protest that some called uncivil, and
she was criticized at least at times for her anti-normative approaches.

Huerta's boldness emerged out of various contexts, audiences,
supporters, and affects and from within as she became empowered
through first her public school education and her family and then community organizing groups, including the UFW. Karma Chávez calls
for rhetorical scholarship to move beyond inclusion and citizenship
politics and to explore difference, unique styles, and alternatives to social norms: "[I]t is imperative that we break from that history, not in
order that Rhetoric may become a more inclusive discipline but so that
it may become something entirely different: a discipline constituted
through non-normative, non-citizen, non-Western perspectives and
ways of knowing and being" (Chávez, 2015, p. 163). Huerta's rhetoric
and her surrounding contexts provide an exemplar for alternative
rhetorics of how intersectional habitus, motherhood, emotionality,
optimism, egalitarianism, courage, and differential bravery may be
enacted in social movements. Huerta did not follow traditional paths,
either personally or as an activist. Her unique styles disrupted rhetorical and social movement norms, flummoxing many who had to work
with her. Dolores Huerta might have been constrained by her styles
and life choices, but, in the end, she has become a Chicana and Latina
icon who represents the long fight for social justice and for our futures.

REFERENCES

Abalos, D. T. (1998). *La comunidad latina in the United States: Personal and political strategies for transforming culture.* Westport, CT: Praeger Publishers.

Ahmed, S. (2004). *The cultural politics of emotion.* New York, NY: Routledge.

——. (2017). *Living a feminist life.* Durham, NC: Duke University Press.

Alarcón, N. (1989). Traductora, traidora: A paradigmatic figure of Chicana feminism. *Cultural Critique, 13,* 57–87.

Anzaldúa, G. (1987). *Borderlands/la frontera: The new mestiza.* San Francisco, CA: Aunt Lute Books.

——. (1990). Haciendo caras, una entrada: An introduction. In G. Anzaldúa (Ed.), *Making face, making soul/Haciendo caras: Creative and critical perspectives by feminists of color* (pp. xv–xviii). San Francisco, CA: Aunt Lute Books.

Arredondo, G. F. (2008). Lived regionalities: Mujeridad in Chicago, 1920–1940. In V. L. Ruiz & J. R. Chávez (Eds.), *Memories and migrations: Mapping Boricua and Chicana histories* (pp. 93–120). Urbana, IL: University of Illinois Press.

Baer, B. L. (1975). Stopping traffic: One woman's cause. *The Progressive, 39*(9), 38–40.

Bardacke, F. (2012). *Trampling out the vintage: Cesar Chavez and the two souls of the United Farm Workers.* New York, NY: Verso.

Beltrán, M. C. (2009). *Latina/o stars in U.S. eyes: The making and meanings of film and tv stardom.* Urbana, IL: University of Illinois Press.

Bitzer, L. F. (1968). The rhetorical situation. *Philosophy and Rhetoric, 25*(1), 1–14.

Black, E. (1970). The second persona. *Quarterly Journal of Speech, 56*(2), 109–119.

Blackwell, M. (2003). Contested histories: *Las hijas de Cuauhtémoc,* Chicana feminisms, and print culture in the Chicano movement, 1968–1973. In G. F. Arredondo, A. Hurtado, N. Klahn, O. Nájera-Ramírez, & P. Zavella (Eds.), *Chicana feminisms: A critical reader* (pp. 59–89). Durham, NC: Duke University Press.

——. (2010). Líderes campesinas: Nepantla strategies and grassroots organizing at the intersection of gender and globalization. *Aztlán: A Journal of Chicano Studies, 35*(1), 13–47.

Blankenship, J., & Robson, D. C. (1995). A "feminine style" in women's political discourse: An exploratory essay. *Communication Quarterly, 43*(3), 353–366.

Borda, J. L. (2002). The woman suffrage parades of 1910–1913: Possibilities and limitations of an early feminist rhetorical strategy. *Western Journal of Communication, 66,* 25–52.

Bourdieu, P. (1990). *The logic of practice.* Stanford, CA: Stanford University Press.

Bratt, P. (Producer & Director), & Bensen, B. (Producer). (2017). *Dolores* [Documentary]. USA: Five Stick Films.

Brennan, T. (2004). *The transmission of affect.* Ithaca, NY: Cornell University Press.

Brown, J. B. (1972). *The United Farm Workers grape strike and boycott, 1965-1970: An evaluation of the culture of poverty theory.* (Unpublished doctoral dissertation, Cornell University, Ithaca, NY).

Brown, M. (2010). *Side by side: The story of Dolores Huerta and Cesar Chavez.* New York: HarperCollins Children's Books.

Bruce, C. (2015). The balaclava as affect generator: Free Pussy Riot protests and transnational iconicity. *Communication and Critical/Cultural Studies, 12*(1), 42–62.

Burke, K. (1966). *Language as symbolic action.* Berkeley, CA: University of California Press.

———. (1969). *A rhetoric of motives.* Berkeley, CA: University of California Press.

Calafell, B. M. (2005). Pro(re-)claiming loss: A performance pilgrimage in search of Malintzin Tenépal. *Text and Performance Quarterly, 25*(1), 43–56.

———. (2007). *Latina/o communication studies: Theorizing performance.* New York, NY: Peter Lang.

Campbell, K. K. (1986). Style and content in the rhetoric of early Afro-American feminists. *Quarterly Journal of Speech, 72*, 436–441.

———. (1989). *Man cannot speak for her: A critical study of early feminist rhetoric* (Vol. 1). New York, NY: Greenwood Press.

———. (1995). Gender and genre: Loci of invention and contradiction in the earliest speeches by U.S. women. *Quarterly Journal of Speech, 81*, 479–495.

———. (2005). Agency: Promiscuous and protean. *Communication and Critical/Cultural Studies, 2*, 1–19.

Cárdenas, J. (1977, December). Chicanas need "Courage and Commitment." *El Popo.*

Carlson, A. C. (1995). Character invention in the letters of Maimie Pinzer. *Communication Quarterly, 43*(4), 408–419.

Carrillo Rowe, A. (2005). Be longing: Toward a feminist politics of relation. *NWSA Journal, 17*(2), 15–46.

———. (2008). *Power lines: On the subject of feminist alliances.* Durham, NC: Duke University Press.

———. (2009). Moving relations: On the limits of belonging. *Liminalities: A Journal of Performance Studies, 5*(5), 1–10.

Carter, S. (2007). Living inside the Bible (belt). *College English, 69*(6), 572–595.

Castillo, A. (1995). *Massacre of the dreamers: Essays on xicanisma.* New York, NY: Penguin/Plume Books.

Chávez, A. (2005). Dolores Huerta and the United Farm Workers. In V. L. Ruiz & V. Sánchez Korrol (Eds.), *Latina legacies: Identity, biography, and community* (pp. 240–254). New York, NY: Oxford University Press.

Chávez, C. A. (2015). "News with an accent": Hispanic television and the re-negotiation of US Latino speech. *Communication and Critical/Cultural Studies, 12*(3), 1–19. http://doi.org/10.1080/14791420.2015.1037778

Chávez, K. R. (2009). Embodied translation: Dominant discourse and communication with migrant bodies-as-text. *Howard Journal of Communications, 20*, 18–36. http://doi.org/10.1080/10646170802664912

———. (2011). Counter-public enclaves and understanding the function of rhetoric in social movement coalition-building. *Communication Quarterly, 59*, 1–18.

———. (2013). *Queer migration politics: Activist rhetoric and coalitional possibilities.* Urbana, IL: University of Illinois Press.

———. (2015). Beyond inclusion: Rethinking rhetoric's historical narrative. *Quarterly Journal of Speech, 101*(1), 162–172.

Chávez, M. (2008). Pilgrimage to the homeland: California Chicanas and international women's year, Mexico City, 1975. In V. L. Ruiz & J. R. Chávez (Eds.), *Memories and migrations: Mapping Boricua and Chicana histories* (pp. 170–195). Urbana, IL: University of Illinois Press.

Cisneros, J. D. (2012). Looking "illegal": Affect, rhetoric, and performativity in Arizona's senate bill 1070. In D. R. DeChaine (Ed.), *Border rhetorics: Citizenship and identity on the US-Mexico frontier* (pp. 133–150). Tuscaloosa, AL: The University of Alabama Press.

Cloud, D. L. (1994). The materiality of discourse as oxymoron: A challenge to critical rhetoric. *Western Journal of Communication, 58*, 141–163.

——. (1999). The null persona: Race and the rhetoric of silence in the uprising of '34. *Rhetoric and Public Affairs, 2*(2), 177–209.

Clough, P. T. (Ed.). (2007). *The affective turn: Theorizing the social.* Durham, NC: Duke University Press.

Coburn, J. (1976). Dolores Huerta: La pasionaria of the farmworkers. *Ms. 5*(5), 11–16.

Cooper, M. M. (2011). Rhetorical agency as emergent and enacted. *College Composition and Communication, 62*(3), 420–449.

Córdova, T. (1999). Anti-colonial Chicana feminism. In R. D. Torres & G. Katsiaficas (Eds.), *Latino social movements: Historical and theoretical perspectives* (pp. 11–41). New York, NY: Routledge.

Coronado, I. (2008). Styles, strategies, and issues of women leaders at the border. In D. J. Mattingly & E. R. Hansen (Eds.), *Women and change at the U.S.-Mexico border* (pp. 142–158). Tucson, AZ: University of Arizona Press.

Councilor, K. C. (2017). Feeding the body politic: Metaphors of digestion in Progressive Era US immigration discourse. *Communication and Critical/Cultural Studies, 14*(2): 139–157. http://doi.org/10.1080/14791420.2016.1274044

Covey, A. (1994). *A century of women.* Atlanta, GA: TBS Books.

Cox, R., & Foust, C. R. (2009). Social movement rhetoric. In A. Lunsford (Ed.), *Sage handbook of rhetorical studies* (pp. 605–627). Thousand Oaks, CA: Sage Publications.

Cram, B. J. (1981). *Women organizers in the United Farm Workers: Their motivation and perceptions of sexism within the union.* (Master's thesis, California State University, Fullerton, CA).

Crenshaw, K. (1991). Mapping the margins: Intersectionality, identity politics, and violence against women of color. *Stanford Law Review, 43*(6), 1241–1299.

Critchley, S. (2012). *Infinitely demanding: Ethics of commitment, politics of resistance.* New York, NY: Verso.

Cruz, P. (Producer), Halfon, L. (Producer), Luna, D. (Producer), Meli, L. (Producer), Pearson, K. (Producer), Smith, R. (Producer), & Luna, D. (Director). (2014). *Cesar Chavez* [Motion Picture]. USA: Lionsgate.

Cultivating creativity: The arts and the farm workers' movement during the 1960s and '70s. (n.d.). Retrieved from http://www.library.sfsu.edu/exhibits/cultivating/intropages/elmalcriado.html

Damasio, A. R. (1999). *The feeling of what happens: Body and emotion in the making of consciousness.* New York, NY: Harcourt Brace & Company.

Daughton, S. M. (1995). The fine texture of enactment: Iconicity as empowerment in Angelina Grimké's Pennsylvania Hall Address. *Women's Studies in Communication, 18*(1), 19–43. http://doi.org/10.1080/07491409.1995.11089786

Dawson, R. (2016, March 24). An open letter to Dolores Huerta. *The Huffington Post.* Retrieved from http://www.huffingtonpost.com/rosario-dawson/an-open-letter-to-dolores-huerta_b_9538994.html?1458825932

de Certeau, M. (1984). *The practice of everyday life.* Berkeley, CA: University of California Press.

DeChaine, D. R. (2002). Affect and embodied understanding in musical experience. *Text and Performance Quarterly, 22*(2), 79–98.

Delgado, F. P. (1995). Chicano movement rhetoric: An ideographic interpretation. *Communication Quarterly, 43*, 446–455.

——. (1999). Rigoberta Menchú and testimonial discourse: Collectivist rhetoric and rhetorical criticism. *World Communication, 28*(1), 17–29.

de Onís, C. M. (2017). What's in an "x"?: An exchange about the politics of "Latinx." *Chiricú Journal: Latina/o Literatures, Arts, and Cultures 1*(2), 78–91.

Dolores Huerta Foundation. (2017). Retrieved from www.doloreshuerta.org

Doss, E. F., & Jensen, R. E. (2013). Balancing mystery and identification: Dolores Huerta's shifting transcendent persona. *Quarterly Journal of Speech, 99*(4), 1–26.

Dow, B. J., & Tonn, M. B. (1993). "Feminine style" and political judgment in the rhetoric of Ann Richards. *Quarterly Journal of Speech, 79*(3), 286–302.

El Malcriado. (n.d.). Retrieved from http://www.farmworkermovement.com/archives

Emirbayer, M., & Mische, A. (1998). What is agency? *American Journal of Sociology, 103*(4), 962–1023.

Enck-Wanzer, D. (2006). Trashing the system: Social movement, intersectional rhetoric, and collective agency in the Young Lords Organization's garbage offensive. *Quarterly Journal of Speech, 92*(2), 174–201.

——. (2010). Gender politics, democratic demand and anti-essentialism in the New York Young Lords. In M. A. Holling & B. M. Calafell (Eds.), *Latina/o discourse in vernacular spaces: Somos de una voz?* (pp. 59–80). Lanham, MD: Lexington Books.

——. (2011). Tropicalizing East Harlem: Rhetorical agency, cultural citizenship, and Nuyorican cultural production. *Communication Theory, 21*(4), 344–367. http://doi.org/10.1111/j.1468-2885.2011.01390

——. (2012). Decolonizing imaginaries: Rethinking "the people" in the Young Lords' church offensive. *Quarterly Journal of Speech, 98*, 1–23.

Faber McAlister, J. (2015). The visual politics of un/veiling the female body in political protest. *Women's Studies in Communication, 38*(4), 357–360.

Fabj, V. (1993). Motherhood as political voice: The rhetoric of the mothers of Plaza de Mayo. *Communication Studies, 44*, 1–18.

Farm union vows pesticide fight. (1969, March 30). Jacques E. Levy Research Collection on Cesar Chavez (Series IV, Box 19, folder 413, File 52: Pesticides). Beinecke Library, Yale University, New Haven, CT.

Felner, J. (1998). For a lifetime of labor championing the rights of farmworkers. Retrieved from http://www.ufw.org/ms.htm

Ferriss, S. & Sandoval, R. (1997). *The fight in the fields: Cesar Chavez and the farmworkers movement.* Orlando, FL: Paradigm Productions.

Flores, L. A. (1996). Creating discursive space through a rhetoric of difference: Chicana feminists craft a homeland. *Quarterly Journal of Speech, 82*(2), 142–156.

Flores, L. A., & Holling, M. A. (1999). Las familias y las Latinas: Mediated representations of gender roles. In M. Meyers (Ed.), *Mediated women: Representations in popular culture* (pp. 339–354). Cresskill, NJ: Hampton Press, Inc.

Flores-Ortiz, Y. G. (1998). Voices from the couch: The co-creation of a Chicana psychology. In C. Trujillo (Ed.), *Living Chicana theory* (pp. 102–122). Berkeley, CA: Third Woman Press.

Foley, E. (1974). "Sorrow in the orchards" her life for years. *Detroit Free Press*, p. 1-C.

Forbes, C. (2004). The radical rhetoric of Caterina da Siena. *Rhetoric Review, 23*(2), 121–140.

Foss, K. A., & Domenici, K. L. (2001). Haunting Argentina: Synecdoche in the protests of the mothers of the Plaza de Mayo. *Quarterly Journal of Speech, 87*(3), 237–258.

Foster, S. (1996). Union leader: Root out racism; Farm workers harvest hope as union rebounds. *Salt Lake Tribune*, p. A1.

Frank, M. (1987). Dolores Huerta: "Sí, se puede—We can do it." Dolores Huerta. Archives of Labor and Urban Affairs, Walter P. Reuther Library of Labor and Urban Affairs, Wayne State University, Detroit, MI.

Fregoso, R. L. (2003a). Reproduction and miscegenation on the borderlands: Mapping the maternal body of Tejanas. In G. F. Arredondo, A. Hurtado, N. Klahn, O. Nájera-Ramírez, & P. Zavella (Eds.), *Chicana feminisms: A critical reader* (pp. 324–348). Durham, NC: Duke University Press.

———. (2003b). *meXicana encounters: The making of social identities on the Borderlands*. Berkeley, CA: University of California Press.

Frydl, K. (2016, February 22). On Dolores Huerta and Bernie Sanders. *The Huffington Post*. Retrieved from http://www.huffingtonpost.com/kathleen-frydl/on-dolores-huerta-and-ber_b_9285182.html

Fulkerson, R. P. (1979). The public letter as rhetorical form: Structure, logic, and style in King's "Letter from Birmingham Jail." *Quarterly Journal of Speech, 65*(2), 121–136.

Gaipa, M. (2007). "A creative psalm of brotherhood": The (de)constructive play in Martin Luther King's "Letter from Birmingham Jail." *Quarterly Journal of Speech, 93*(3), 279–307.

Gangotena, M. (2004). The rhetoric of *la familia* among Mexican Americans. In A. González, M. Houston, & V. Chen (Eds.), *Our voices: Essays in culture, ethnicity, and communication* (4th ed.), (pp. 92–103). Los Angeles, CA: Roxbury Publishing Company.

Ganz, M. (2009). *Why David sometimes wins: Leadership, organization, and strategy in the California farm worker movement*. New York, NY: Oxford University Press.

García, A. M. (Ed.). (1997). *Chicana feminist thought. The basic historical writings*. New York, NY: Routledge.

García, M. T. (2007). *The gospel of César Chávez: My faith in action*. Lanham, MD: Sheed & Ward.

———(Ed.). (2008). *A Dolores Huerta reader*. Albuquerque, NM: University of New Mexico Press.

———. (2015). *The Chicano generation: Testimonios of the movement*. Oakland, CA: University of California Press.

Garcia, M. [Matt]. (2012). *From the jaws of victory: The triumph and tragedy of Cesar Chavez and the farm worker movement*. Berkeley, CA: University of California Press.

Gay, R. (2014). *Bad feminist: Essays*. New York, NY: HarperCollins Publishers.

———. (2015). Confessions of a bad feminist. TED Talk. Retrieved from http://www.ted.com/talks/roxane_gay_confessions_of_a_bad_feminist

Godoy, M. (2017, September 17). Dolores Huerta: The civil rights icon who showed farmworkers "Sí se puede." Texas Public Radio [transcript]. Retrieved from http://tpr.org/post/dolores-huerta-civil-rights-icon-who-showed-farmworkers-si-se-puede#stream/0

Goltz, D. B., & Pérez, K. (2012). Borders without bodies: Affect, proximity, and utopian imaginaries through "lines in the sand." In D. R. DeChaine (Ed.), *Border rhetorics: Citizenship and identity on the US-Mexico frontier* (pp. 163–178). Tuscaloosa, AL: University of Alabama Press.

González Martínez, E. (2002). Dutiful hijas: Dependency, power and guilt. In D. Hernández

& B. Rehman (Eds.), *Colonize this! Young women of color on today's feminism* (pp. 142–156). New York, NY: Seal Press.

Granovetter, M. S. (1978). Threshold models of collective behavior. *American Journal of Sociology, 83*(6), 1420–1443. Retrieved from http://www.jstor.org/stable/2778111

Greene, R. W. (1998). Another materialist rhetoric. *Critical Studies in Mass Communication, 15*, 21–41.

———. (2004). Rhetoric and capitalism: Rhetorical agency as communicative labor. *Philosophy and Rhetoric, 37*(3), 188–206.

Gregg, R. B. (1971). The ego-function of the rhetoric of protest. *Philosophy and Rhetoric, 4*(2), 71–91.

Griffin, C. L., & Chávez, K. R. (2012). Introduction: Standing at the intersections of feminisms, intersectionality, and communication studies. In K. R. Chávez & C. L. Griffin (Eds.), *Standing in the intersection: Feminist voices, feminist practices in communication studies* (pp. 1–31). Albany, NY: State University of New York Press.

Gring-Pemble, L. M. (1998). Writing themselves into consciousness: Creating a rhetorical bridge between the public and private spheres. *Quarterly Journal of Speech, 84*, 41–61.

Griswold del Castillo, R., & Garcia, R. A. (1995). *César Chávez: A triumph of spirit*. Norman, OK: University of Oklahoma Press.

Guerra, J. C. (2004). *Putting literacy in its place: Nomadic consciousness and the practice of transcultural repositioning*. Chicano Studies Institute, University of California, Santa Barbara. Retrieved from http://escholarship.org/uc/item/52q817fq

Hahner, L. A. (2012). Constitutive intersectionality and the affect of rhetorical form. In K. R. Chávez & C. L. Griffin (Eds.), *Standing in the intersection: Feminist voices, feminist practices in communication studies* (pp. 147–168). Albany, NY: State University of New York Press.

Hammerback, J. C., & Jensen, R. J. (1980). The rhetorical worlds of César Chávez and Reies Tijerina. *Western Journal of Speech Communication, 44*, 166–176.

———. (1994). Ethnic heritage as rhetorical legacy: The plan of Delano. *Quarterly Journal of Speech, 80*, 53–70.

———. (1998). *The rhetorical career of César Chávez*. College Station, TX: Texas A&M University Press.

Hammerback, J. C., Jensen, R. J., & Gutierrez, J. A. (1985). *A war of words: Chicano protest in the 1960s and 1970s*. Westport, CT: Greenwood Press.

Hardt, M. (2007). Foreword: What affects are good for. In P. T. Clough & J. Halley (Eds.), *The affective turn: Theorizing the social*. Durham, NC: Duke University Press.

Hayden, S. (1999). Negotiating femininity and power in the early twentieth century West: Domestic ideology and feminine style in Jeannette Rankin's suffrage rhetoric. *Communication Studies, 50*, 83–102.

———. (2003). Family metaphors and the nation: Promoting politics of care through the Million Mom March. *Quarterly Journal of Speech, 89*, 196–215.

Holling, M. A. (2000). *Extending critical rhetoric and feminist theory: Rhetorical constructions of Chicana subject/ivity, identity, and agency* (Unpublished doctoral dissertation, Arizona State University, Tempe, AZ).

———. (2006). El simpático boxer: Underpinning Chicano masculinity with a rhetoric of familia in Resurrection Blvd. *Western Journal of Communication, 70*(2), 91–114.

———. (2012). A dispensational rhetoric in "The Mexican Question in the Southwest." In

D. R. DeChaine (Ed.), *Border rhetorics: Citizenship and identity on the US-Mexico frontier* (pp. 65–85). Tuscaloosa, AL: University of Alabama Press.

Huerta, D. (1962). Please excuse my long delay. NFW Association (Series I, General Correspondence, Box 2, Folder 11). Archives of Labor and Urban Affairs, Walter P. Reuther Library of Labor and Urban Affairs, Wayne State University, Detroit, MI.

———. (1962). This letter has been a week in the making. United Farm Workers (Box 2, Folder 12). Archives of Labor and Urban Affairs, Walter P. Reuther Library of Labor and Urban Affairs, Wayne State University, Detroit, MI.

———. (1962). You have probably thought that the FWA. United Farm Workers (Box 2, Folder 14). Archives of Labor and Urban Affairs, Walter P. Reuther Library of Labor and Urban Affairs, Wayne State University, Detroit, MI.

———. (1963). I hope this letter finds you and yours in the best of health. United Farm Workers (Box 2, Folder 11). Archives of Labor and Urban Affairs, Walter P. Reuther Library of Labor and Urban Affairs, Wayne State University, Detroit, MI.

———. (1964). Hope this letter finds you all in the best of health. NFW Association (Series I, General Correspondence, Box 2, Folder 11). Archives of Labor and Urban Affairs, Walter P. Reuther Library of Labor and Urban Affairs, Wayne State University, Detroit, MI.

———. (1964, February 29). I received you [sic] penitent letter. NFW Association (Series I, General Correspondence, Box 2, Folder 11). Archives of Labor and Urban Affairs, Walter P. Reuther Library of Labor and Urban Affairs, Wayne State University, Detroit, MI.

———. (1964). Since I had not heard from you. United Farm Workers (Box 2, Folder 13). Archives of Labor and Urban Affairs, Walter P. Reuther Library of Labor and Urban Affairs, Wayne State University, Detroit, MI.

———. (1966, April 10). Speech given in Sacramento at the conclusion of the Delano-Sacramento pilgrimage. NCPB/KQED News, San Francisco Bay Area Television Archive at San Francisco State University, San Francisco, CA. Retrieved from https://diva.sfsu.edu/collections/sfbatv/bundles/185999 and https://diva.sfsu.edu/collections/sfbatv/bundles/189795

———. (1969, July 15). Statement of Dolores Huerta, vice-president, United Farm Workers Organizing Committee, AFL-CIO. UFW Office of the President, Cesar Chavez (Box 36, Folder 12). Archives of Labor and Urban Affairs, Walter P. Reuther Library of Labor and Urban Affairs, Wayne State University, Detroit, MI.

———. (December 196[x]). This is the fourth attempt. United Farm Workers (Series I, General Correspondence, Box 2, Folder 12). Archives of Labor and Urban Affairs, Walter P. Reuther Library of Labor and Urban Affairs, Wayne State University, Detroit, MI.

———. (1970, April 27). Memorandum. UFW Office of the President (Series III Correspondence, Box 36, Folder 11). Archives of Labor and Urban Affairs, Walter P. Reuther Library of Labor and Urban Affairs, Wayne State University, Detroit, MI.

———. (1970, July 11). Handwritten note responding to memo from Chávez. UFW Office of the President (Series III Correspondence, Box 36, Folder 11). Archives of Labor and Urban Affairs, Walter P. Reuther Library of Labor and Urban Affairs, Wayne State University, Detroit, MI.

———. (1973). Testimony of the United Farm Workers AFL-CIO. Dolores Huerta (Box 2). Archives of Labor and Urban Affairs, Walter P. Reuther Library of Labor and Urban Affairs, Wayne State University, Detroit, MI.

———. (1973, January 25). Dolores Huerta talks about Republicans, César Chávez, children, and her home town. *La Voz del Pueblo*, pp. 3–4.

———. (1973, March 24). East coast boycott report. Dolores Huerta (Box 2). Archives of Labor and Urban Affairs, Walter P. Reuther Library of Labor and Urban Affairs, Wayne State University, Detroit, MI.

———. (1974, May). Stanford University, transcript of speech given by Dolores Huerta. UFW Office of the President, Cesar Chavez, Part 2 (Box 46, Folder 12). Archives of Labor and Urban Affairs, Walter P. Reuther Library of Labor and Urban Affairs, Wayne State University, Detroit, MI.

———. (1974, October 21). Keynote address before the Annual Convention of the American Public Health Association, New Orleans, LA. UFW Office of the President, César Chávez Collection, Part 2 (Box 46, Folder 11). Archives of Labor and Urban Affairs, Walter P. Reuther Library of Labor and Urban Affairs, Wayne State University, Detroit, MI.

———. (1976, July 9-14). Martin Luther King Farm Workers Fund Campesino Centers Conference Minutes. Unprocessed Dolores Huerta Materials (Box 7/25). Archives of Labor and Urban Affairs, Walter P. Reuther Library of Labor and Urban Affairs, Wayne State University, Detroit, MI.

———. (1980). Testimony for the Assembly Select Committee on Farm Labor, School of Law, University of California, Los Angeles, CA. Dolores Huerta Collection. Archives of Labor and Urban Affairs, Walter P. Reuther Library of Labor and Urban Affairs, Wayne State University, Detroit, MI.

———. (1987, July 31). Plenary, Cherríe Moraga, Anna Nieto Gómez, Dolores Huerta (Lecture-Eng, 19, Tapes 6 & 7). Center for Chicano Studies Special Collections, University of California, Los Angeles, Los Angeles, CA.

———. (2002, March 9). Speech for Mexican American Political Association, Rialto Chapter, Rialto, CA. [Author's notes and transcription].

———. (2003, April 24). *A life's work in the building of community.* Speech at the 16th Annual Tomás Rivera Conference, Zacatecas Restaurant, Riverside, CA. [Author's notes and transcription].

———. (2006, April). Speech at the University of Texas at El Paso, El Paso, TX. [Author's notes and transcription].

———. (2012). Comments on Presidential Medal of Freedom. Retrieved from http:// doloreshuerta.org/dolores-huerta/

———. (2013, October 16). *Descúbrete: Empowerment through wings of knowledge.* Speech at the 12th Annual Hispanic Heritage Celebration at the El Paso Community College Administrative Services Center, El Paso, TX. [Author's notes and transcription].

———. (n.d.). At long last I am sending you another letter. NFW Association (Series II, Box 4, Folder 20). United Farm Workers. Archives of Labor and Urban Affairs, Walter P. Reuther Library of Labor and Urban Affairs, Wayne State University, Detroit, MI.

———. (n.d.). Capitol Capers. United Farm Workers. Archives of Labor and Urban Affairs, Walter P. Reuther Library of Labor and Urban Affairs, Wayne State University, Detroit, MI.

———. (n.d.). Enclosed are dues for a new member Salvador Salas and for Filemon Lepe. NFW Association (Series I, General Correspondence, Box 2, Folder 11). United Farm Workers. Archives of Labor and Urban Affairs, Walter P. Reuther Library of Labor and Urban Affairs, Wayne State University, Detroit, MI.

———. (n.d.). Enclosed is an application for an estate loan. United Farm Workers. Archives of Labor and Urban Affairs, Walter P. Reuther Library of Labor and Urban Affairs, Wayne State University, Detroit, MI.

———. (n.d.). I hope this letter finds you well and recuperated from the Convention. United Farm Workers. Archives of Labor and Urban Affairs, Walter P. Reuther Library of Labor and Urban Affairs, Wayne State University, Detroit, MI.

———. (n.d.). I'm goinf [sic]. United Farm Workers (Box 2, Folder 14). Archives of Labor and Urban Affairs, Walter P. Reuther Library of Labor and Urban Affairs, Wayne State University, Detroit, MI.

———. (n.d.). The importance of union organizing. UFW Office of the President: Cesar Chavez Collection, Part 2 (Box 46, Folder 12). Archives of Labor and Urban Affairs, Walter P. Reuther Library of Labor and Urban Affairs, Wayne State University, Detroit, MI.

———. (n.d.). Just a few short lines. United Farm Workers (Box 2, Folder 13). Archives of Labor and Urban Affairs, Walter P. Reuther Library of Labor and Urban Affairs, Wayne State University, Detroit, MI.

———. (n.d.). Problems in organizing farmworkers. Statement for the U.S. Senate SubCommittee. UFW Information and Research Department (Box 17, Folder 7). Archives of Labor and Urban Affairs, Walter P. Reuther Library of Labor and Urban Affairs, Wayne State University, Detroit, MI.

———. (n.d.). Received your concise communication. United Farm Workers. Archives of Labor and Urban Affairs, Walter P. Reuther Library of Labor and Urban Affairs, Wayne State University, Detroit, MI.

———. (n.d.). Thank you very much for the last informative letter which you sent. United Farm Workers (Series I, General Correspondence, Box 2, Folder 12). Archives of Labor and Urban Affairs, Walter P. Reuther Library of Labor and Urban Affairs, Wayne State University, Detroit, MI.

———. (n.d). Well, dear leader, the time has come to stop this chatter. United Farm Workers. Archives of Labor and Urban Affairs, Reuther Library of Labor and Urban Affairs, Wayne State University, Detroit, MI.

———. (n.d.). Yes, I am still breathing. United Farm Workers (Box 2, Folder 14). Archives of Labor and Urban Affairs, Walter P. Reuther Library of Labor and Urban Affairs, Wayne State University, Detroit, MI.

Hull, G. T., Scott, P. B., & Smith, B. (Eds.). (1982). *Black women's studies: All the women are white, all the blacks are men, but some of us are brave.* New York, NY: The Feminist Press at the City University of New York.

Hull, G. T., & Smith, B. (1982). Introduction: The politics of Black women's studies. In G. T. Hull, P. B. Scott, & B. Smith (Eds.), *Black women's studies: All the women are white, all the blacks are men, but some of us are brave* (pp. xvii–xxxii), New York, NY: The Feminist Press at the City University of New York.

Hurtado, A. (1996). Strategic suspensions: Feminists of color theorize the production of knowledge. In N. Goldberger, J. Tarule, B. Clinchy, & M. Belenky (Eds.), *Knowledge, difference, and power: Essays inspired by women's ways of knowing* (pp. 372–392). New York, NY: Basic Books.

———. (1998). *Sitios y lenguas*: Chicanas theorize feminisms. *Hypatia, 13*, 134–161.

Japp, P. M. (1985). Esther or Isaiah? The abolitionist-feminist rhetoric of Angelina Grimké. *Quarterly Journal of Speech, 71*, 335–348.

Jensen, R. J., Burkholder, T. R., & Hammerback, J. C. (2003). Martyrs for a just cause: The eulogies of Cesar Chavez. *Western Journal of Communication, 67*(4), 335–356.

Jensen, R. J., & Hammerback, J. C. (1980). Radical nationalism among Chicanos: The rhetoric of José Angel Gutiérrez. *The Western Journal of Speech Communication, 44*, 191–202.

———. (1982). "No revolutions without poets": The rhetoric of Rodolfo "Corky" Gonzáles. *The Western Journal of Speech Communication, 46*, 72–91.

———(Eds.). (2002). *The words of César Chávez.* College Station, TX: Texas A&M University Press.

Just, S. N., & Berg, K. M. (2016). Disastrous dialogue: Plastic productions of agency-meaning relationships. *Rhetoric Society Quarterly, 46*(1), 28–46.

Karampoumiotis, P. D., Sreenivasan, S., Szymanski, B. K., & Korniss, G. (2015). The impact of heterogeneous thresholds on social contagion with multiple initiators. *PLoS ONE, 10*(11), 1–15. http://doi.org/10.1371/journal.pone.0143020

Lake, R. A. (1983). Enacting Red power: The consummatory function in Native American protest rhetoric. *Quarterly Journal of Speech, 69,* 127–142.

Lechuga, M. (2017). Coding intensive movement with technologies of visibility: Alien affect. *Capacious: Journal for Emerging Affect Inquiry, 1*(1): 83–97.

Levy, J. E. (1969). Dolores Huerta interview [transcribed]. From Series I: Principal Cesar Chavez tape collection transcripts (Box 5, Folder 183, File 11, pp. 1–153). Jacques E. Levy Collection on Cesar Chavez, WA MSS S-2406, Beinecke Library, Yale University, New Haven, CT.

———. (2007). *Cesar Chavez: Autobiography of la causa.* Minneapolis, MN: University of Minnesota Press.

A life of sacrifice for farm workers. (1990, July). Dolores Huerta (Main Biographical Folder). Archives of Labor and Urban Affairs, Walter P. Reuther Library of Labor and Urban Affairs, Wayne State University, Detroit, MI.

A life-time commitment. (1979, June 29–July 5). *Pacific Sun,* p. 6.

López, A. (2002). In praise of difficult chicas: Feminism and femininity. In D. Hernández & B. Rehman (Eds.), *Colonize this! Young women of color on today's feminism* (pp. 119–132). New York, NY: Seal Press.

Lozano-Reich, N. M., & Cloud, D. L. (2009). The uncivil tongue: Invitational rhetoric and the problem of inequality. *Western Journal of Communication, 73*(2), 220–226.

Lugones, M. (2003). *Pilgrimages/peregrinajes: Theorizing coalition against multiple oppressions.* Lanham, MD: Rowman & Littlefield Publishers, Inc.

———. (2010). Toward a decolonial feminism. *Hypatia, 25*(4), 742–759.

Lunsford, A. A. (1999). Toward a mestiza rhetoric: Gloria Anzaldúa on composition and postcoloniality. In G. A. Olson & L. Worsham (Eds.), *Race, rhetoric, and the postcolonial* (pp. 43–78). Albany, NY: State University of New York Press.

Lyotard, J-F., & Thébaud, J-L. (1985). *Just gaming.* Minneapolis, MN: University of Minnesota Press.

Mallon, F. E. (1995). *Peasant and nation: The making of postcolonial Mexico and Peru.* Berkeley, CA: University of California Press.

Marcotte, A. (2016, February 22). Dolores Huerta takes on Bernie's base: Nevada caucus flap speaks volumes about the frustrations of Sanders' supporters. *Salon.com.* Retrieved from http://www.salon.com/2016/02/22/dolores_huerta_takes_on_bernies_base_nevada_caucus_flap_speaks_volumes_about_the_frustrations_of_sanders_supporters/

Martinez, J. M. (2000). *Phenomenology of Chicana experience and identity: Communication and transformation in praxis.* Lanham, MD: Rowman and Littlefield.

Martínez Guillem, S. (2017). Precarious privilege: Indignad@s, daily disidentifications, and cultural (re)production. *Communication and Critical/Cultural Studies, 14*(3), 238–253. https://doi.org/10.1080/14791420.2017.1310387

McCormick, S. (2008). Mirrors for the queen: A letter from Christine de Pizan on the eve of civil war. *Quarterly Journal of Speech, 94*(3), 273–296.

McGee, M. C. (1980a). The origins of "liberty": A feminization of power. *Communication Monographs, 47,* 23–45.

———. (1980b). The "ideograph": A link between rhetoric and ideology. *Quarterly Journal of Speech, 66,* 1–16.

McKinnon, S. L., Asen, R., Chávez, K. R., & Howard, R. G. (2016). Introduction: Articulating text and field in the nodes of rhetorical scholarship. In S. L. McKinnon, R. Asen, K. R. Chávez, & R. G. Howard (Eds.), *Text + field: Innovations in rhetorical method* (pp. 1–21). University Park, PA: Pennsylvania State University Press.

Molina, N. (2014). *How race is made in America: Immigration, citizenship, and the historical power of racial scripts.* Berkeley, CA: University of California Press.

Molina Guzmán, I. (2010). *Dangerous curves: Latina bodies in the media.* New York, NY: New York University Press.

Molina Guzmán, I., & Valdivia, A. N. (2004). Brain, brow, and booty: Latina iconicity in U.S. popular culture. *The Communication Review, 7,* 205–221. http://doi.org/10.1080/10714420490448723

Montoya, M. E. (1995). *Máscaras, trenzas, y greñas*: Un/masking the self while un/braiding Latina stories and legal discourse. In Richard Delgado (Ed.), *Critical race theory: The cutting edge* (pp. 529–539). Philadelphia, PA: Temple University Press.

Mora, P. (1993). *Nepantla: Essays from the land in the middle.* Albuquerque, NM: University of New Mexico Press.

Moraga, C., & Anzaldúa, G. (Eds.). (1981). *This bridge called my back: Writings by radical women of color.* New York, NY: Kitchen Table/Women of Color Press.

Morales, S. (Director). (2009). *A crushing love: Chicanas, motherhood, and activism* [Documentary]. New York, NY: Women Make Movies.

Morris, C. E. (2002). Pink herring and the fourth persona: J. Edgar Hoover's sex crime panic. *Quarterly Journal of Speech, 88*(2), 228–244.

Morris, C. E., & Browne, S. H. (2013). *Readings on the rhetoric of social protest* (3rd Ed.). State College, PA: Strata Publishing Inc.

Muñoz, J. E. (2000). Ethnicity and affect in Ricardo Bracho's *The sweetest hangover (and other STDs). Theatre Journal, 52*(1), 67–79.

Nájera-Ramírez, O. (2003). Unruly passions: Poetics, performance, and gender in the ranchera song. In G. F. Arredondo, A. Hurtado, N. Klahn, O. Nájera-Ramírez, & P. Zavella (Eds.), *Chicana feminisms: A critical reader* (pp. 184–210). Durham, NC: Duke University Press.

National Farm Worker Ministry. (2016). Retrieved from *http://nfwm.org/wp-content/uploads/2014/02/12.9.13-h2a-short-farm-workers-and-migration.pdf; http://nfwm-yaya.org/wp-content/uploads/2011/11/pdf_Timeline-of-Agricultural-Labor.pdf*

NBC News. (2014, September 19). Even Dolores Huerta gets jabbed in Latinos' immigration quarrel. NBC News. Retrieved from *http://www.nbcnews.com/news/latino/even-dolores-huerta-gets-jabbed-latinos-immigration-quarrel-n206541*

Nevarez, G. (2014, September 19). Dolores Huerta sees end-game strategy in Obama's delay on immigration. Retrieved from Voxxi.com.

NietoGomez, A. (1997). La Feminista. In A. M. García (Ed.), *Chicana feminist thought: The basic historical writings* (pp. 86–92). New York, NY: Routledge.

Ono, K. (2012). Borders that travel: Matters of the figural border. In D. R. DeChaine (Ed.), *Border rhetorics: Citizenship and identity on the US-Mexico frontier* (pp. 19–32). Tuscaloosa, AL: University of Alabama Press.

Ortega, M. (2004). "This thin edge of barbwire": Selves from land in the middle. *Latino Studies, 2,* 298–303.

Ott, B. L., & Aoki, E. (2001). Popular imagination and identity politics: Reading the future in *Star Trek: The next generation*. *Western Journal of Communication, 65*(4), 392–415.

Palczewski, C. (1996). Bodies, borders, and letters: Gloria Anzaldúa's "Speaking in tongues: A letter to 3rd world women writers." *The Southern Communication Journal, 62*, 1–16.

———. (2001). Contesting pornography: Terministic catharsis and definitional argument. *Argumentation and Advocacy, 38*, 1–17.

Paredez, D. (2009). *Selenidad: Selena, Latinos, and the performance of memory*. Durham, NC: Duke University Press.

Pawel, M. (2006a). UFW: A broken contract; Decisions of long ago shape the union today. *Los Angeles Times*, January 10, retrieved from http://www.latimes.com/local/la-me-history10jan10-story.html

———. (2006b). UFW: A broken contract; Farmworkers reap little as union strays from its roots. *Los Angeles Times*, January 8, retrieved from http://www.latimes.com/local/la-me-ufw8jan08-story.html

———. (2006c). UFW: A broken contract; Linked charities bank on the Chavez name. *Los Angeles Times*, January 9, retrieved from http://www.latimes.com/local/la-me-nonprofits9jan09-story.html

———. (2009). *The union of their dreams: Power, hope, and struggle in Cesar Chavez's farm worker movement*. New York, NY: Bloomsbury Press.

———. (2014). *The crusades of Cesar Chavez: A biography*. New York, NY: Bloomsbury Press.

Pérez, E. (1998). Irigaray's female symbolic in the making of Chicana lesbian *sitios y lenguas* (sites and discourses). In C. Trujillo (Ed.), *Living Chicana theory* (pp. 87–101). Berkeley, CA: Third Woman Press.

Pesquera, B. M., & de la Torre, A. (1993). Introduction. In A. de la Torre & B. M. Pesquera (Eds.), *Building with our hands: New directions in Chicana studies* (pp. 1–11). Berkeley, CA: University of California Press.

Pezzullo, P. C. (2003). Resisting "National Breast Cancer Awareness Month": The rhetoric of counterpublics and their cultural performances. *Quarterly Journal of Speech, 89*, 345–365.

Pezzullo, P. C., & de Onís, C. M. (2017). Rethinking rhetorical field methods on a precarious planet. *Communication Monographs, 85*, 103–122. https://doi.org/10.1080/03637751.2017.1336780

Ramírez, C. S. (2009). *The woman in the zoot suit: Gender, nationalism, and the cultural politics of memory*. Durham, NC: Duke University Press.

Rand, E. J. (2008). An inflammatory fag and a queer form: Larry Kramer, polemics, and rhetorical agency. *Quarterly Journal of Speech, 94*(3), 297–319.

Reid-Brinkley, S. R. (2012). Mammies and matriarchs: Feminine style and signifyin(g) in Carol Moseley Braun's 2003–2004 campaign for the presidency. In K. R. Chávez & C. L. Griffin (Eds.), *Standing in the intersection: Feminist voices, feminist practices in communication studies* (pp. 35–58). Albany, NY: State University of New York Press.

Renegar, V. R., & Sowards, S. K. (2009). Contradiction as agency: Self-determination, transcendence, and counter-imagination in third wave feminism. *Hypatia, 24*(2), 2–20.

———. (2018). Feminist transgressions: Vulnerability, bravery, and the need for a more imperfect feminism. In J. Manning & J. Dunn (Eds.), *Trans-gressions*. New York, NY: Routledge.

Rice, J. E. (2008). The new "new": Making a case for critical affect studies. *Quarterly Journal of Speech, 94*(2), 200–212. http://doi.org/10.1080/00335630801975434

Riley, D. (2005). *Impersonal passion: Language as affect.* Durham, NC: Duke University Press.

Rincón, B. (1997). La Chicana: Her role in the past and her search for a new role in the future. In A. M. García (Ed.), *Chicana feminist thought: The basic historical writings* (pp. 24–28). New York, NY: Routledge.

Rodríguez, C. E. (2004). *Heroes, lovers, and others: The story of Latinos in Hollywood.* New York, NY: Oxford University Press.

Rorty, R. (1989). *Contingency, irony, and solidarity.* Cambridge, UK: Cambridge University Press.

Rose, M. (1988). *Women in the United Farm Workers: A study of Chicana and Mexicana participation in the labor union, 1950 to 1980* (Unpublished doctoral dissertation, University of California, Los Angeles, CA).

——. (1990a). Traditional and nontraditional patterns of female activism in the United Farm Workers of America, 1962 to 1980. *Frontiers, XI*(1), 26–32.

——. (1990b). "From the fields to the picket line: Huelga women and the boycott," 1965–1975. *Labor History, 31*(3), 271–293.

——. (1994). Gender and civic activism in Mexican American barrios in California: The Community Service Organization, 1947–1962. In J. Meyerowitz (Ed.), *Not June Cleaver: Women and gender in postwar America, 1945–1960* (pp. 177–200). Philadelphia, PA: Temple University Press.

——. (1995). "Woman power will stop those grapes": Chicana organizers and middle-class female supporters in the farm workers' grape boycott in Philadelphia, 1969–1970. *Journal of Women's History, 7*(4), 6–36.

——. (2001). César Chávez and Dolores Huerta: Partners in "la causa." In R. W. Etulain (Ed.), *César Chávez: A brief biography with documents* (pp. 95–106). New York, NY: Bedford/St. Martin's.

——. (2002). Dolores Huerta: Passionate defender of la causa. Retrieved from http://chavez.cde.ca.gov/ModelCurriculum/Teachers/Lessons/Resources/Documents/Dolores_Huerta_Essay.pdf

——. (2004). Dolores Huerta: The United Farm Workers Union. In E. Arnesen (Ed.), *The human tradition in American labor history* (pp. 211–229). Wilmington, DE: SR Books.

Ruiz, V. L. (1982). *UCAPAWA, Chicanas, and the California food processing industry, 1937–1950.* (Unpublished doctoral dissertation, Stanford University, Stanford, CA).

——. (1998). *From out of the shadows: Mexican women in twentieth-century America.* New York, NY: Oxford University Press.

Ruiz, V. L., & Chávez, J. R. (Eds.). (2008). *Memories and migrations: Mapping Boricua and Chicana histories* (pp. 93–120). Urbana, IL: University of Illinois Press.

Salas, E. (2008). "The floating borderlands": Identity, farmwork, and políticas in Washington state. In V. L. Ruiz & J. R. Chávez (Eds.), *Memories and migrations: Mapping Boricua and Chicana histories* (pp. 151–169). Urbana, IL: University of Illinois Press.

Saldívar-Hull, S. (2000). *Feminism on the border: Chicana gender politics and literature.* Berkeley, CA: University of California Press.

Sandoval, C. (2000). *Methodology of the oppressed.* Minneapolis, MN: University of Minnesota Press.

Schwarze, S. (2006). Environmental melodrama. *Quarterly Journal of Speech, 92*(3), 239–261.

Schwarze, S., Peeples, J., Schneider, J., & Bsumek, P. (2014). Environmental melodrama, coal, and the politics of sustainable energy in *The last mountain*. *International Journal of Sustainable Development, 17*(2), 108–122.

Shaw, R. (2008). *Beyond the fields: Cesar Chavez, the UFW, and the struggle for justice in the 21st century*. Berkeley, CA: University of California Press.

Shome, R. (1996). Postcolonial interventions in the rhetorical canon: An "other" view. *Communication Theory, 6*(1), 40–59.

———. (2003). Space matters: The power and practice of space. *Communication Theory, 13*(1), 39–56. http://doi.org/10.1111/j.1468-2885.2003.tb00281.x

Sims, P. (1974, January 30). Growers cower when Dolores sits at bargaining table. *Philadelphia Inquirer*, p. 3-B.

Sowards, S. K. (2006). Rhetoric of the perpetual potential: A case study of the environmentalist movement to protect orangutans in Indonesia. In S. Depoe (Ed.), *Environmental communication yearbook, volume 3* (pp. 115–135). Mahwah, NJ: Lawrence Erlbaum Associates.

———. (2010). Rhetorical agency as haciendo caras and differential consciousness through lens of gender, race, ethnicity, and class: An examination of Dolores Huerta's rhetoric. *Communication Theory, 20*, 223–247.

———. (2012). Rhetorical functions of letter writing: Dialogic collaboration, affirmation, and catharsis in Dolores Huerta's letters. *Communication Quarterly, 60*(2), 295–315.

Sowards, S. K., & Renegar, V. R. (2006). Reconceptualizing rhetorical activism in contemporary feminist contexts. *Howard Journal of Communications, 17*, 57–74.

Speer, R. (April 19, 1977). Dolores Huerta on UFW. *Wildcat News & Review*, pp. 1, 4.

———. (April 26, 1977). Dolores Huerta on "People's Movement." *Wildcat News & Review*, pp. 1, 5.

Squires, C. R. (2002). Rethinking the Black public sphere: An alternative vocabulary for multiple public spheres. *Communication Theory, 12*(4), 446–468.

Stephen, L. (1997). *Women and social movements in Latin America: Power from below*. Austin, TX: University of Texas Press.

Stewart, C. J. (1997). The evolution of a revolution: Stokely Carmichael and the rhetoric of black power. *Quarterly Journal of Speech, 83*(4), 429–446.

———. (1999). Championing the rights of others and challenging evil: The ego function in the rhetoric of other-directed social movements. *The Southern Communication Journal, 64*(2), 91–105.

Tonn, M. B. (1996). Militant motherhood: Labor's Mary Harris 'Mother' Jones. *Quarterly Journal of Speech, 82*, 1–21.

Trujillo, C. (1998). La virgen de Guadalupe and her reconstruction in Chicana lesbian desire. In C. Trujillo (Ed.), *Living Chicana theory* (pp. 214–231). Berkeley, CA: Third Woman Press.

UFW. (2016, September 22). UFW petitions EPA to ban chemical that harms farm workers & children. Retrieved from http://ufw.org

UFW History. (2000). Retrieved from http://www.ufw.org/ufw.htm

Valdivia, A. (2008). Is my butt your island? The myths of discovery and contemporary Latina/o communication studies. In A. Valdivia (Ed.), *Latina/o communication studies today* (pp. 3–26). New York, NY: Peter Lang Publishing Inc.

Valenzuela Arce, J. M. (2003). . . . *And to suffer again*: New approaches to melodrama. (R.

M. Gamez, Trans.). In G. F. Arredondo, A. Hurtado, N. Klahn, O. Nájera-Ramírez, & P. Zavella (Eds.), *Chicana feminisms: A critical reader* (pp. 220-227). Durham, NC: Duke University Press.

Vargas, Z. (2000). Citizen, immigrant, and foreign wage workers: The Chicana/o labor refrain in U.S. labor historiography. In R. I. Rochín & D. N. Valdés (Eds.), *Voices of a new Chicana/o history* (pp. 153-165). East Lansing, MI: Michigan State University Press.

Vats, A. (2014). Racechange is the new Black: Racial accessorizing and racial tourism in high fashion as constraints on rhetorical agency. *Communication, Culture & Critique, 7*(1), 112-135. http://doi.org/10.1111/cccr.12037

Vonnegut, K. S. (1992). Listening for women's voices: Revisioning courses in American public address. *Communication Education, 41*(1), 26-39.

Wallace, M. (1982). A Black feminist's search for sisterhood. In G. T. Hull, P. B. Scott, & B. Smith (Eds.), *Black women's studies: All the women are white, all the blacks are men, but some of us are brave* (pp. 5-12). New York, NY: The Feminist Press at the City University of New York.

Wander, P. (1984). The third persona: An ideological turn in rhetorical theory. *Central States Speech Journal, 35*(4), 197-216.

Warren, S. E. (2012). *Dolores Huerta: A hero to migrant workers.* Las Vegas, NV: Amazon Children's Publishing.

West, I. (2008). Debbie Mayne's trans/scripts: Performative repertoires in law and everyday life. *Communication and Critical/Cultural Studies, 5*(3), 245-263. http://doi.org/10.1080/14791420802206841

Weston, K. (1991). *Families we choose: Lesbians, gays, kinship.* New York, NY: Columbia University Press.

Williams, N. (1990). *The Mexican American family: Tradition and change.* Dix Hills, NY: General Hall, Inc.

Yamada, M. (1990). Masks of woman. In G. Anzaldúa (Ed.), *Making face, making soul/ Haciendo caras: Creative and critical perspectives by feminists of color* (pp. 114-116). San Francisco, CA: Aunt Lute Books.

Yinger, W. (1975). *Cesar Chavez: The rhetoric of nonviolence.* Hicksville, NY: Exposition Press.

Yoshino, K. (2006). *Covering: The hidden assault on our civil rights.* New York, NY: Random House.

Zaeske, S. (1995). The "promiscuous audience" controversy and the emergence of the early woman's rights movement. *Quarterly Journal of Speech, 81,* 191-207.

——. (2002). Signatures of citizenship: The rhetoric of women's antislavery petitions. *Quarterly Journal of Speech, 88*(2), 147-168.

Zavella, P. (1987). *Women's work and Chicano families: Cannery workers of the Santa Clara Valley.* Ithaca, NY: Cornell University Press.

INDEX

Farrell, Mike, 150
fasting, 11, 30, 114, 126, 148
Felner, J., 98
feminism, 5, 44–45, 48, 74, 87, 102, 129, 142, 148, 149. *See also* women
Fernández, Juan, 35
Ferrera, America, 141
Flores, Lisa, 48, 52, 74, 93, 158
Food and Justice (magazine), 150
Foss, Karen A., 101
Foust, Christina, 161
Fregoso, Rosa Linda, 97
Freshpict, 135
FWA. *See* Farm Workers Association (FWA)

Galarza, Ernesto, 23
"Game, The," 134, 137
Gandhi, Mahatma, 107, 126
Gangotena, Margarita, 95–96
Ganz, Marshall, 16, 17, 18, 19, 23, 24, 27, 28, 29, 48, 56, 132, 134, 137
García, Mario, 22, 54, 71, 107, 126, 152
Garcia, Matt, 24, 27, 134, 137, 138–139, 158
Garcia, Richard A., 44, 107, 109
Gay, Roxane, 123
gay rights movements. *See* LGBTQ movements
gender, 77–78, 82, 84, 91, 92, 93, 94, 101, 103. *See also* feminism; Latinas; women
gestionar, 104
Godoy, María, 142
Gonzales, Dolores, 62
Gonzáles, Rodolfo "Corky," 4n1, 76, 146
Govea, Jessica, 6, 29, 95, 138
Granovetter, Mark, 117, 131
Green, Al, 23, 57
Greene, Ronald Walter, 160–161
Gregg, Richard, 67, 68, 70, 76
Griffin, Cindy, 123
Gring-Pemble, Lisa, 52, 53, 54, 75
Griswold del Castillo, Richard, 44, 107, 109
gritos, 3, 86, 106, 113, 115–116
Guerra, Juan, 82, 83
Gunterman, Joe, 50
Gutiérrez, José Angel, 7, 146

habitus, 33–34, 35, 38–39, 41; constraining factors of, 46, 48, 49, 155, 160; defined, 6, 12, 32; intersectional, 49, 77, 131, 133, 153, 154, 158, 162; and rhetorical agency, 49, 80. *See also* class; ethnicity; gender; language; race
haciendo caras, 78, 80, 81, 82–83, 106, 109, 110, 133, 154, 157
Hahner, Leslie A., 79
Hammerback, John, 7, 7n2, 26, 116, 126, 146
Hartmire, Chris, 56, 57, 138, 148
Hayworth, Rita, 86n5
Head, Celeste, 108
Head, Ralph, 39
health care, 2, 3, 13, 20, 96, 130, 140, 150–151
Higgins, George, 135
Hoffa, Jimmy, 27
Hoffman, Gaby, 141–142
Holling, Michelle, 9, 48, 71, 93, 119, 156, 158
hope, 108, 109, 127–128, 131, 140, 144, 154, 155, 156
housing conditions, 21, 22, 24, 140
Huelga School, 137, 138
Huerta, Dolores: and boycotts, 2, 3, 25–26, 42, 60–61, 108, 149; and Chávez's support, 42–44, 47, 48; and conflict with Chávez, 73–74, 94, 135–137; and constraining factors, 158–159, 160, 161; criticisms of, 133, 135–136, 138–139, 141–142; and discrimination, 4–5, 10, 37, 141, 150; early life and activism of, 35–38, 39–41, 158; and financial struggles, 71–72, 97, 107–108, 158; and founding of FWA, 2, 16, 20, 23, 31, 41–42, 55, 104; and gender, 5, 44–45, 46–47; and habitus, 33–34, 47–48, 49; iconic status of, 142, 143, 144, 145, 152, 153, 156, 162; and intersectionality, 147–148, 149–152; and leadership in UFW, 2, 23, 30, 42, 46, 140; legacy of, 1–2, 9, 14, 49, 143, 147, 152, 162; and letters to Chávez, 13, 50–51, 52–53, 54, 75–76; and lobbying, 28, 55, 68–69, 72–73; marriages of, 15, 39, 40, 42, 97, 122; as a mother, 2–3, 11, 39, 40, 42,

WITHDRAWN

CPSIA information can be obtained
at www.ICGtesting.com
Printed in the USA
LVHW031840060421
683591LV00003B/674

9 781477 317679